Praise for Jeff Foster's
After Effects and Photoshop

Choosing to write a book about either Adobe Photoshop or Adobe After Effects poses quite a challenge. Taking on the task of writing a book that covers both multiplies that challenge, but also offers a unique perspective into the creative possibilities these applications have not only individually, but in tandem. For anyone who uses both applications, this is a must-read.

> —DANIEL BROWN, Sr. Evangelist, Digital Video, Adobe Systems Inc.

With the book you hold in your hands, Jeff Foster has created the one indispensble, and definitive, production guide to two of the world's greatest symbiotic tools: After Effects and Photoshop. One has to be an expert in Photoshop to really make After Effects fly, the two programs being joined at their very core. And one also needs a professional understanding of traditional cinematic and animation timing and effects—as well as directing material in 3D space—to fully take advantage of the capabilities of Adobe's most powerful siblings. Jeff has this expertise in spades, and he combines his many years of professional experience with his gift for training and inspiring others in this immensely practical and straightforward book and DVD package. Buy it—from the first project, it will dramatically expand your creative possibilities.

> —JACK H. DAVIS, coauthor, the *Photoshop Wow!* books, the *One-Click Wow!* books, and *How to Wow: Photoshop for Photography*

This book really speaks a motion-designer's language, from the layout to the projects to Jeff's step-by-step style—it all comes together in a book that needs to be on every motion graphic designer's shelf. Well done!

> —SCOTT KELBY, President, National Association of Photoshop Professionals

The only thing that could add to the awesome power of After Effects and Photoshop on my computer would be a single kick-ass book on how to use both programs together—and this book is it. If you're holding this book in your hands, buy it now! You can thank me later.

> —BOB SELF, animator/educator

Jeff shares his big bag of tricks an(
that extra edge. Covering a mix o,
appreciated by both aspiring and
> —STEVE TIBORCZ, After Eff

r Effects W
Exit Only
toshop Roa

After Effects®
and Photoshop®

Animation and Production Effects for DV and Film

Second Edition

Jeff Foster

WILEY PUBLISHING, INC.

Wiley Publishing, Inc.

Acquisitions Editor: Willem Knibbe
Developmental Editor: Heather O'Connor
Technical Editor: Mark Ahn
Copy Editor: Kathy Carlyle
Compositor: Happenstance Type-O-Rama
Production Manager: Tim Tate
Associate Publisher: Dan Brodnitz
Vice President and Executive Group Publisher: Richard Swadley
Vice President and Executive Publisher: Joseph B. Wikert
Media Development Specialist: Kate Jenkins
Media Project Supervisor: Shannon Walters
Media Development Coordinator: Laura Atkinson
Proofreader: Nancy Riddiough
Indexer: Ted Laux
Cover Designer and Illustration: Richard Miller, Calyx Design
Cover Image: Jeff Foster

Copyright © 2006 by Wiley Publishing, Inc., Indianapolis, Indiana

Published simultaneously in Canada

First edition copyright © 2004 SYBEX Inc.

ISBN-13: 978-0-7821-4455-0
ISBN-10: 0-7821-4455-1

For general information on our other products and services or to obtain technical support, please contact our Customer Care Department within the U.S. at (800) 762-2974, outside the U.S. at (317) 572-3993 or fax (317) 572-4002.

Wiley also publishes its books in a variety of electronic formats. Some content that appears in print may not be available in electronic books.

Library of Congress Cataloging-in-Publication Data is available from the publisher.

Manufactured in the United States of America

10 9 8 7 6 5 4 3 2 1

Dear Reader,

Thank you for choosing *After Effects and Photoshop,* *Second Edition.* This book is part of a family of premium quality Sybex graphics books, all written by outstanding authors who combine practical experience with a gift for teaching.

Sybex was founded in 1976. Thirty years later, we're still committed to producing consistently exceptional books. With each of our graphics titles we're working hard to set a new standard for the industry. From the paper we print on, to the writers and photographers we work with, our goal is to bring you the best graphics books available.

I hope you see all that reflected in these pages. I'd be very interested to hear your comments and get your feedback on how we're doing. To let us know what you think about this or any other Sybex book, please send me an e-mail at: sybex_publisher@wiley.com. Please also visit us at www.sybex.com to learn more about the rest of our growing graphics line.

Best regards,

DAN BRODNITZ
Vice President and Publisher
Sybex, an Imprint of Wiley

Acknowledgments

I would like to thank the great editorial and development team at Sybex for all your help and encouragement in producing this book—it just wouldn't be complete without your input and guidance. My college English professor must think I can really write like this! And to the production team, thank you for making this book and DVD look great!

I also want to thank my professional design and instructional colleagues for your guidance, ideas, and support. I couldn't have done this book without the still image content and support from Stephanie Robey at PhotoSpin.com. Thanks! And many thanks to the Adobe After Effects and Photoshop development teams for your help and for listening to us "users." Thanks for making these great products so fun to use!

I would especially like to thank my family and friends for your continued love, understanding, and support—especially when I've been too tired and grouchy to talk to. I love you all!

About the Author

Jeff Foster has authored and contributed to several Adobe how-to books, including the *Photoshop Web Magic* series and *Special Edition: Using Photoshop* series. He has appeared regularly as a member of the Instructor Dream Team at PhotoshopWorld and as a featured speaker at Macworld User Conferences and the NAB (National Association of Broadcasters) Post Production Conference. He has served as an instructor and course curriculum developer for Westwood College, and he has taught at several other colleges and universities around Southern California. He provides consulting, training, and design services for corporate clients, production studios, and TV stations nationally.

Foster has been creating traditional and digital images, photography, illustration, motion graphics, and special effects for digital video and film for more than two decades. His vast portfolio includes clients such as McDonnell Douglas, Motorola, Spike TV, Fox Television, Universal Studios, and Disney.

Foreword

Print is dead. There... I said it. (It needed to be said.)

Now, I'm not saying that we will never see books in print again, nor that people all over the world will suddenly stop reading printed material. I'm just stating that the desktop publishing revolution has seen its glory days. We're on to a new revolution... the Digital Video Revolution!

We are living in an age where visual communication is king. Television has become the #1 outlet for the world to receive information. Filmmakers, actors, and TV personalities have been elevated to a status that in previous centuries was reserved only for royalty. DVDs have become the fastest growing new technology of all time. All these methods of communication and distribution involve visual imagery.

As a video guy working in the new millennium, I find that there are plenty of books that pay attention to how a single image looks on paper, but almost no resources on how to make images look great while moving across time. Thank goodness Jeff Foster has written a book that focuses on how to get your images looking great in Adobe Photoshop and then give them life in Adobe After Effects. Every designer in the world has used Photoshop, and many consider themselves experts at it. However, few have focused on mastering the art of using Photoshop with other programs as Jeff has.

Jeff Foster has been a leader in the field of motion graphics, animation, and special effects for 20 years. I first met Jeff as an instructor at PhotoshopWorld years ago, and I have continued to run into him because he is in such demand as an instructor. As this book shows, Jeff has a knack for tutorials that make difficult concepts easy to understand. As an Adobe Certified Expert, Jeff also has the technical knowledge needed to troubleshoot difficult projects, and he shares this knowledge freely with anyone who attends his classes, reads his books, or visits his entertaining website, PixelPainter.com.

Motion graphics requires technical discipline and artistic discipline. From displacement maps to parenting, layering to compositing, keying to rotoscoping... I can't imagine a better guide to navigate a user through the labyrinth of technical detail and design decisions than Jeff Foster. I consider myself lucky to call Jeff my colleague, my instructor, and most importantly my friend. As you work through this book, he will also be a friend to you, especially as you further your knowledge of After Effects and Photoshop.

Now turn the page and *Go Be Creative!*

ROD HARLAN
Executive Director, Digital Video Professionals Association
www.DVPA.com, www.DVPA.org, www.RodHarlan.com

Contents

"You can take virtually any two-dimensional image and bring it to life, applying some traditional and progressive techniques to your own projects."

Introduction

After Effects and Photoshop were made for each other. Well, not exactly, but Adobe has been closing the gap between the two applications more and more with each revision they make. This book is based on how both applications work in concert with each other—and how you can get the most out of that union.

Industry professionals have been using Photoshop for image manipulation and compositing for years. After Effects has become a staple for serious motion graphics designers and desktop digital video compositors who want to use a more powerful tool than just a nonlinear editor. I've been using these applications together for design and production for years and have shown some of my techniques to classrooms and audiences, to help demystify animation and special effects techniques.

There are already hundreds of books on Photoshop and a few on After Effects, so why is this book so important? Although many of these books teach you *how to use* the applications and make great stuff, they often fail to tell you why. *This* is a production effects and animation book. I wanted to get down to showing you some animation basics, so you can take virtually any two-dimensional image and bring it to life by applying some traditional as well as progressive techniques to your own projects. But most important, I wanted to make you start thinking more creatively and look at a simple image or video clip and ask yourself, "How can I animate this and make it more exciting?" Some of the examples in this book you may recognize; others are new concepts and techniques that are starting to show up on television and at the movies.

I often use techniques in some chapter examples that are similar to ones I've used in previous chapters in the book. This is very intentional, as I feel that the best way to reinforce knowledge is to apply it in real-world projects. This is how I've taught college courses and corporate training as well. People learn best by doing—and most people retain their learned knowledge if they understand the *why* as well as the *how* to do something.

Note: Most of the projects in this book require the most recent, professional versions of these applications. At the minimum, you'll need After Effects 7.0 and Photoshop CS2 with ImageReady. You might be able to complete some of the projects step-by-step with an older version; you just won't be able to open them up from the DVD. You will also find older versions of the After Effects project files at www.pixelpainter.com. Apple's QuickTime Pro is also necessary for a few projects.

Who Should Use This Book

This book was written for people who already have a basic understanding and working knowledge of how the After Effects, Photoshop, and ImageReady applications work. It does not necessarily show you what all of the tools do; rather, it shows how to use them to create animations, composites, and special effects. Many great books are available that show you how to scan an image, remove red eye, log video footage, optimize your movies, and apply compression. *After Effects and Photoshop: Animation and Production Effects for DV and Film* does not. I decided that communicating the message of this book is more important than hiding the techniques inside a technical book. This book teaches you to think creatively and get excited about animation and special effects in your production!

Although I chose to use a Mac for all of the screen shots in this book, all of the projects and examples can be done on a PC running Windows. Adobe has put a lot of effort into making the CS2 and After Effects 7 software products look, feel, and function identically, regardless of which operating system you use.

What's Inside

After Effects and Photoshop was designed to walk you through basic animation principles and help you understand how to most effectively use After Effects, Photoshop, and ImageReady together in animating, video compositing, and effects production.

Part I: Connecting Photoshop, ImageReady, and After Effects gives you the simplest, fastest techniques of animation and describes how these programs interact.

> **Chapter 1: Basic ImageReady Animation, Tweening, and Layer Styles** demonstrates how Photoshop and ImageReady work together as a powerful animation tool, producing work that can be imported into After Effects.
>
> **Chapter 2: Photoshop Layers and After Effects** explores the ability to transfer Photoshop layers to separate comp layers in After Effects and then edit the original as desired without having to replace or reimport layers.
>
> **Chapter 3: 3-D Layers from Photoshop Layers** teaches you some of the many detailed After Effects camera and light controls that enable you to create realistic 3-D motion from static image layers.

Part II: Applying Animation Concepts is the heart and soul of basic character animation, applied to two-dimensional image objects and characters.

> **Chapter 4: Cause and Effect** shows you how gravity, friction, inertia, and collision all affect how a character moves and responds.
>
> **Chapter 5: Exaggeration Equals Characterization** takes all of the principles of Chapter 4 and tosses them out the window in fun and creative ways!

Part III: Clean-Up, Mattes, and Objects gives you a look at the nuts and bolts of production effects and compositing scenes, matte painting, and chroma keying.

Chapter 6: Blue-Screen Garbage Mattes provides simple techniques for cleaning up chroma key footage prior to compositing.

Chapter 7: Rotoscoping Techniques with Photoshop gives you step-by-step instruction on how to do frame-by-frame retouching on footage to clean up or remove items in a scene.

Chapter 8: Shooting a Clean Blue/Green Screen introduces cameras, lights, and action! It provides production tips for getting the best results when shooting a good green screen.

Chapter 9: Matte and Keying Plug-Ins shows you a side-by-side comparison of the most popular keying plug-in products on the market—and tells which one is best for different applications.

Chapter 10: Static Matte "Painting" in Photoshop explores traditional matte painting techniques in a digital medium—creating realistic composites and scene locations.

Chapter 11: Motion Matte "Painting" in Photoshop covers how to create matching mattes that move with the camera, as well as motion tracking simulation.

Chapter 12: Making Movies from Stills gives you an overview of a new animation technique that creates simulated 3-D camera motion from still images.

Part IV: Advanced Movie Magic covers production techniques for creating a more professional-looking video or film project.

Chapter 13: Scale and Speed teaches you perspective and scale in motion and how it relates to the speed of an object in motion.

Chapter 14: Color, Light, and Focus explores techniques for fooling the eye into thinking that composited objects are clearly part of the original footage.

Chapter 15: Atmosphere, Film, and Noise Effects shows you how to create moving layers of noise, clouds, and smoke without the application of third-party plug-in effects.

Chapter 16: Motion Titling Effects gives you a different look at creating titling and animating text that gets attention! It includes tips for creating lower thirds.

Chapter 17: Custom Scene Transitions helps you expand your scene-to-scene transitioning capabilities into a professional, creative level—including using 3-D layer animations as transitions.

The Appendix is full of references for other After Effects and Photoshop training and reference resources, as well as contact information for third-party vendors and suppliers of stock images, video footage, and plug-in effects used in this book.

The Companion DVD

The enclosed DVD-ROM includes all the source materials and project files required to complete every example in this book, plus it contains finished QuickTime movies showing all the effects.

I've also collected a vast array of stock footage and third-party After Effects plug-ins for you to experiment with and enjoy!

How to Contact the Author

You can reach me through my website at www.pixelpainter.com. I welcome all of your comments and questions and would like to hear from you! If you have a comment, question, or concern about the book, please feel free to contact me directly and I will do my best to respond with help or a resolution in a timely manner.

After Effects® and Photoshop®

Animation and Production Effects
for DV and Film

Second Edition

Connecting Photoshop, ImageReady, and After Effects

I

When you think about creating animation and motion graphics, Photoshop and ImageReady aren't necessarily the first applications that come to mind. Surprisingly, a lot of animation capability to create frame-by-frame animations and effects is available—and that capability is expanded when you use these programs in combination with After Effects. These chapters will walk you through some of the basics of the tools and options available and how best to utilize their functions.

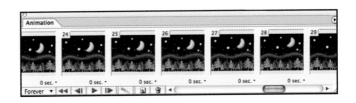

Basic ImageReady Animation, Tweening, and Layer Styles

Photoshop and ImageReady work together as an image creator, editor, and animation tool. While Photoshop is the preferred tool to create content, ImageReady will put it into motion. Some of the projects in this chapter can be totally created in ImageReady. These animations can be exported as uncompressed QuickTime movies that you can import into After Effects. We will cover some animations that just can't be created any other way (for example, animated layer styles).

1

Chapter Contents

Turning Photoshop Layers into Frames

If you create an animation using different layers in Photoshop, such as a distorted or "Liquified" object, then there's a simple way to convert each layer into a single frame of animation. You might choose to create an animation in Photoshop because some tools and brushes are not readily available in ImageReady (Figure 1.1).

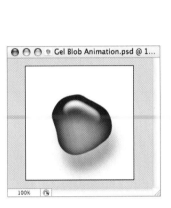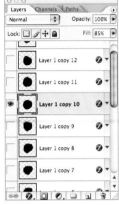

Figure 1.1

Several layers created for an animation sequence

After you jump from Photoshop to ImageReady, select the Make Frames From Layers option from the Animation palette menu. This will insert the background layer as Frame 1 and the subsequent layers as frames in order of layer hierarchy (see Figure 1.2). Because in most cases you won't want the background layer to be inserted as a frame in the animation, simply delete Frame 1 from the Animation palette. This will eliminate the background color/texture behind the animated pieces in the example animation. Choose Select All Frames from the Animation palette menu and make the background layer visible.

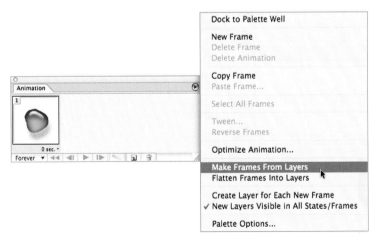

Figure 1.2

Selecting Make Frames From Layers from the Animation palette menu

Now the animation sequence is in place and is ready for any adjustments in timing or output options and previewing in the default web browser for quick reference (see Figure 1.3). Even though the animation will appear as an animated GIF, it will run at normal playback speed, though it's not in full resolution. It will give you a better idea of the actual flow and real-time animation than the Playback button in ImageReady, and you don't have to export the animation to a QuickTime movie just to preview the animation sequence timing.

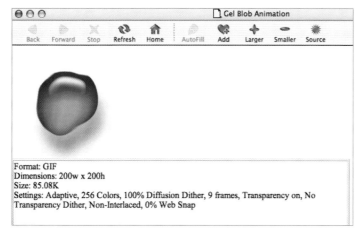

Figure 1.3
Previewing the animation in the default web browser

Note: Look for finished examples of many of the book's projects and animations on the enclosed DVD.

The Animation Palette in ImageReady

Most common animation techniques, such as moving and blending object and text layers in a sequence, are best left for video compositing tools such as Adobe After Effects. Still, there are many animation techniques that can be done quickly and easily with ImageReady and that require very little programming or timeline editing. These techniques are covered in detail throughout this book, and references will be made to the Animation palette.

The Animation palette (Figure 1.4) is the heart of creating animations in ImageReady. It's a very intuitive layout for frame-by-frame animation sequences, with advanced features such as tweening and frame generation from layers. Getting familiar with the features and buttons on the palette will help speed up your animation process.

Ⓐ Frame delay time Ⓔ Duplicates current frame
Ⓑ Looping options Ⓕ Deletes selected frames
Ⓒ Playback controls Ⓖ Palette menu
Ⓓ Tweens animation frames

Figure 1.4 Features of the Animation palette

We'll create a simple one-layer animation to familiarize you with the Animation palette. To begin, create a single object on a new layer. Move the object on a single layer, using the Animation palette, and click the Duplicates current frame button.

After duplicating the frame, and with the frame selected in the palette, use the Move tool to relocate the object on the layer to another area in the window. The Animation palette will show the updated frame. Shift+click the two frames in the palette to select them, and click the Tweens Animation Frames button to bring up the Tween dialog box (Figure 1.5) to add a few frames "in between" the selected frames. Select the All Layers and Position options, and set the number of frames to add. In this example, only five frames were added.

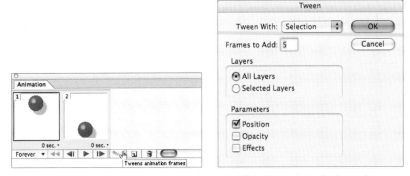

Figure 1.5 Select two frames on the Animation palette and click the Tweens Animation Frames button to select how many frames to add.

Note: You can find more information about tweening in the Animation palette later in this chapter. See "Pre-Animation: Painless Tweening in ImageReady."

Continue duplicating frames, moving the object layer and tweening to create a simple animation that can be played back from the palette for preview. Select the Play button on the Animation palette to preview the animation, or use the Preview In Default Browser button on the toolbar to view in real time.

To adjust the playback speed of all frames, choose the Select All Frames option from the palette menu, and select the frame delay to set (see Figure 1.6). The frames can be adjusted individually as well.

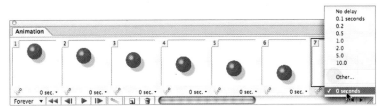

Figure 1.6 Adjusting the frame delay

Exporting Animation Files from ImageReady

There are two basic ways to save your animations out of ImageReady: as QuickTime movies or as animated GIF files. Of course, it helps to know going into your project what kind of animation you're creating—the frames per second, pixel dimensions, color depth, etc. Exporting the animations requires testing and previewing to get the timing correct. You can do this quickly by selecting the default web browser; although the color depth will be limited to an optimized 256-color palette, you will still be able to gain a sense of your final timing.

To export an animated GIF, choose the Save Optimized As option and then select Images Only as the format, as shown in Figure 1.7. Make sure you set the color depth and dithering prior to exporting, which is how you adjust the size of the finished GIF file. Your exported file will look just as it did when you previewed it in the web browser.

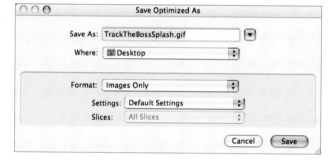

Figure 1.7

Exporting an animated GIF
file with Save Optimized As

Exporting a QuickTime movie file is a bit different, however. The timing of each frame will be reflected in QuickTime Player as the repetition of certain frames to make up the frame rate. If you have only a few frames and want to stretch out the time, then it may be a good idea to increase the frame timing in the Animation palette first.

Note: Importing and exporting frames from QuickTime movies requires the inexpensive commercial product QuickTime Pro, not just the free QuickTime Player.

To export the movie, select File → Export → Original Document to bring up the dialog box. Select QuickTime Movie from the Format selector, name the file, click Save, and then set the Compression Settings from the pop-up dialog box (see Figure 1.8).

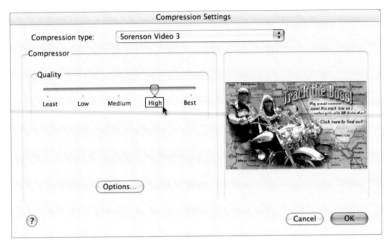

Figure 1.8
Exporting a QuickTime
movie file from
ImageReady

Open the QuickTime movie file and play back the animation (see Figure 1.9). If you need to make adjustments in time or size, just go back into ImageReady and reexport when you have finished.

Figure 1.9
Playing back the animation
in QuickTime Player

In some cases, you'll want to use the animation frames as individual images that you can work on or import into another application. You can do this simply by selecting File → Export → Animation Frames As Files, where you can select different file-naming and compression options from the dialog window. (See Figure 1.10.)

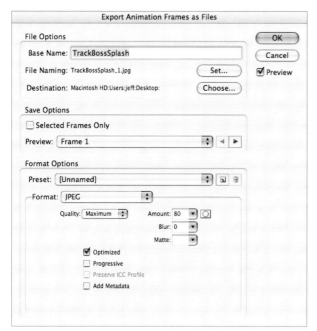

Figure 1.10

From ImageReady, you can save frames as individual files in a sequence easily.

Pre-Animation: Painless Tweening in ImageReady

Tweening is the process of automatically adding frames between two selected frames (called key frames) to create a designated number of steps of motion, opacity, or applied effects so that you can create a smooth, continuous animation sequence. The more key frames you have, the more control you will have over your animation's tweening.

Knowing what the final animation will be used for will help you to determine the speed and length of the animation sequence you are creating. Using more frames for tweening makes your animation not only smoother but also longer. It takes some practice to determine the correct number of tweened frames to add for each sequence, as well as the delay time that each frame is made visible. If you are creating an animation for a DV (digital video) or a QuickTime movie, it will be around 15–30 frames per second, depending on the final movie frame rate required.

Note: I usually choose to tween animations in ImageReady, rather than using After Effects, because I want to animate the layer styles or text effect shapes. Simply moving the Photoshop layers in After Effects won't create the same effects.

Tweening Motion

You don't have to be an experienced animator to be rewarded with simple motion tweening. By simply tweening a single object layer that is positioned on opposite sides of the frame window, you can make an animation in just a couple of steps. To see how, open MotionTweening.psd from the Chapter 1 folder on this book's companion DVD.

In this example, I started with a multilayered Photoshop file, with simple shapes (including trees, hills, stars, and a moon) on layers. The layers were placed in order from closest (at the top of the layers stack) to farthest (at the bottom) in the frame. With the moon layer tucked down behind the hills layer, I jumped to ImageReady, where the default position is automatically created as Frame 1 on the Animation palette, as shown in Figure 1.11.

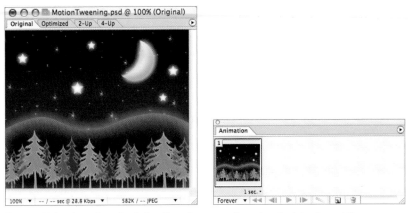

Figure 1.11 Jumping to ImageReady from Photoshop creates Frame 1 on the Animation palette.

Click the Duplicate Selected Frame button on the Animation palette to create a new frame (Frame 2). The moon layer then moves up into the sky (see Figure 1.12), which becomes the current position for Frame 2. Select the two frames in the Animation palette, and click the Tweens animation frames icon to open the Tween dialog box (Figure 1.13). Select the number of frames to add for your animation, and set the Tween Parameters to Position.

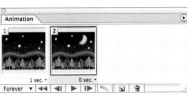

Figure 1.12
Duplicate the first frame, and move the object to its destination point.

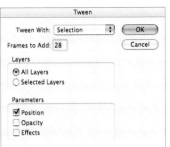

Figure 1.13
Set the number of tweened frames to insert.

The tweened frames are added between the original selected frames. Click the Play button on the Animation palette to preview the motion path that is created by tweening, as shown in Figure 1.14.

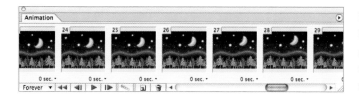

Figure 1.14

Use the Playback controls on the Animation palette to preview the motion created by tweening the two frames.

For a quick preview of the animation (and timing), select the Preview In Default Browser button on the toolbar. This opens the browser window and plays the animation as an animated GIF, so the color depth will be limited to 256 colors. However, you will gain a sense of how the animation will move in real time. Export the completed animation as a noncompressed QuickTime file for your final movie, or you can view my version (MotionTweening.mov in the Chapter 1 folder) on the DVD.

Tweening Effects

Tweening your effects is a matter of dealing with custom layer styles and text warping effects to create fun and interesting animations. You can create several effect tweens, such as the motion of warped text and the transition of layer styles, although they do not work with Photoshop filters or plug-ins.

For this example, let's create a simple warped-text animation using only the Tween Effects feature in ImageReady, so we won't need to jump to Photoshop.

1. Using the Text tool in ImageReady, start with a single text layer.
2. Apply a Warp Text effect to the text layer in an exaggerated position, as in Figure 1.15; this becomes Frame 1 of the animation.

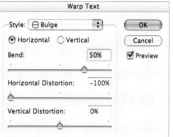

Figure 1.15 Create a single text layer and apply Warp Text to it for the starting frame of the animation.

3. Duplicate the frame, and open the Warp Text dialog box again. Reverse all of the parameters of the warp, as shown in Figure 1.16. This becomes the state of Frame 2, or the second key frame.

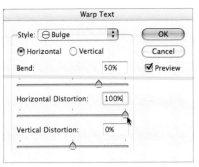

Figure 1.16 Duplicate Frame 1, and reverse the parameters of the Warp Text for the second key frame of the animation.

4. Select the two frames on the Animation palette, and click the Tween button to open the Tween dialog box (Figure 1.17). Select the number of frames you want to add and choose the Effects check box.

5. Duplicate the tweened frames, and move them to the right of the second key frame. Select the Reverse Frames option from the Animation palette menu to create a closed "loop" animation (Figure 1.18). Preview the finished animation in the default web browser.

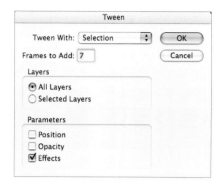

Figure 1.17

Tween the Effects between the two key frames.

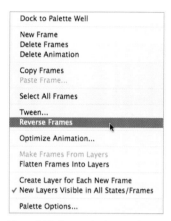

Figure 1.18 Reverse the frame order to create a closed loop animation.

Applying Depth and Realism to Animations

To create the illusion of depth in a two-dimensional image, you need to have a basic understanding of lighting and shading. Knowing the direction of light on an object is not as important as understanding that all shading, including shadow falloff, must be applied on the opposing sides. For example, if you have a sphere that has a light source at the 10 o'clock position projected onto it, then naturally you will want the shaded side of the sphere to appear at the 4 o'clock position. The shadow from this sphere would then fall upon whatever planes or objects are 180° from the light source.

Fortunately, the layer styles in Photoshop automatically handle all of this (when Use Global Light is selected). There may be times when you might want to take control over the automatic settings to force a highlight or shadow onto an area of your image to create an illusion of forced perspective.

Using the text animation in the preceding project, apply a layer style to the text. I applied Lime Green Glass Button, from the Styles palette (if you don't see that style in your list, append the Glass buttons from the Styles palette pull-down menu to get it). By changing the color to green and reducing the opacity to 50% (see Figure 1.19, which shows the Photoshop layer style settings and the result in ImageReady), I then modified the drop shadow layer to act more as a refracted light gel.

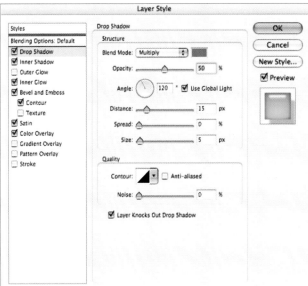

Figure 1.19
Modify a default layer style to refract light and enhance transparency and dimension.

Styles in Motion: Neon Text

This project will familiarize you with different layer style options and animating a sequence in ImageReady by only making changes to the layer style settings. Creating neon effects involves two elements: the tubing and the light glow. When the light is off, the tubing still has a 3-D surface and casts a shadow if any ambient light is present. When the light is on, it casts a glow but no shadows.

 Note: Intermediate or advanced Photoshop users may want to open the file NeonText.psd on the DVD and skip ahead to the animation section of this project.

1. Start by creating a text or object layer in Photoshop that will simulate the shape of the neon tubing (see Figure 1.20).

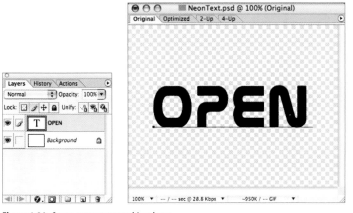

Figure 1.20 Create a new text or object layer.

2. Click the Add Layer Style button on the Layers palette to open the Layer Style dialog box. The first step is to give the shape a base color, so select the Color Overlay option and choose a color by clicking on the colored rectangle. In this example, I used the default red color for my base.

3. Select the Bevel And Emboss option, and adjust the Depth to 200% and set the Size to 6 pixels. Change the Highlight color to a lighter shade of the base color you're using (mine is a pale pink) and change the Shadow color to a darker shade (a dark red in my example). Adjust the Opacity of each to achieve a balance between the base color and the highlights.

4. Set the altitude of the light source high so that it creates the highlight on the top surface of the tubing, as shown in Figure 1.21.

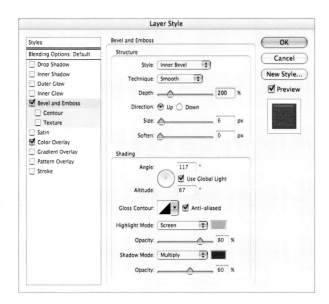

Figure 1.21
Apply the Bevel And
Emboss option and
change settings to create
a tubing effect.

5. Apply the Inner Glow option. Change the color to a lighter version of your base color (in my example, it's a pale pink). Set the size to approximately 10 pixels—adjust for the size/resolution of your image and object layer. Change the Contour from the default to Ring-Double.

6. Select the Outer Glow option, and set the color to a slightly lighter variation of your base color. Set the Opacity to 50% and the Blend Mode to Normal. Adjust the Size to 15 pixels to achieve an even spread of "light" around the object (see Figure 1.22).

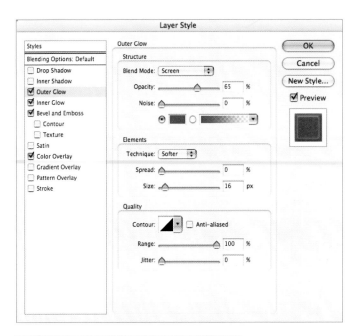

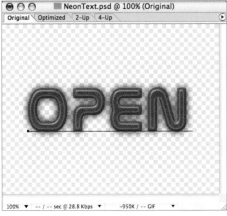

Figure 1.22
Use Outer Glow to make the neon shed some light!

7. Click OK and apply a dark background texture to a layer below the neon object layer.

Your final image should have a soft glow around the edges of the tubing (See Figure 1.23). You may need to make some adjustments to the glow opacity and size if the image appears too weak or strong for a realistic effect.

Figure 1.23
The completed image
should have a soft glow
around the edges.

We will now create the "off" version of the tubing by making a few changes in the Layer Style dialog box:

1. Duplicate the neon tube object layer and open the Layer Style dialog box. Deselect the Inner Glow and Outer Glow options by clicking their check boxes off.

2. Set the Opacity of the Color Overlay to approximately 30% and apply a slight Drop Shadow, as shown in Figure 1.24. Depending on your background color, you will need to adjust the opacity of the shadow's intensity to make it just barely visible.

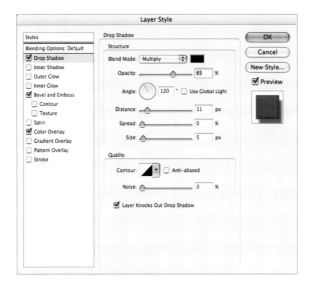

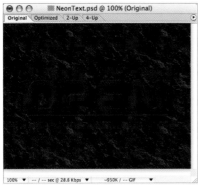

Figure 1.24
Applying a drop
shadow in the "off"
version of the tubing
will give the object a
3-D effect against
the background.

3. Jump to ImageReady to animate the sequence of the light flashing on and off. For a believable effect of the neon light turning on and off, there should be a bit of flicker, which can easily be created in the timeline.

4. Start with the first frame in the Animation palette and make only the "off" layer visible. In the second frame, make the "on" layer visible.

5. Duplicate these two frames three times (creating a total of eight frames—off/on, off/on, and so on).

6. On the seventh frame, make the "on" layer visible and set the Opacity to 50%. This will make it appear as if it is fading as it turns off completely.

7. Set the timing on each frame by clicking on the delay setting (as shown in Figure 1.25). Set the first and sixth frames to 2 seconds, while setting the remaining frames to No Delay. This will cause a slight flicker as the light goes on and off.

Figure 1.25 Adjust the timing of the frames to create a realistic "flicker" in the neon light.

Note: As with all animation projects created in ImageReady, you can preview the animation in a web browser to gain a feel of the timing. Then choose Export Original Document and create a QuickTime movie of your completed animation sequence.

Light in Motion: Leaf Shadow

Obviously, there are several methods you can use to move layered objects around in ImageReady to create animation. Some of those methods can be used to animate with layer styles that will give realistic 3-D effects. Lighting and shadows in motion or moving textures across an object are just a few ways you can create motion with a single object or text layer. This project will guide you through creating lights, shadows, depth, and motion. With this method, you will modify only the layer styles in Photoshop and animate their settings in ImageReady. You can follow along by opening LightMotion.psd from the Chapter 1 folder on the companion DVD.

Using the Global Light directional settings, you can create incredibly realistic 3-D animations with layer styles. This project shows that an image with only one layer and a single layer style applied can be animated in ImageReady to create the illusion that a light source is moving from the bottom to the top of the frame.

Start with a text layer or an object floating in a layer in Photoshop. Apply a Drop Shadow to the object layer in the Layer Styles dialog box, setting the Distance far away from the object, as shown in Table 1.1. I changed the Angle to create the illusion of the light source coming from the bottom and moving to the top and also made the shadow a bit bolder by adjusting the Spread (see Figure 1.26).

▶ **Table 1.1** Layer Style settings for a drop shadow

Setting	Value	Result
Angle	–120°	Creates the illusion of the light source coming from the bottom and moving to the top.
Distance	30 pixels	Positions the light far away from the object.
Spread	20%	Makes the shadow bolder, exaggerating the shadow depth.

Figure 1.26 Create dramatic drop shadows for your object layer.

Apply a solid Color Overlay to the object layer and a Pattern Overlay for texture if you want. I applied a Pattern Overlay of Gouache Watercolor and set the Color Overlay Blending Mode to Overlay, allowing the texture to show through the solid color.

Apply a Bevel And Emboss to the layer, with a Half Round Contour. Set the options as shown in Table 1.2 and in Figure 1.27. In addition, I added a light background texture to give it depth and interest.

▶ **Table 1.2** Bevel And Emboss Layer Style settings

Setting	Value
Depth	250%
Size	Approx. 10 pixels
Light Source Direction	Leave as is, Up
Altitude	65°

Jump to ImageReady—your first frame will automatically be positioned in the current state. Duplicate the first frame, and change the angle of the Drop Shadow to +120°, making sure that the Use Global Light selection is checked (see Figure 1.28).

Select both frames on the Animation palette, and click the Tween button. Select only the Effects option, and set the number of frames you want to add to your animation. I chose 28 for a smooth 1-second animation at 30 fps (see Figure 1.29).

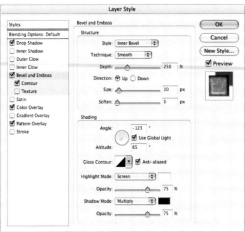

Figure 1.27
Apply a Color Overlay and Emboss to the layer to give it depth and dimension.

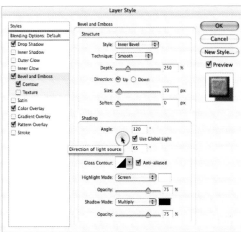

Figure 1.28
Note how the light angle and the drop shadows affect the surface of the image.

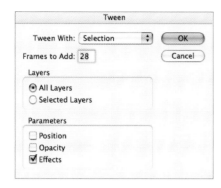

Figure 1.29
Tweening the effects with several
frames will give you a longer,
smoother animation.

You can set the delay timing to slow down or freeze the animation in the time-line on the Animation palette. I chose to add .1 Sec a few frames toward the end of the animation sequence to "ease in" to the last frame, and then hold on the last frame for 2 seconds before looping again (Figure 1.30). See the final animation, LightMotion.mov, in the Chapter 1 folder on the companion DVD.

Figure 1.30
Speed up or slow down the animation further by setting the
delay timing for each frame.

Pattern in Motion: Rolling Eye

You don't always need a 3-D application to create realistic 3-D animations or effects. Starting with a single photograph, you can extract portions of it and apply them as a layer-style pattern on a shape layer that can be animated to appear as if it was rendered with light sources and reflections.

Start this project by opening the file EyeballAnim.jpg in Photoshop, from the Chapter 1 folder on the DVD (see Figure 1.31). Duplicate the background layer and hide the background. Select only the eyeball from the center of the eye and cut it from the image layer, as shown in Figure 1.32. You may want to use the Lasso tool to select the eyeball, or for more accuracy, use the Eraser tool to remove the portion of the image on that layer.

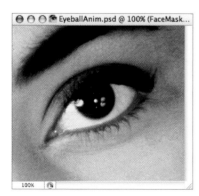

Figure 1.31
The eyeball image file
found on the DVD

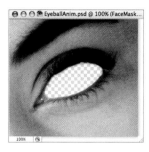

Figure 1.32
Delete the eyeball portion of the image, revealing the transparency behind it.

Make the background visible again, and click on it to activate the layer. Select the transparency of the modified layer (⌘+click/Ctrl+click in the Layers palette and invert the selection) and copy/paste the eyeball section from the background. This will create a new layer with just the eyeball on it. Hide the other layers and start painting around the eyeball to create a large, soft circle (see Figure 1.33). Be sure to clone over areas like the light reflections and highlights on the pupil of the eye and add interesting details, artifacts, and noise back into the eyeball texture. Select All, and chose Edit → Define Pattern to add this new texture to the Pattern library. This will become the pattern that will be applied to the final shape via the layer style.

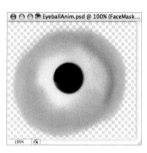

Figure 1.33
Paint out reflections and put details back into the eyeball "texture map."

Create a new layer. With the Elliptical Marquee tool, draw out a circle larger than the eye socket and fill it with white, as shown in Figure 1.34. This will be the shape that the pattern and layer style will be applied to.

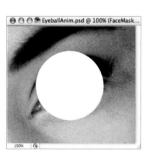 

Figure 1.34
Create a circular filled shape to apply the pattern style to.

Making only the filled-circle layer visible, open the Layer Style editor and add a Bevel And Emboss with a 1/4 Round Contour shape. Use a dark purple for the Shadow Mode, and turn the Highlight Mode down to 0% Opacity. Set the Size to 65 pixels and Soften to 7 pixels. Set the Depth to 150%. Change the Angle to 130° with the Altitude at 30°. This is the basic geometry of the eyeball sphere.

Select Pattern Overlay and the eyeball pattern you just added to the pattern library. The selected pattern will already be the correct size, so leave the scale at 100% (see Figure 1.35).

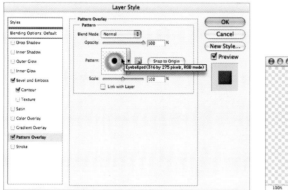
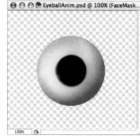

Figure 1.35 Apply an Emboss and the eyeball pattern to the circle shape layer.

Make the background and top face layers visible. Open the Layer Style editor again, and choose the Pattern Overlay option. Drag the pupil of the eyeball into position approximately where the original was.

Create a new layer. Using the Paintbrush tool and a small soft-edged brush, paint the original white highlights on the eyeball. Click the Layer Visibility of the eyeball layer on and off to make sure you're getting all of the original highlights in approximately the correct positions. Apply an Outer Glow layer style to the highlights, change them to a pink "melon" color, and set the Size to 3 pixels (see Figure 1.36). This will give a natural glow around the reflected lights on the surface of the eyeball and help to give it a "wet" look.

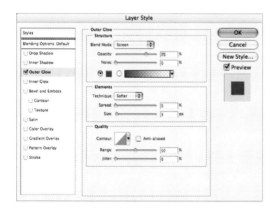

Figure 1.36 Add highlights to a layer above the eyeball to give a wet look to the surface of the eye.

Select the top face layer and apply an Outer Glow layer style. Change it to a pink flesh color, and set the Blend Mode to Multiply. Set the Opacity to 50% and add 6% Noise. Make the size 20 pixels (Figure 1.37). This will help blend the edges of the eye socket tissue into the eyeball and throw some ambient reflection onto the surface of the eye.

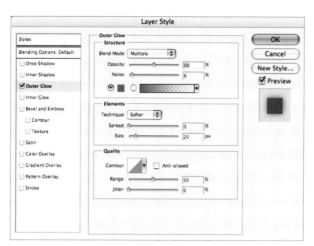

Figure 1.37 Apply an outer glow to the eye socket to help blend the tissue colors with the eyeball.

Jump to ImageReady and duplicate Frame 1. Select Frame 2 and jump back to Photoshop. Open the Layer Style editor on the eyeball layer, and choose the Pattern Overlay option. Drag the pattern over toward the inside (toward the nose), as shown in Figure 1.38. Notice how the highlights remain in place, as they would in nature. Make sure you don't move the eyeball pattern too much, or it will look comical instead of realistic. *(Which might be fun, actually!)*

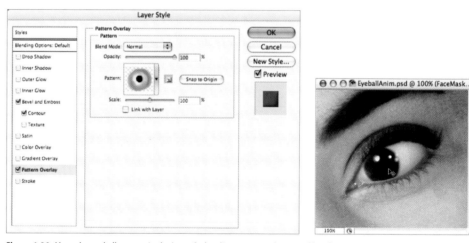

Figure 1.38 Move the eyeball pattern in the Layer Style editor to create the second key frame position in the animation sequence.

Jump to ImageReady and duplicate Frame 2. Select Frame 3 and jump back to Photoshop. Repeat the process in the previous step, moving the eye to the outside position, and return to ImageReady (see Figure 1.39).

Select Frames 1 and 2 in the Animation palette and chose the Tween option. Select only the Effects check box and add three frames (see Figure 1.40). Select the last two frames and repeat, adding five to seven frames. Create new key frames and repeat the process of moving the eyeball pattern around, and make new, creative movements of the eyeball.

Figure 1.39 Repeat the process, moving the eye to the outside position.

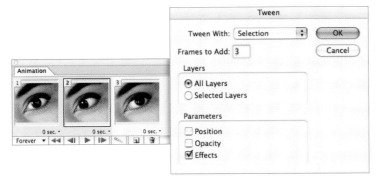

Figure 1.40 Tween between the key frames to create the eyeball movement animation.

Preview the final animation in the default web browser. You can make adjustments in timing before saving or exporting your final QuickTime movie. More frames create longer, smoother animations. Just remember that at 30 fps, the frames must have no delay added to them individually or extra frames will be added when exporting as a QuickTime movie. However, if you want a pause on any frame, the movie will export additional frames to match closely the adjusted timing you set in the frame delay.

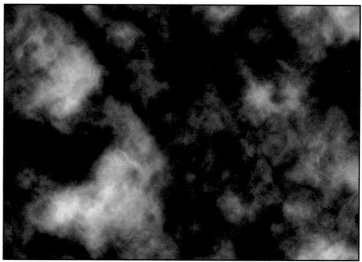

Photoshop Layers and After Effects

At the root of the partnership of After Effects and Photoshop is the ability to transfer Photoshop layers to separate comp layers in After Effects and then edit the original as desired without having to replace or reimport layers. What may be 20 static layers in Photoshop can become 20 moving layers in After Effects.

This chapter briefly explores that union between the two applications so you can design your projects with this workflow in mind. See Chapters 10–12 for more projects utilizing this concept.

2

Chapter Contents
Basic Layer Transfers
Transferring Layers with Style Effects
Displacement Maps: Static Layers in Motion

Basic Layer Transfers

Virtually any Photoshop file with multiple layers can be imported into After Effects with all of the layers separated—but there are a few rules to consider before attempting this process. If you don't properly organize and name your project files and name the layers correctly, you may end up with a real mess!

When you are creating your Photoshop layers, be sure to name them sequentially (1, 2, 3, etc....) or alphabetically (a, b, c, etc....), with Layer 1 or Layer A being the top layer (see Figure 2.1). This will ensure that the layers will remain in the correct order when you import the file into After Effects. I've created some real problems for myself by forgetting to do this, and I've ended up with Background as my top layer of a 20-layer project!

Figure 2.1

Correct naming will ensure that your project's layers will remain in the correct order when transferred.

You can import your Photoshop files into After Effects either as a footage file, which merges all of the layers together (or allows you to select just one layer in the file), or as a composition, which leaves the layers intact (see Figure 2.2). Once the file is imported into your project, you will have a composite layer and a folder that contains all of the individual layers.

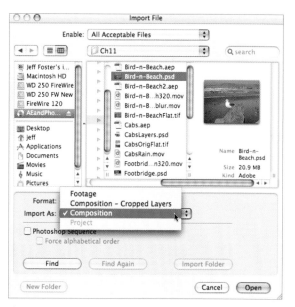
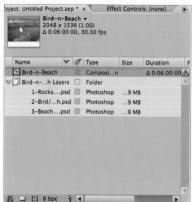

Figure 2.2 Importing the Photoshop file as a composition will keep the layers intact.

To maintain the correct positioning of the layers, drag the entire folder to the Comp view window or the Timeline window (Figure 2.3). If you try to select all of the layers inside the folder and drag them independently, they will center in the Comp view window instead of maintaining their correct positions in relation with one another.

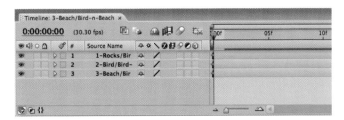

Figure 2.3 Move the imported file folder to maintain proper layer position and hierarchy.

> **Note:** If you are importing a layered Photoshop file as a composition and are *not* going to need the layers scaled down drastically for an extreme zoom, then simply double-click the composition file After Effects creates for you in the Project window. All of your layers will remain intact and in the proper hierarchy.

You can easily edit a file once it's imported into After Effects. Click on any layer in the Project window and select Edit > Edit Original (⌘/Ctrl+E). This will launch Photoshop and open the file for editing.

Once you've made your edits in Photoshop, save the file. Go back to your After Effects project, and select the layer(s) of the edited file and choose File > Reload Footage from the menu (Shift+⌘+L/Shift+Ctrl+L). This will update the entire project with the edited layers, so there's no need to reimport the file or start over again with a new project.

Transferring Layers with Style Effects

After Effects doesn't utilize layer styles the way Photoshop does, so it's important to know how to transfer layers and keep the applied effects in place. In most cases, merely merging the layer with the style effect applied to a new blank layer will do the trick.

Although they are not editable in After Effects, there are only four layer styles that will transfer correctly visually: Drop Shadow, Bevel And Emboss, Color Overlay, and Inner Shadow (Figure 2.4).

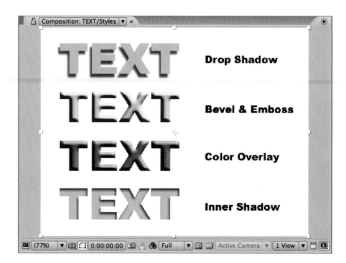

Figure 2.4
When the layers are transferred to After Effects, only four layer style effects appear correctly.

When the Photoshop file is imported into After Effects as a composition, it will give you all of the actual Photoshop layers, plus a composition layer for each layer that has an effect applied to it. It will also give you a composition layer for every layer set you have in your file; however, all of the layers in the layer set composition will not be separately movable (Figure 2.5).

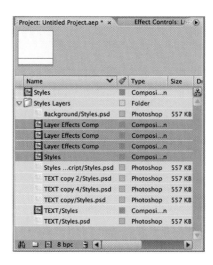

Figure 2.5
Composition layers are created when importing layers and layer sets with style effects applied.

When applying effects that won't transfer—especially when several effects are applied to one layer—you will need to create a new layer and link it with the style layer. Select Merge Layers from the Layers palette menu, and the effects will be rendered and rasterized, as shown in Figure 2.6. In this example, the layer with style effects applied was duplicated to demonstrate how both layers will transfer to After Effects.

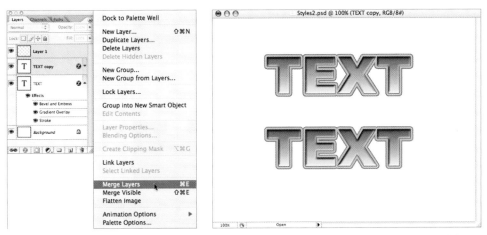

Figure 2.6 Merge styled layers with new blank layers to render the effects in one layer and retain all transparency of the layer's content.

Importing this example file with one rendered layer and one layer with the style effects applied shows how the effects will not transfer correctly unless rendered first (see Figure 2.7).

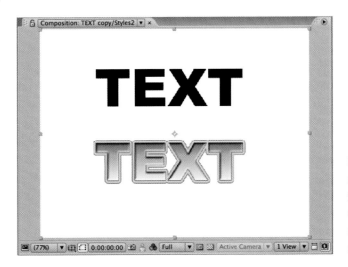

Figure 2.7
After importing the Photoshop file with both a style effect layer (black) and a rendered layer, you can see what the preferred method would be.

However, if you don't render the layers first, you can import the file as footage and merge the layers. This will render all of the style effects on the fly, but it will also flatten the file so no editable layers will remain (see Figure 2.8).

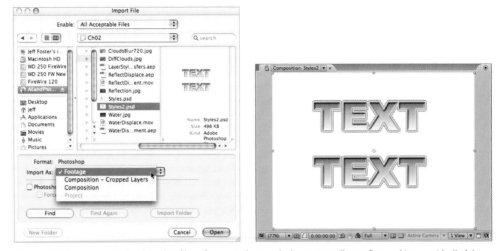

Figure 2.8 When you import the Photoshop file as footage and merge the layers, you will get a flattened image with all of the style effect layers rendered.

Displacement Maps: Static Layers in Motion

One way to animate a static image is to apply a moving displacement map layer to the image layer. Using this technique, you can make still waters ripple, static flags wave, or trees in the background sway in the wind. This requires creating a grayscale displacement map image that will be animated in a loop and applied to the image layer you want to affect.

In this first project study of displacement maps, we will be using the file Water.jpg, found on the DVD (Figure 2.9). Notice that this is a perspective angle photograph—which will be important as we create the displacement map image.

 Note: For comparison and examples, you can view the completed QuickTime sample movies for this chapter, found on the DVD.

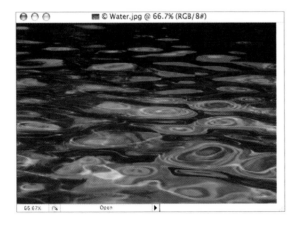

Figure 2.9
The source image that will be put into motion with a displacement map

Creating a Displacement Map

The After Effects Displacement Map Effect plug-in uses varying levels of gray in the map image. Lighter areas of the image will move the image up and to the right, while the darker areas will move portions of the image down and to the left. How much it gets moved is controlled not only by the effect settings in After Effects but also by how much contrast is in the displacement map source image.

To create the displacement map for this project, we'll start with a new image file in Photoshop that is 720 × 720 pixels, Grayscale. Apply the Clouds filter to the image (Filter > Render > Clouds). This will create the contrasting light-to-dark areas in a random pattern.

We will need to tile this image horizontally for use as a moving displacement map. To make a seamless tile, apply the Offset filter (Filter > Other > Offset), and set the Horizontal offset to +350 pixels with the Wrap Around option selected. There will be a sharp vertical division line down the center of the image that needs to be edited out. Using the Clone Stamp tool with a large soft-edged brush, select areas of the image that will most likely cover up the hard edge line and blend them in with the rest of the image (Figure 2.10).

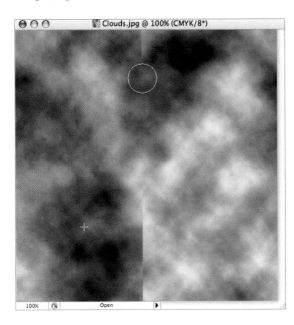

Figure 2.10

After applying the Offset filter to the cloud image, use the Clone Stamp tool to eliminate the hard vertical line down the center.

The more contrast a map image has, the more severe the motion will be. Because you don't want violent movement in the water image you're using, apply a 10-pixel Gaussian Blur to soften the image and take away any sharp contrast.

Note: An alternative method of normalizing an image used for a displacement map would be to adjust the midtone marker in Levels; this also gives you a real-time preview of the amount of contrast in the image. However, this method will not smooth out the edges of transition from the contrasting shapes, as a Gaussian Blur will.

The water image you're applying the displacement map to is a perspective view, so you can control the amount of motion toward the back of the scene (or top of the image window) by adding a Solid Color Fill layer with a soft gradient mask (Figure 2.11). When selecting the color of the Fill layer, choose 50% gray (128 RGB), because this will read 0% as a displacement map color, while white is +100% and black is –100%. To further force the illusion of depth, resize the height of the image to 480 pixels, for a final dimension of 720 × 480 pixels.

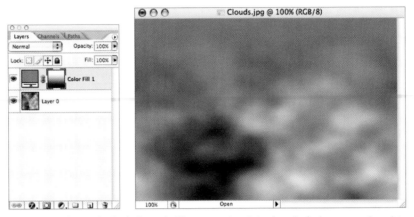

Figure 2.11 Softening the cloud effect and adding a neutral gradation from the farthest perspective point will create a sense of depth in the motion of the final composite.

Applying a Displacement Map

Follow these steps to apply the map to an image:

1. Create a new project in After Effects and make a new composition, selecting the preset, NTSC DV, 720 × 480, and 5 seconds in length.

2. Import the file Water.jpg from the DVD and the Cloud map image you just created (or use the provided map image, CloudsBlur720.jpg on the DVD). Center the Cloud map image in the Comp 1 window by dragging it from the Project window to the Timeline (Figure 2.12).

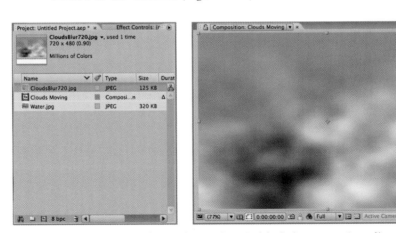

Figure 2.12 Create a new project and import the source image and the displacement map image files.

3. Now that everything is imported into After Effects, we will set the displacement map in motion. Select the CloudsBlur720.jpg layer in the Timeline window, and apply the Offset filter (Effects > Distort > Offset). Make sure the Current Time Indicator in the Timeline window is set to Frame 1, and select the Time-Vary Stopwatch on the Shift Center option in the Effects window. This will allow beginning and end points for the motion of the displacement map image.

4. Move the Current Time Indicator on the Timeline to the last frame position (5 seconds). In the Effects window, drag the horizontal position of the Shift Center option to the right, increasing the movement to at least 1,000 pixels. This is the distance the image will move (or offset) while the tile wraps around and appears to be a continuous loop (Figure 2.13).

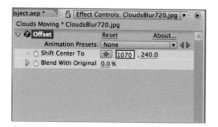

Figure 2.13

Adjusting the number of pixels the displacement map will move will speed up or slow down the animation.

You can choose a RAM Preview to test the speed at which your loop is moving. To slow it down, simply adjust the amount of motion set at the last frame in the Effects window. To speed it up, increase the number of pixels it will move.

5. Once you are satisfied with the speed of your animation, create a pre-composition by selecting Layer > Pre-compose, with the options Move All Attributes Into The New Composition and Open New Composition selected (Figure 2.14). This will treat the displacement map as a continuous loop animation in one layer of Comp 1.

Figure 2.14

Create a pre-comp for the displacement map animation loop.

6. Hide the Pre-comp layer in the Timeline by clicking the small eye icon. The displacement map does not need to be visible for the effect to work.

7. With the Comp 1 project window open, center the Water.jpg image in the composition window. Adjust the size of the image just slightly larger than the live area of the project window frame (Figure 2.15). This will assure that enough of the image around the edges will be pulled in by the movement of the displacement map effect.

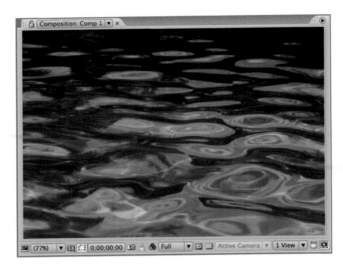

Figure 2.15

Adjust the image layer to allow source material to be pulled and pushed out of the frame by the displacement map.

8. Apply the displacement map effect to the Water image layer by selecting Effects > Distort > Displacement Map. Select the source displacement map image from the selector, choosing the pre-comp layer name (Figure 2.16). Use Luminance for both the Horizontal and Vertical displacements, and set the maximum pixel movement to 15 for both. Increase or decrease these numbers to control the amount of movement you want to have in your animation.

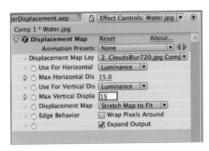

Figure 2.16

Apply the displacement map pre-comp layer to the image layer, and adjust for the amount of displacement the map source image will affect. Be sure to select Stretch To Fit instead of Center Map.

Run a RAM Preview to test the animation of the displacement map effect and adjust the speed and pixel displacement as necessary (Figure 2.17). Notice how the neutral gray toward the top of the image has less of the effect applied, aiding the illusion of depth in the scene.

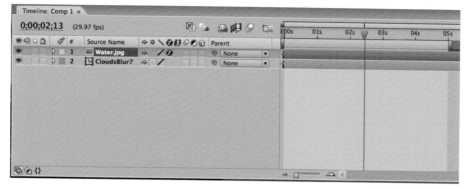

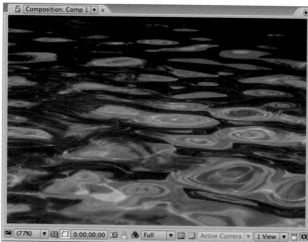

Figure 2.17

A RAM Preview will allow you to test the amount of displacement and the speed of the motion effect.

Masking and Adjusting a Displacement Map

Using different techniques in creating your displacement map for varying needs, you must keep in mind the scale of the source image and how much displacement you want to apply to generate motion.

In the image Reflect.jpg found on the DVD, we just want to put a slight motion in the water without affecting the shoreline (Figure 2.18). We need a denser displacement map for this project because we don't want to create a lot of violent motion in the water.

Starting with a new file, 720 × 480 pixels, Grayscale, apply the Difference Clouds filter (Filter > Render > Difference Clouds). Repeat the filter application at least a dozen times (⌘/Ctrl+F) until you have a detailed swirl pattern with a lot of contrast (Figure 2.19). Next, add a new layer and apply the Clouds filter to it. Adjust the opacity of the layer to 50%, and the resulting image is softened but the details still show through the surface (Figure 2.20).

Figure 2.18 This image will require a displacement map with more density for a smaller scale water surface texture, plus a mask to keep from affecting the shoreline or the trees in the background.

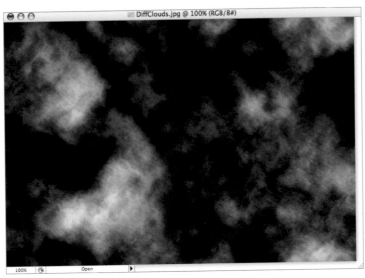

Figure 2.19 Reapplying the Difference Clouds filter over itself several times creates an intricate swirl pattern.

Using the new displacement map you just created and the Reflect.jpg image from the DVD, create a new project in After Effects and follow the steps in the previous project for setting up and importing. Similarly to the previous displacement map project, follow the steps to create an animated pre-composition of the displacement map layer. Use the same Offset settings for the speed of the animation loop.

Apply the displacement map effect to the reflection image, selecting the pre-composition layer as the displacement source, and use Luminance for both Horizontal and Vertical displacement. For this project, leave the default settings for pixel movement, as we need a more subtle effect applied to the image, and the scale is much lower.

Figure 2.20 A 50% Cloud layer added above the swirl pattern softens it without losing detail.

We now need to mask the upper portion of the displacement map so the effect is applied only to the water in the image. Open the displacement map composition in the Composition window. Add a solid color layer (Layer > New > Solid), and set the color to 50% gray (128 R, 128 G, 128 B). To quickly apply an adjustable mask, we'll use a fixed Linear Wipe transition (Effect > Transitions > Linear Wipe). Set the Wipe Angle to 0° and the Transition Completion to 30%. This will place the edge of the effect close to the tree line, but adding a Feather of 75 pixels will make a smooth transition into the water and scale back the amount of movement in the water near the shoreline (Figure 2.21).

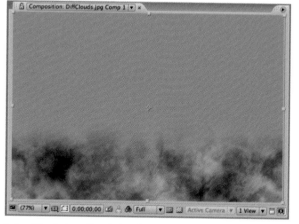

Figure 2.21 Adding a solid layer and applying a static transitional wipe will mask the effect of the displacement map to the image.

Run a RAM Preview to test the animation of the displacement map effect and adjust the speed and pixel displacement as necessary.

3-D Layers from Photoshop Layers

3

After Effects has the ability to turn any layer into a 3-D layer, allowing you to spin and move the layers, cameras, and lights—just like a 3-D application. After Effects has many detailed camera and light controls to create realistic 3-D motion. Even though you can't import primitive shapes or extrusions, you can do many things to fool the eye with photographic shapes cut out from Photoshop layers and rendered in a 3-D scene in After Effects.

Chapter Contents

Basic 3-D Layers in Motion
Animation with a Camera in Motion
Duplicating Layers in Motion

Basic 3-D Layers in Motion

Setting up a basic 3-D animation in After Effects requires having some basic knowledge of multiple views, moving layers in three-dimensional space, and using the X-, Y-, and Z-axes. It's really much easier than it sounds, and this project will introduce you to some of those basic controls. You may want to follow along with the completed After Effects file, 3-DText.aep, on the DVD.

1. Start a new project file in After Effects and import two single-layer Photoshop files, FilmReel.psd and MovieText.psd, from the companion DVD (look in the 3-D_MovieText subfolder of the Chapter 3 folder). Import them as Composite files to preserve the transparent layers, or select the individual layers instead of Merged Layers if importing as Footage.

2. Create a new composition, 640 × 480 NTSC (6 seconds in length), drag the film reel composition file from the Project window onto the Comp 1 window, and resize the layer to 70% (Figure 3.1).

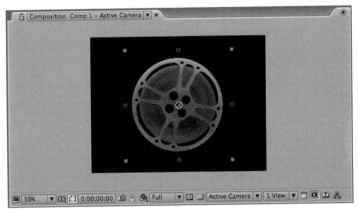

Figure 3.1 Import and place the film reel composition, and resize the layer.

3. Select the film reel layer, right-click/Ctrl+click it in the Comp 1 window, and select 3-D Layer from the contextual menu. This will convert the layer to a 3-D layer, using the transparent space of the Photoshop layer as the defining edges in 3-D. (You can, instead, click the 3-D Layer box on the Timeline to convert layers.) This layer can now be moved in all three directions, as shown with the X-, Y-, and Z-axis arrows in the middle of the layer (Figure 3.2).

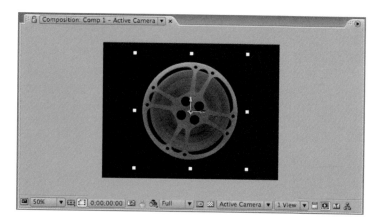

Figure 3.2
Converting the layer into a 3-D layer will allow it to be moved along the X-, Y-, and Z-axes.

4. To make the third dimension more predominant, we'll add the ability for this layer to cast shadows when we shine a light on it. Drop down the settings for the layer in the Timeline window, and open Material Options. Turn on the Casts Shadows option.

5. Duplicate the layer in the Timeline window (⌘/Ctrl+D), select both layers, and press the A key to reveal the Anchor Point settings on both layers.

6. Right-click/Ctrl+click the Comp 1 window tab to bring up the contextual menu, and select Switch 3-D View > Left.

7. On the top layer, set the Z-axis Anchor Point to –20. On the bottom layer, set the Z-axis Anchor Point to +20. This will separate the two layers at the center point, creating a simulated film reel (Figure 3.3).

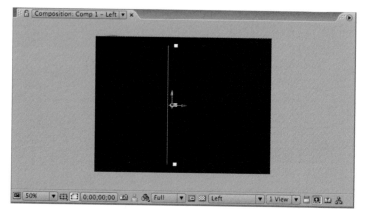

Figure 3.3 Offset the anchor points at the center core to simulate two halves of a film reel.

Parenting the Layers and Adding Text

Now we will connect the two halves of the film reel so they will move in sync with each other.

1. Select the top layer and the Parent pull-down menu in the Timeline. Select the second layer as its parent—the top layer will now copy anything that is applied to the bottom layer. They will now rotate around the center of their perspective anchor points, as if they were actually connected.

2. Press the R key to reveal the Rotate settings for the bottom layer, and click the Y-Rotation Stopwatch to set the first marker at the beginning of the Timeline.

3. Move the Indicator down to the 6-second mark on the Timeline. Set the Y-axis rotation to 3 × +0.0°—this will make the film reel spin three complete revolutions in 6 seconds (Figure 3.4).

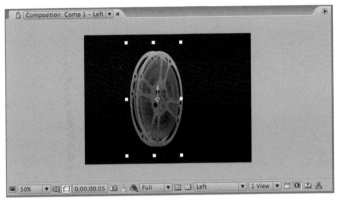

Figure 3.4 With the film reels connected through parenting, they will move together on their anchor points and appear as one object when rotated.

4. Add the movie text layer to the Comp 1 window and scale it down to 85%, centered in the window. Right-click/Ctrl+click it in the Comp 1 window, and select 3-D Layer from the contextual menu.

5. Right-click/Ctrl+click the Comp 1 window tab to bring up the contextual menu, and select Switch 3-D View > Left. Drop down the settings for the layer, and open the Material Options. Turn on the Casts Shadows option.

6. Move the Indicator in the Timeline down to the point where you see the movie reel at a perfect 90° angle. You will see how the movie reel slices right through the text layer. Select the movie text layer, and drag the Z-axis arrow to the right until the layer is just out of reach of the movie reel (Figure 3.5).

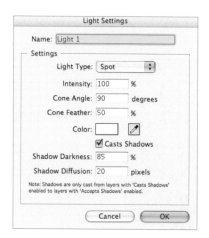

Figure 3.5

Make the movie text layer a 3-D layer and move it out of the rotating motion path of the film reel.

7. Up to this point, there isn't any real light source shining on the scene, so no shadows are visible yet. Create a spotlight for the scene by selecting Layer > New > Light. When the Light Settings dialog pops up, choose Spot as the Light Type and select the Casts Shadows check box. Adjust the Shadow Darkness to 85% and the Shadow Diffusion to 20 pixels (Figure 3.6).

Figure 3.6

Create a spotlight for the scene that will cast shadows and add depth and realism.

Note: For more natural-looking light, add a little yellow or orange tint to the light source. It will warm up your scene as if lit by incandescent light—or even natural sunlight. If you leave it white, your scene will retain a bluish cast and appear cold.

Positioning Lights and Layers

From this point, we will be working in several views on our scene to help us position our lights and layers: the main Active Camera view and Top, Front, and Left side views. Select the Comp View Layout and choose 2 Views. Right-click/Ctrl+click on each window and select the view you want to preview. This will create two comp windows on your screen, so if you're working on a smaller monitor, things might get a bit crowded. Just resize the windows to see the entire comp area and stack them up if necessary. You should leave one of them in the Active Camera view all the time, because you will need to see the effects from all of your movements. At times you will need to adjust the scale of the preview window to be able to see some of the objects that move outside the view window, such as lights, cameras, and layers that fly in and out.

1. Open a side view window, right-click/Ctrl+click the Comp 1 window tab to bring up the contextual menu, and select Switch 3-D View > Left. You can also use the view tab on the bottom right side of the Comp window to change views.

2. Drag the light up to the right of the object layers, and then drag the Point Of Interest handle down to the center of the movie reel. Open the Front view window, and drag the X-axis arrow to pull the light slightly off-center and to the right. This will provide a shadow that will be down and to the left of the movie text layer as it rests in front of the film reel (Figure 3.7). You may want to zoom out in the Comp window so you can see where you are moving the light beyond the boundaries of the frame.

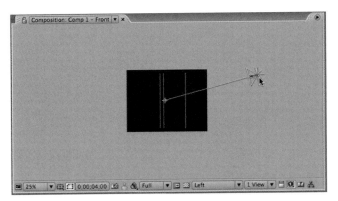

Figure 3.7

Move the light into position to create a shadow that is cast on the lower-left side of the film reel.

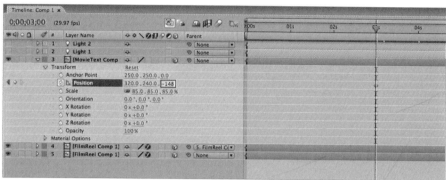

Figure 3.8 Set the final rest position of the movie text layer at the 3-second mark.

3. Once the light is set into position, hide the layer so the redraw time won't slow down with each move you make of the Timeline Indicator. Move the Indicator down to the 3-second mark, select the movie text layer in the Timeline, and click the Position Stopwatch. This will set the final position of the movie text fly-in animation (Figure 3.8).

4. Move the Indicator to the first frame on the Timeline, and set the Z-axis of the movie text layer to −890. This makes the layer disappear from the Active Camera window. When you view the Left side window, you will see it's just out of camera range (Figure 3.9). This gives the appearance that the text will fly in from behind the camera and pull into the spotlight before resting in front of the film reel.

5. To enhance the realism in this effect, we will add motion blur to the movie text layer as it first enters the frame and pulls into the spotlight. At Frame 1 on the Timeline, apply the Directional Blur filter to the movie text layer, Effect > Blur and Sharpen > Directional Blur. Adjust the Blur Length to 10 pixels and leave the default angle at 0° (Figure 3.10).

6. Set the Effects Stopwatch on the Timeline, and move the Indicator down to the 3-second mark. Change the Blur Length to 0, because the movie text layer is no longer in motion at this point.

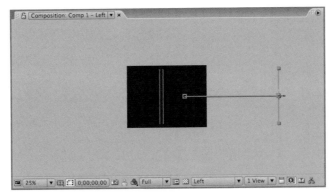

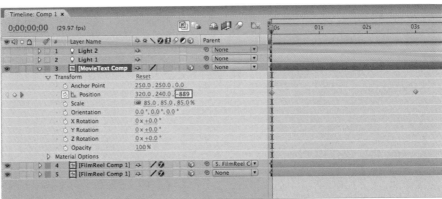

Figure 3.9 Move the movie text layer along the Z-axis to pull it out of the frame so it will appear to fly in from behind the camera.

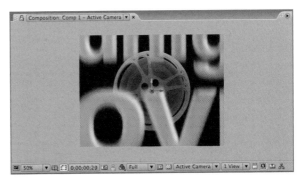

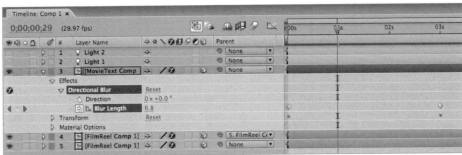

Figure 3.10 Adding motion blur to the movie text will enhance the fly-in motion.

Use a RAM Preview to check that all of the motion is working properly. Although the light and shadows are in the right place at this point, the scene seems a bit muddy—so we'll add some warm ambient light to brighten up the highlights and shadows. Select Layer > Light, and choose an Ambient light, set at 35% Intensity without casting shadows. To help adjust the color to a darker orange, make sure the shadows are warmed up a bit as well (Figure 3.11). Notice the big difference a small amount of ambient light can have on the entire animation! You can watch the example QuickTime movie 3DFilmText-320.mov found on the DVD for reference.

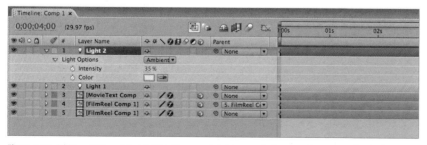

Figure 3.11 Adding a little ambient light to the scene brightens up the layers and warms up the shadows.

Animation with a Camera in Motion

Now that you've experienced working with rotating and moving 3-D layers on an axis, positioning lights, and changing work views, it's time to explore working with cameras. Instead of just moving the 3-D layers, you can move the camera to zoom in on or fly by a scene with static layers. When you combine this effect with layers in motion, you have a more exciting animation.

We are going to build this scene at a 90° angle—where the ground will actually be a distant back wall and the camera will move toward it horizontally, as will the "falling" leaves.

1. Create a new project file in After Effects. Import a few files (Branch.psd, Leaf1.psd, Leaf2.psd, and Leaf3.psd) from the 3-D_Leaves subfolder in the Chapter 3 folder on the DVD. Import them as composite files to retain the layer transparency. Import the file Grass.jpg as a footage file because it is flat and does not have a transparent layer.

2. Create a new composition, 640 × 480 NTSC—6 seconds in length. Drag the grass file from the Project window onto the Comp 1 window, and scale it to 85%.

Note: You can also open the After Effects project file (3D_Leaves.aep) and follow along with this tutorial; the finished QuickTime movie is also available on the DVD.

3. Right-click/Ctrl+click the image in the Comp 1 window and select 3D Layer. Set the Z-axis position to 1800 (Figure 3.12). This will place the grass layer far enough from the window view to appear just slightly larger than the frame window.

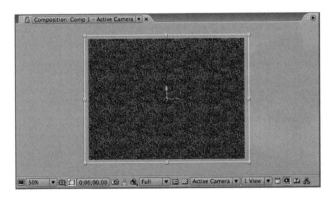

Figure 3.12
Set the grass background away from the frame view in Frame 1 as the zoom-out position.

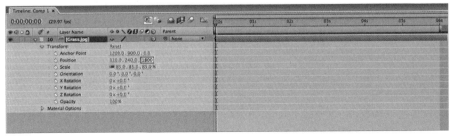

Setting Up a Camera

Let's create a camera to move:

1. Choose Layer > New > Camera. At this point, many options are available to customize your camera; but for this project, just select the 50mm Preset option and click OK (Figure 3.13).

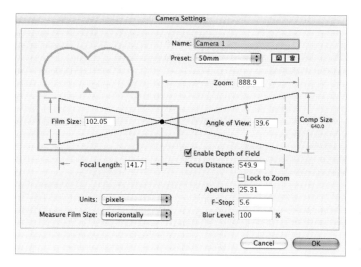

Figure 3.13

Create a simple camera with a 50mm lens that can be moved through the scene.

This places the camera on the Timeline as a layer—so all of the same settings and controls for position, rotation, options, and more are controlled in time—just like any other layer.

2. Open the Left side view; you will see the triangle of the camera's field of view (Angle Of View). To make sure you keep everything aligned properly, show rulers (⌘/Ctrl+R) and drag down a guideline to the center of the motion path. Drag the Point Of Interest circle from the camera down to the center of the grass layer (Figure 3.14).

3. Open the Timeline settings for the camera layer, and click the Position Stopwatch at Frame 1. This sets the current position of the camera at the beginning of the animation.

4. Move the indicator to the 5-second mark, set the Z-axis on the camera to 900, and select the Easy Ease In Keyframe Assistant (Figure 3.15). This should place the camera FOV triangle in the Left side view right up next to the grass layer at the end of its motion path. The new Active Camera view should show the grass zoomed in close.

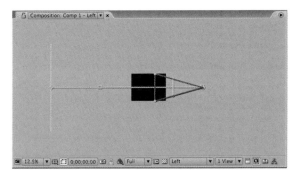

Figure 3.14 The camera works like any other layer that can be moved in the Timeline.

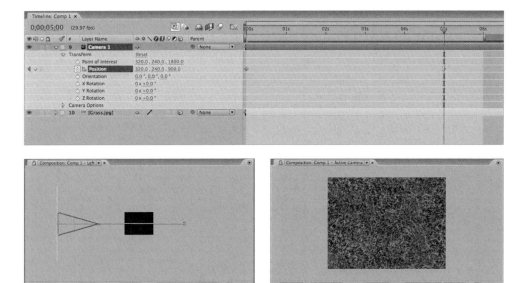

Figure 3.15 The motion of the camera is a simple straight line that will travel "through" the tree branches and toward the ground.

Preparing the Layers

We have a lot of work to do, scaling and positioning layers. The branches will be placed in 3-D space in our scene, and the leaves need to be animated to "fall" to the ground as the camera moves in.

1. Drag the branch composition file to the Comp 1 window and convert it to a 3-D layer, as we did to the grass layer. Because this layer will remain static as the camera passes by, just place it into position by setting the Z-axis to –500

(Figure 3.16). Check the Left side view to see the placement in reference to the camera—which should be so close that it shows only the edges of a few leaves.

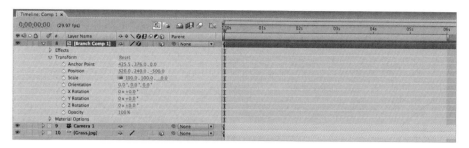

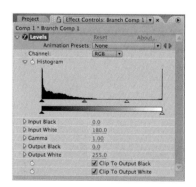

53
■
ANIMATION WITH A CAMERA IN MOTION

Figure 3.16
Place the static branch layer close to the camera so it will brush by in the animation.

2. The branch layer is a bit dark in contrast to the lush green grass, so we'll adjust the levels on the layer. Select Effect > Color Correction > Levels, and set the Input White setting to 180.0 (Figure 3.17). When we add the lights later in this project, the leaves will appear more natural in the scene.

3. Duplicate the branch layer and position the duplicate below the first branch layer. Open the Transform settings for Branch Layer 2, and set the Z Rotation to +180.0° and the Position to 223.0, 178.6, –120.0. Check the distance from the first layer and the camera in the Left side view.

4. We want this layer to be a little darker than the first branch layer, because the light will be shining on the lower branches more in this project. Set the Input White to 220.0 (Figure 3.18). This will also add more depth to the view from the camera as it passes by.

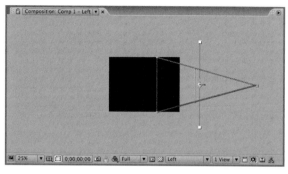 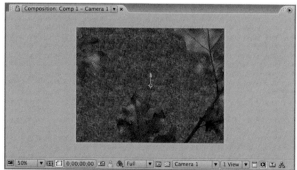

Figure 3.17 Adjust the levels of the branch layer to enhance the leaf colors.

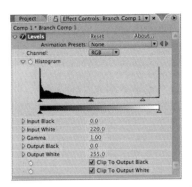
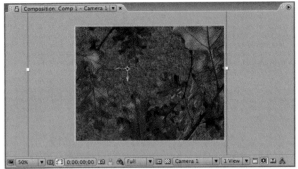

Figure 3.18 Adjust the levels of Branch Layer 2 slightly darker than the first to add depth to the camera view.

5. Duplicate Branch Layer 2, and reposition it lower in relation to the other branch layers: Z Rotation +345.0°; Position 324.6, 254.1, 290.0. This will be our "bottom" branch on the tree as the camera passes through, and it will create another layer of depth. Notice how the layers are stacked in the Left side view (Figure 3.19). Select the Levels settings and adjust the Input White level to the default 255.0.

Note: Don't worry about where the leaf layer is. As a 3-D layer, it doesn't matter where it will be placed in the Timeline hierarchy, and it will be animated in the Z-axis as well.

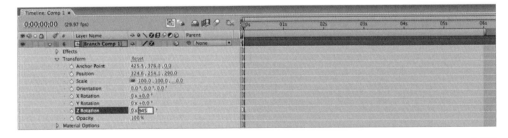

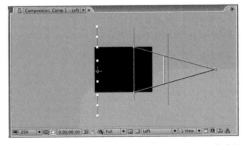
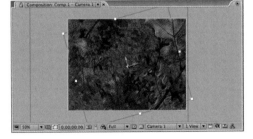

Figure 3.19 Reposition the third branch layer to give added depth to the tree layers.

Scrub the Timeline Indicator to preview the camera's motion path (Figure 3.20). You will notice that the camera appears to be heading straight for the ground through the tree branches. There is no other scaling or zooming in this effect—only natural camera motion.

Figure 3.20
Preview the camera's motion path by "scrubbing" the Current Time Indicator back and forth on the Timeline.

6. Drag the Leaf 1 composition to the Comp 1 window, convert it to a 3-D layer, and set the scale to 40%. Open the Material Options settings on the Timeline and turn on the Casts Shadows option.

7. Move the Indicator to the 5-second mark on the Timeline, and set the position of the Z-axis to 1790.0 (Figure 3.21). This places the leaf just 10 pixels above the grass layer in its resting position, and it will appear more natural when the lights are added and a slight shadow is cast on the grass layer beneath it. This leaf will be the first one to hit the ground, so subsequent leaves will land about 10 pixels higher on each occurrence so that they overlap slightly.

8. Rotate and drag the layer off-center and to the lower left so there will be room for the other leaves to fall into the frame. You can use the Move and Rotation tools or enter these numeric settings: Z Rotation −80.0°; Position 227.9, 306.1, 1790.0.

Figure 3.21
Position the leaf just above the grass layer in its resting position as the first leaf to hit the ground in the animation.

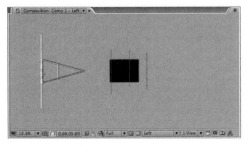

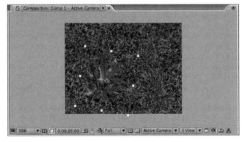

Repeat this procedure with the remaining two leaf layers, converting them to 3-D layers and repositioning them at the 5-second mark (Figure 3.22). Open the Material Options settings on the Timeline and turn on the Casts Shadows option. Check Table 3.1 for the position and rotation settings of these layers, or use the Move tool to position them manually to your liking. The most important setting to watch is the Z-axis position so the layers don't intersect with one another or get hidden behind another layer.

▷ **Table 3.1** Leaf Layer Resting Position at 05;00

Transform	Leaf Layer 2	Leaf Layer 3
Position	466.5, 103.4, 1780.0	359.2, 232.2, 1770.0
Z Rotation	0.0°	+15.0°

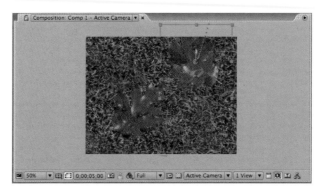

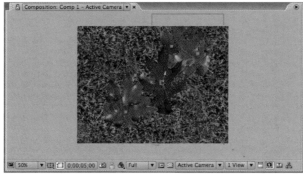

Figure 3.22
Position the second and third leaf layers just above the first so they appear to overlap.

Animating the Layers

Now that we've determined the resting positions of the leaf layers, let's put them into motion! I've created some simple animations of the leaves falling to the ground slightly ahead of the camera's motion path and will list all of the settings in tables for each leaf. Take note that even though we've created the resting positions for the leaf layers, they will all end their motion path at different intervals, so make sure to follow the key frames as indicated in the tables.

The Rotation Tool: The "Axis of Evil"?

As handy as the Rotation tool is, you must take care in its use, because it is often unwieldy and can spin your camera or object around in ungodly directions—right in the middle of your motion path! Make a slight movement too far in one direction and you've inadvertently added a complete revolution or overcorrected in the opposite direction. This happens the most with lights and cameras—where you may not discover the error until you do a RAM Preview of your animation. I have opted for the numeric input right on the Timeline, or you can use the drag method on the axis number on the Timeline. This gives you precise control and instant feedback in the Comp view windows—and, I hope, not spinning in all directions!

The first step to applying these settings for the animation paths is to start with the last frame of each layer's motion path (the leaf's resting position on the Timeline) and click the layer's Position and Rotation Stopwatches. Also, look for the appropriate Keyframe Assistants for Ease In settings. A blank cell in a table denotes no key frame marker for that setting.

We'll start with Leaf Layer 1 settings (Figure 3.23/Table 3.2). Notice the finished motion path that is created. Scrub the Timeline Indicator to preview the motion the leaf makes to the ground.

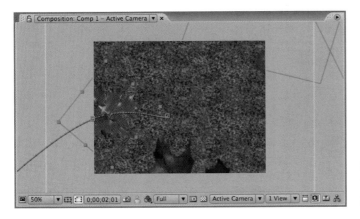

Figure 3.23
The motion path for Leaf Layer 1

▷ **Table 3.2** Leaf Layer 1 Keys

Transform	00;16	01;26	03;13
Position	−104.7, 561.8, 100.0	−1.5, 280.0, 877.0	227.9, 306.1, 1790.0
Z Rotation	−19.0°		−80.0°
Keyframe Assistant			Easy Ease In

The animation settings for Leaf Layer 2 (Figure 3.24/Table 3.3) and Layer 3 (Figure 3.25/Table 3.4) follow consecutively.

Figure 3.24
The motion path for
Leaf Layer 2

▶ **Table 3.3** Leaf Layer 2 Keys

Transform	00;25	01;16	02;11	03;00	03;23	04;03
Position	779.5, −158.3, 266.3	543.0, 10.8, 200.0		436.3, 23.8, 1102.9		466.5, 103.4, 1780.0
X Rotation			−11.0°		+12.0°	+0.0°
Y Rotation				+18.0°	−9.0°	+0.0°
Z Rotation		+26.0°				+0.0°
Keyframe Assistant						Easy Ease In

Figure 3.25
The motion path for Leaf
Layer 3

▶ **Table 3.4** Leaf Layer 3 Keys

Transform	00;00	02;00	03;03	04;08	04;23	05;00
Position	593.2, 342.3, 100.0	544.8, 298.7, 0.0		369.0, 294.2, 1306.1		359.2, 232.2, 1770.0
X Rotation		−16.0°	−16.0°	+4.0°		+0.0°
Y Rotation		−10.0°	+17.3°	−6.8°	−2.0°	+0.0°
Z Rotation		−18.0°	−18.0°		+10.0°	+15.0°
Keyframe Assistant						Easy Ease In

Now that the animations have been created, use a RAM Preview or scrub the Indicator in the Timeline to verify that all of the settings are correct.

Adding Lights

We'll add lights to the scene, which will add depth and dimension to the animation.

1. First add a spotlight (Layer > New > Light) and choose Spot Light, 100% Intensity, and a warm yellow light color.

2. Open the Left side view and drag the light up and to the right of the camera's position at Frame 1. Drag the Point Of Interest circle to the center of the grass layer, at the same point as the camera's Point Of Interest (Figure 3.26).

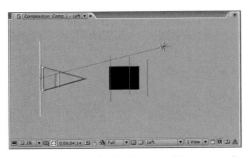

Figure 3.26 The spotlight adds shadows and dimension to the scene.

3. Move the Indicator to the 5-second mark, and open the Light 1 layer Options settings in the Timeline. Click the Shadow Stopwatches, and set the options as follows:

- At 02;00, Shadow Darkness 0%
- At 02;19, Shadow Darkness 35%
- At 05;00, Shadow Darkness 70% and Shadow Diffusion 10.0 pixels

After applying the settings, scrub the Indicator to see how the shadows increase as the leaves near the ground.

4. You'll most likely notice that the scene has a lot of contrast between the shadows and the lit areas, which has actually made the animation look a bit muddy. Select Layer > New > Light, and choose Ambient Light at 35% Intensity and a yellow-orange color (Figure 3.27). Adding a warm ambient light to the scene will soften the shadows and brighten the colors of the leaves—especially in the foreground at the beginning of the animation.

Figure 3.27 Adding a warm ambient light will brighten the animation and soften the shadows.

Duplicating Layers in Motion

Adding motion to more of the objects in the animation, as well as moving the camera and light source, can liven up a 3-D scene. By duplicating some layers in motion and redistributing them along the Timeline, you can create a complex animation in little time.

This project uses a camera on a single motion path through a scene with static and moving 3-D layers and a spotlight moving in an arc from left to right. You can open the file 3-DMoney.aep from the 3-D_Money subfolder on the DVD to follow along with this project to familiarize yourself with the process. Again, I've provided a sample of the final QuickTime movie.

Create a new project file in After Effects, and import the single-layer Photoshop file, BillsBackground.psd, from the Chapter 3 folder on the DVD. Create a new composition, 640 × 480 NTSC—6 seconds in length. Import the two multilayered Photoshop files, CoinStacks.psd and Bills.psd, as composition—cropped layers. This will trim the unwanted transparent space around the layer objects so they can be properly scaled and placed.

Drag the background file onto the Comp 1 window, and convert it to a 3-D layer. Open the Left side view, and drag the Z-axis arrow to the left about 1000 pixels from the center. Alternatively, you can open the background layer setting on the Timeline and enter 1000 in the Z-axis position (Figure 3.28).

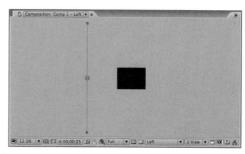

Figure 3.28 Position the stacked bills image as a 3-D layer in the background.

Duplicate the background layer and position it upward in the Y-axis position, next to the original layer. Apply the Position settings, –1928 in the Y-axis and 1008 in the Z-axis in the Timeline (Figure 3.29). This will place the duplicated layer just slightly behind the original so the seam won't show in the final rendering.

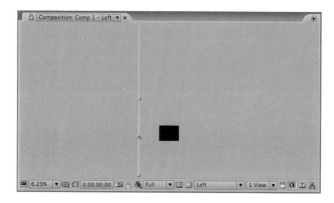

Figure 3.29

To create one long background to move the camera along, duplicate the background layer and position it on top of the original.

Create a new camera layer, with the 50mm preset. From the Left side view window, reposition the camera and its Point Of Interest down toward the background layer, to get an idea of the starting angle for the animation (Figure 3.30). The exact location is not critical at this point, because we'll be animating the camera later in this chapter.

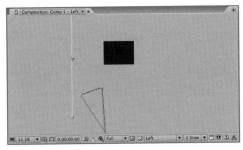
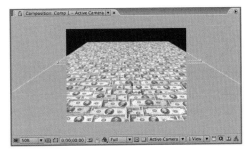

Figure 3.30 Angle the camera down at the background layer by dragging the Point Of Interest handle.

Drag the four stacked coin layers from the Project window to the Comp 1 window, from inside the CoinStacks folder in the Project window. While they are all still selected, convert them to 3-D layers and select the Casts Shadows Materials option. Then rotate all four selected layers 90° in the X-axis by opening up the Rotation settings on the Timeline.

Set the scale of the four layers to 60%. Deselect and hide the penny, nickel, and dime layers. Then enter the following Transform settings for the stacked quarters layer position at Frame 1 (Figure 3.31):

- Position 91.0, 586.2, 906.0
- Scale 60.0%
- X Rotation +90.0°

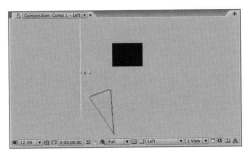
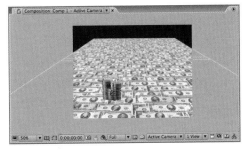

Figure 3.31 Position the stacked coin layers against the background layer.

Position the remaining three stacked coin layers to the settings shown in Table 3.5. This will set the first location of these layers before we duplicate and relocate them in the scene.

▶ **Table 3.5** Settings for the Stacked Dimes, Nickels, and Pennies Layers

Transform	Dimes	Nickels	Pennies
Position	428.0, 708.7, 923.1	536.0, 416.3, 909.6	172.0, 388.5, 896.1
Scale	60.0%	60.0%	60.0%
X Rotation	+90.0°	+90.0°	+90.0°

Now that you have the initial stacked coin layers in place, you can duplicate them and reposition them around the background. Be sure to space them out so they aren't too close together, and leave plenty of room for the other elements to pass through in animation (Figure 3.32). All of your movements can be done in either the Left side view window or the X- and Y-axis settings of each layer on the Timeline. Be sure not to change the Z-axis settings, or your coin stacks may be cut off at the bottom or appear to float in the air above.

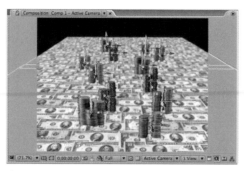 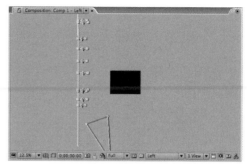

Figure 3.32 Duplicate and reposition the coin layers, distributed around the background.

Putting the Camera in Motion

We'll animate the camera by creating a motion path for it. This will determine the speed of the animation as well as the timing for the remaining motion elements. Because we've added the stacked coins and placed them about the background, we can determine the path down the middle for the camera.

I've created this motion path to emulate physical camera motion. The camera's motion path is smooth, as if it is on a dolly track, but then it swoops down and back up again at the end as if on a crane (Figure 3.33). Follow the keyframe settings in Table 3.6 to re-create this motion track. Scrub the Indicator on the Timeline to preview the camera motion path.

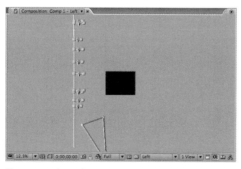 

Figure 3.33 Create the camera's motion path through the scene.

Table 3.6 Camera 1 Motion Path Keys

Transform	00;00	01;15	03;00	04;15	05;00	05;26
Point Of Interest	272.0, 288.0, 848.0	272.0, −712.0, 896.0	272.0, −1864.0, 888.0			272.0, −2416.0, 1048.0
Position	272.0, 1856.0, 311.1	272.0, 984.0, 815.1	272.0, 16.0, 863.1	272.0, −1288.0, 871.1	272.0, −1688.0, 575.1	272.0, −2096.0, 575.1
Keyframe Assistant						Easy Ease In

We'll add the bills in and animate them, and then we'll duplicate and reposition as we did with the static coin layers. Select and drag all three bill layers from the Project window to the Comp 1 window. Convert them to 3-D layers and select the Casts Shadows Material option. Apply the motion path settings for each bill as outlined in Tables 3.7, 3.8, and 3.9. Note the placement of the bill animations in the Left side view and how they land in between the gaps of the stacked coins (Figure 3.34).

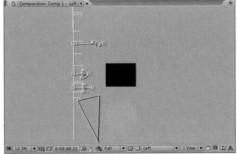

Figure 3.34 Animate the bill layers to land in between the stacks of coins.

Table 3.7 Ten Dollar Bill Motion Path

Transform	00;00	01;00	01;08
Position	−504.0, 507.4, 596.0	484.0, 507.4, 998.0	540.0, 507.4, 998.0
X Rotation	+15.0°	+0.0°	
Y Rotation	−10.0°	+0.0°	
Keyframe Assistant		Easy Ease In	

Table 3.8 Twenty Dollar Bill Motion Path

Transform	00;00	00;15	01;00	01;09
Position	680.3, 214.9, 998.2	287.2, 215.1, 801.6	625.2, 215.1, 998.0	687.2, 215.1, 998.0
X Rotation	+0.0°	+15.0°	+0.0°	
Y Rotation	+0.0°	−6.0°	+0.0°	
Keyframe Assistant		Easy Ease		

▶ **Table 3.9** Five Dollar Bill Motion Path

Transform	00;00	01;22	01;24	02;00
Position	78.0, −409.6, 350.0	284.0, −409.6, 949.0		284.0, −409.6, 998.0
X Rotation	+0.0°	8 x +0.0°	6 x +17.0°	+0.0°

Duplicate the animated bill layers and redistribute them along the Timeline, filling in the gaps between the stacked coin layers. Scrub the Indicator to test the timing of the animations to see that there isn't any interference with subsequent animations (Figure 3.35).

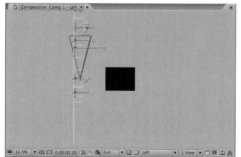

Figure 3.35 Duplicate and reposition the animated bill layers, distributed along the Timeline and in between the stacks of coins.

Adding Lights

Once the animations are positioned and the timing is satisfactory, it's time to shed some light on this animation. We'll need a spotlight to cast shadows and an ambient light to warm and brighten up the scene.

Create a new spotlight layer, with 100% Intensity and a warm yellow light. Select the Casts Shadows check box, and set the Shadow Darkness to 85% and the Shadow Diffusion at 20 pixels. Open the Left side view and move the light over the back tip of the camera, and then drag the Point Of Interest handle down to the middle of the background layer (Figure 3.36). I've set the light's Point Of Interest to 320.0, 208.0, 1801.0 and the Position to 346.7, −418.7, −846.2.

Open the Front view window and move the spotlight over to the left side of the scene, so the light will cast shadows off to the right in the Active Camera window. To set the spotlight in motion, click the Position Stopwatch in the Timeline and move the

Indicator down toward the end of the animation. Move the spotlight to the right side, and pull the adjustment handles in the Left side view window to create an arc in the spotlight motion path (Figure 3.37).

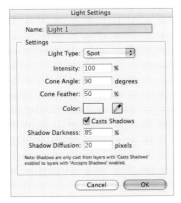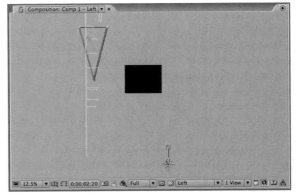

Figure 3.36 Create a warm spotlight and position it above the camera, pointed toward the middle of the scene.

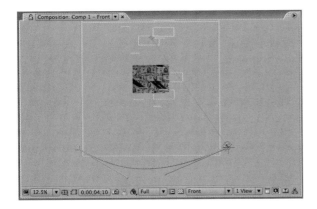

Figure 3.37

Move the spotlight to the upper left to cast shadows off to the right in the beginning of the animation.

Add an ambient light layer, 35% Intensity, and a warm orange color. Adjust the Intensity level if the scene is too bright or too dim. To create a greater depth of field from the camera in motion, adjust the camera layer's Aperture to 50 pixels—a higher number provides a greater depth of field, while a lower number offers less depth (Figure 3.38).

Figure 3.38

Adding a warm ambient light and increased depth of field adds to the realism of the animation.

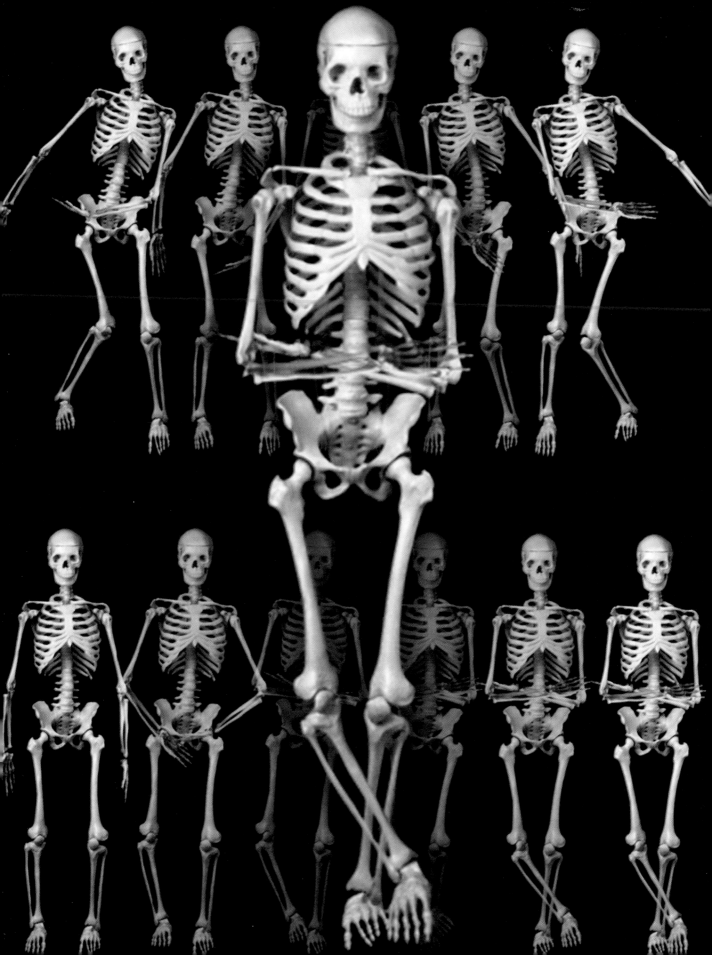

Applying Animation Concepts

II

When the focus of an animation is on the animated objects or characters, it's important to create a smooth, believable motion. On the other hand, there are times when a humorous animation is required—which can require extremely exaggerated and distorted characters and motion to emphasize the actions being made (have you watched any classic cartoons lately?). The next two chapters cover the various aspects of both the real and fantasy worlds of physical motion and animation.

Chapter 4   **Cause and Effect**
Chapter 5   **Exaggeration Equals Characterization**

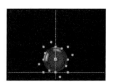

Cause and Effect

The effects of gravity, recoil, drag, friction, inertia, and collision are around us every day. We'll explore some common principles applied to animation that will give the viewer a sense of realistic motion. This is all part of telling the story of what your characters or moving objects are supposed to be doing. To help you better understand these principles and apply them to your own animations, the projects in this chapter will include realistic effects, timing, and more.

Chapter Contents

Gravity: The Freefall

A study in gravity is more than just dropping objects off the Tower of Pisa. In animation, it involves several other factors that include velocity and wind drag—but ultimately, all objects in the natural world will find their way down. Falling objects need smooth motion. Don't use a sharp turn unless there's a clear reason for it, such as an outside force that changes the object's direction. A smartly placed blur will help sell the motion.

The first project we'll create in our study of gravity starts with a single image on a Photoshop layer. The orange will appear as if it is rolling on a surface and then drops off suddenly. Because there is some momentum to the rolling orange, it will not drop straight down along the very edge of the surface but will roll forward off the corner and then down at an arc.

1. Import the sliced orange file, OrangeSlicedSmall.psd on the DVD, into a new After Effects project as a composition—which retains the transparency around the orange.

2. Open the composition into a Comp window, and change the composition settings to 640 × 480 NTSC.

Note: If you want to follow along with a completed After Effects project file, you'll find GravityFall.aep as well as the completed QuickTime movie on the DVD in the Chapter 4 folder. I've included finished QuickTime versions of all the projects of this chapter.

3. Click the orange and move it to the upper half of the window. Make the rulers visible (View > Show Rulers; ⌘/Alt+R) and drag down a guideline to the bottom of the orange's surface. Drag out a guideline from the left side to just past the halfway point. These guides will act as our surface and the edge of the drop-off (Figure 4.1).

4. Click the orange layer in the Timeline window, and drag the Current Time Indicator to the 1-second mark. Move the orange in the Comp window to the center of the vertical guide and touch the bottom edge with the horizontal guide.

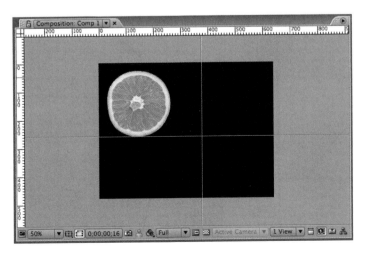

Figure 4.1
The guidelines will help us correctly animate the orange rolling off an imaginary table surface.

5. Press the P key on the keyboard to show the Position settings. Click the Stopwatch, and return the Indicator back to zero (or home key). Drag the orange in the Comp window off the left side of the window, keeping it in line horizontally with the previous position by holding down the Shift key while dragging the layer.

6. Press the R key to select the Rotation settings, and click the Stopwatch to set the current degree of rotation. Move the Indicator to the 1-second mark, and set the rotation to +180°.

7. Select RAM Preview to note the path your orange is moving, and make sure it is rotating the right amount for the motion path it's traveling. If it looks as if it's spinning on the surface, then adjust the degree of rotation at the 1-second mark to a lesser rotation. If it appears to be dragging on the surface, then increase the degree of rotation (Figure 4.2).

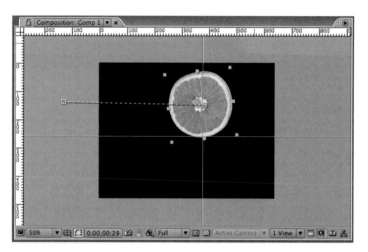

Figure 4.2
Adjust the rotation of the orange along the horizontal guide so that the orange appears to be rolling on a flat surface.

8. Return to the Timeline window and move the Indicator to 01:03 (three frames past the 1-second mark). In the Comp window, drag the orange down to the right of the intersection of the guidelines; use that intersection as an imaginary corner to the table, and place the orange at a 45° angle right on the corner. Set the rotation to an additional 45°.

9. Because there is no more contact with the table surface, the orange will drop down in a freefall, and it will spin approximately another 45° in the duration. Move the Indicator on the Timeline window to 01:10; then continue to move the orange down to the right and off the bottom of the Comp window, creating a

slight arc from its departure from the table surface. Add an additional 45° to the rotation at the bottom point (Figure 4.3). Run a RAM Preview to see the motion path the orange takes.

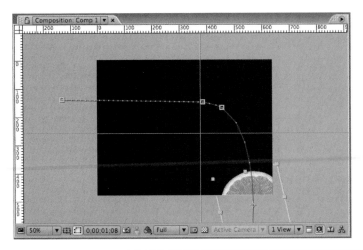

Figure 4.3
The orange continues a slight rotation and at a slight arc because of the momentum created from rolling before the freefall.

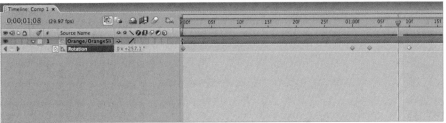

This animation is now functional, but it still lacks visual realism during the freefall. To enhance this, we will add a motion blur (Directional Blur) to the orange layer.

10. Move the Indicator on the Timeline window to the 01:03 mark, where the starting point of the freefall will begin the motion blur. Select Effect > Blur & Sharpen > Directional Blur, click the Stopwatch for the Blur Length settings in the Timeline window, and leave the default setting of zero at this point.

11. Move the Indicator to the 01:05 mark, click the Direction Stopwatch, and set the Direction to –60° and the Blur Length to 24 pixels (Figure 4.4).

12. Because the orange is still spinning slightly during the freefall, it is important to adjust the blur direction to keep it in a vertical motion blur. Move to the 01:10 mark and increase the Direction and Blur Length. I've selected a Direction of –105°, but you can adjust yours to get the arc you want. In addition to the rotation, the freefall of the orange is at a maximum toward the bottom of the Comp window, so I increased the Blur Length to 50 pixels.

Run a RAM Preview, and take note of any discrepancies in the animation motion path, rotation, or motion blur. Make minor adjustments accordingly. If the overall timing is an issue, then open up all of the settings in the Timeline window and select/drag an entire column of markers to the right or left to make adjustments (Figure 4.5).

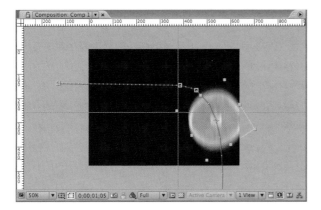
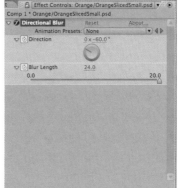
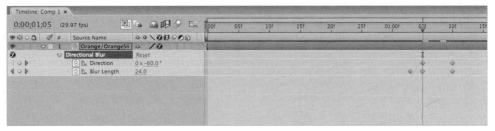

Figure 4.4 Adding a Directional Blur to the freefall portion of the animation will provide smoothness and realism, similar to the natural motion blur in video or film footage.

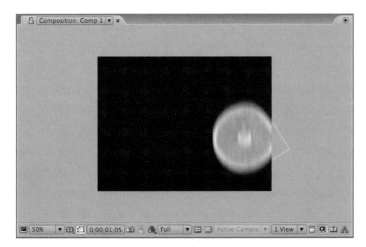

Figure 4.5 Make global adjustments to the timing of the animation with an entire column of Timeline markers.

Gravity: Smooth Landing

In Pixar's *Toy Story*, after Buzz Lightyear soars around the bedroom, Sheriff Woody says, "That's not flying—it's falling with style!" We can tell the difference, visually, between something that's flying under power and something that's falling or gliding. Using a paper airplane for this project helps us to visualize a different effect of gravity. The factors of wind resistance and loft keep the airplane from making a dramatic freefall as the orange does. (However, I have seen some horribly designed paper airplanes that defy all principles of flight and behave more like a brick than an airplane!)

The image I chose for this project was originally a flattened TIFF file with an alpha channel, which I used to extract the plane for the background. I added a feathered selection for creating a slightly blurred shadow layer in Photoshop. The finished two-layered file, PaperAirplane.psd, can be found on the DVD.

Create a new project in After Effects and import the airplane file as a composition. Change the composition dimensions to 640 × 480 NTSC, and then change the Background Color to white. Move the airplane in the Comp window to the upper-left corner along the top, just outside the window's boundaries. Move the shadow to the left side, just outside the window and down about 150 pixels from the airplane (Figure 4.6).

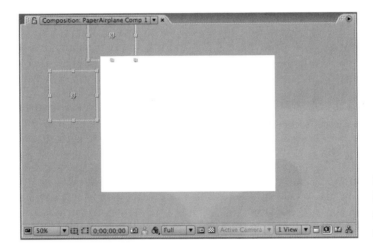

Figure 4.6
Position the two layers outside the Comp window for their final approach.

Select both layers on the Timeline window and hit the P key to get the position settings; click the Stopwatch for both layers and move the Indicator to around the 1-second mark. Move the airplane in the Comp window down past the center of the window, and drag the shadow a little bit under it. Move the Indicator down about 10 frames, and continue to drag the airplane and shadow together along the same direction as the combined landing angle about 50 pixels (Figure 4.7). The shadow will need to enter the window before the plane in order to create the illusion of a top light source; nudge the position marker for the airplane layer down a few frames so its movement starts later. To give the shadow a better sense of depth, set the beginning opacity to 0% (press the T key and set the Stopwatch) and set the landing opacity to 65% on out to the end.

Because this animation is of a fairly slow descent, we want the airplane to experience a little lift upon landing. This is where the motion and mass of the airplane cause a slight bit of air compression against the floor surface, which causes it to nose up very slightly and scoot across the floor before the drag on the floor surface makes it come to a complete stop. A simple, slight upward rotation at the end of the flight path provides this effect.

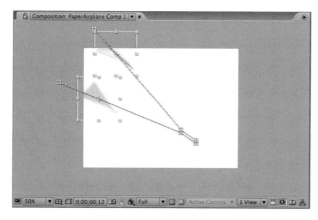

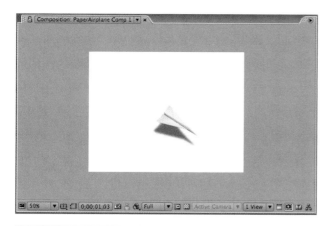

Figure 4.7
Creating a believable flight/land-ing path requires an eye for per-spective and attention to timing.

Select both layers in the Timeline window. Starting just before the 1-second mark and the actual landing of the plane, create a Rotation marker set to 0°. Halfway between the landing point and the end of the skid, set a Rotation marker for both layers to –10° (Figure 4.8). The effect is very subtle, but it reinforces the illusion of the plane actually landing on a hard, smooth surface.

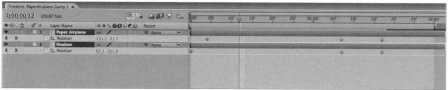

Figure 4.8
A slight rotation at the end of the flight path establishes the per-spective of the floor surface to the plane.

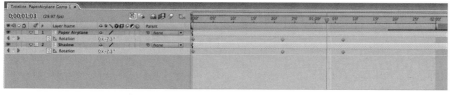

Gravity and Collision: The Bounce and Hang Time

"It's not a fear of falling—it's the sudden stop at the end that scares me!" We've heard that from many characters, and it reflects the fact that the movement of different materials is affected by more than just their mass and the atmosphere. If you drop something heavy, solid, and inflexible, it will either break or it will make a dent in whatever it lands on or collides with. Soft, semi-flexible objects, such as tomatoes, could explode from the pressure, depending on the amount of gravitational force applied (how high was it dropped from?).

In between these extremes, gravity causes a force on impact that makes a flexible object, such a basketball, repel with nearly equal pressure in the opposite direction. This is known as a bounce, and when the downward force is continued in a similar method repeatedly (dribbling the ball, for example), the motion is continued for a sustained period of time—at least until someone's arm gets really tired!

So what happens when you bounce the ball really hard and watch it until it bounces again? There is an effect at the top of the bounce cycle called *hang time*, where the upward energy that thrusts the ball into the air ceases and gravity takes over again. When there is no continued downward thrust of the ball, then the energy gets absorbed with each bounce, and the ball is repelled less with every bounce until it comes to a complete stop.

Let's defy the natural laws of physics for a moment and create a 1-second animation loop so we can study the bounce effect and the hang time at the top of the bounce:

1. Create a new project in After Effects and import the file Basketball_Small.psd from the DVD as a composition. Resize the composition to 640 × 480 NTSC.

2. Make the rulers visible, and drag down two guidelines to set the bottom and top bounce points. Drag the ball up to the top guideline, and click the Position Stopwatch in the Timeline window.

3. Move the Indicator on the Timeline to 00:15 (Frame 15), and drag the ball straight down to the bottom guideline.

4. Go to the 1-second mark and drag the ball back up to the top (Figure 4.9).

Set the work area slider to the 1-second mark, and run a RAM preview of the loop. At this point, it looks more like a game of Pong than it does a bouncing ball. To simulate the hang time at the highest point of the bounce, we'll slow down the animation at both ends of the loop.

5. Select the first marker in the Timeline and apply the Easy Ease Out Keyframe Assistant. Select the last marker at the end of the animation and apply Easy Ease In. Adjust the speed in the Keyframe Velocity dialog box (Figure 4.10). Increase the percentage to slow down the delay, and lower it to increase the delay.

6. To add visual realism to the bounce, we need to add motion blur, increasing in effects through the quickest part of the animation. Apply the Directional Blur filter to the ball layer (Effect > Blur & Sharpen > Directional Blur). Move the

Indicator on the Timeline to the Frame 10 position, and press the E key to reveal the Directional Blur Effect settings. Click the Stopwatch to create a marker, and set the Blur Length to 25 pixels, leaving the Direction in the default position of 0°.

7. Move the Indicator back to the Frame 2 position and set the Blur Length to 0. Move the Indicator to the Frame 18 position and set the Blur Length to 0 there also (Figure 4.11).

Run a RAM Preview to see the timing of the hang time and motion blur effect, and make any necessary adjustments.

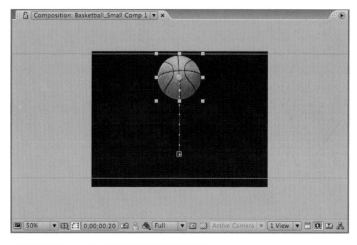

Figure 4.9
Set the animation to loop in a 1-second bounce.

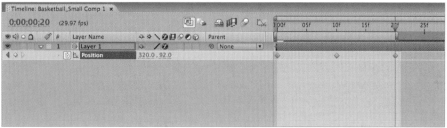

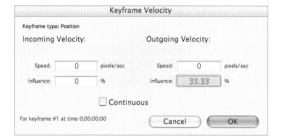

Figure 4.10
Applying an Ease In/Out to both ends of the animation loop will create the illusion of hang time.

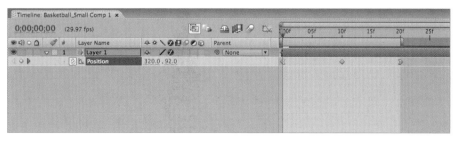

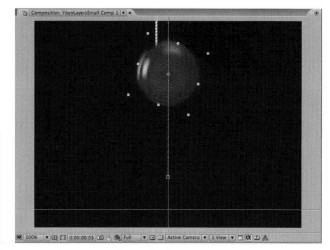

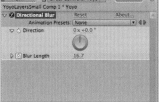

Figure 4.11 Adding motion blur through the fastest part of the animation for visual realism

Gravity and Recoil: The Yo-Yo

Somewhat similar to an upside-down bounce, the recoil of a yo-yo has a slight pause at the end of the motion path when the string is extended. The difference is that the yo-yo is jerked back instead of returning solely under its own power, so the timing is slightly different.

The yo-yo image used in this project, YoyoLayersSmall.psd on the DVD, is a two-layered Photoshop file, created from the original flat TIFF image file. The shiny highlights on the yo-yo were selected and copied to a new layer. The original yo-yo layer beneath was retouched to remove the highlights, because it will be rotated underneath the highlight layer in After Effects (Figure 4.12).

1. Create a new project in After Effects, and import the yo-yo PSD file as a composition. Open the composition in the Comp window and resize the composition to 640 × 480 NTSC. Make the rulers visible, and drag down a horizontal guideline to set the bottom point. Drag out a vertical guideline to the center of the Comp window.

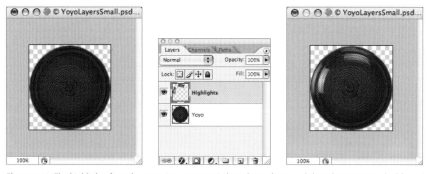

Figure 4.12 The highlights from the yo-yo image are copied to a layer above, and then they are retouched from the lower image so it can rotate.

2. Drag the yo-yo and highlight together past the top of the window so they are out of the frame, and click the position Stopwatch in the Timeline window for both layers. Open the Rotation setting in the Timeline for the yo-yo layer and click the Stopwatch.

3. Move the Indicator on the Timeline to Frame 20, and drag the two layers straight down to the lower guide. Then move the Indicator to the 1-second mark, and drag the two layers back up out of the top of the window. Set the Rotation of the yo-yo layer to 8 × 0.0°. This will keep the yo-yo rotating at the same speed the full duration of the animation, but the highlights on the layer above will remain static.

4. Select the Position marker at Frame 20, apply the Easy Ease In Keyframe Assistance, and adjust the Influence percentage in the Keyframe Velocity dialog to 100% (Figure 4.13). This will create the slight hesitation at the end of the unwinding and allow a quick "snap" back up.

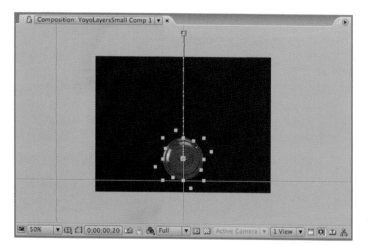

Figure 4.13

Applying an Ease In will help to define the pause and snap of the yo-yo in motion.

5. Import the file String.psd from the DVD as footage, selecting only the string layer, and drag it into the Comp window. Arrange it to be on the bottom in the Timeline window. Move the Indicator so the yo-yo is visible, and line up the string layer vertically with the yo-yo's motion path, to the left of the yo-yo's center winding core. Press the P key to select the position settings, and click the Stopwatch to set the Frame 0 position.

6. Move the Indicator to the 1-second mark, and move the string layer over to the right side of the winding. This will give the side-to-side motion of the string unwinding and rewinding back onto the yo-yo.

7. Move the Indicator to the center point of the animation where the yo-yo gets to the bottom of the path, and move the string to the inside left side of the center core. Then move the Indicator ahead about two frames, and move the string layer to the right side of the inside center core. This is the point where the string comes to the end of the unwinding and jumps to the other side to begin rewinding (Figure 4.14).

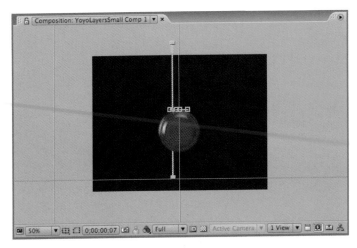

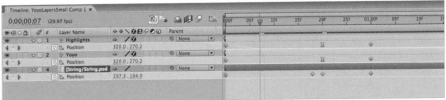

Figure 4.14
Move the string from left to right to simulate the unwinding and rewinding motion.

Note: Because the unwinding and rewinding of a string around the core of the moving object generate the yo-yo's recoil motion, no spring tension is involved in the string. The string in the animation doesn't move up and down with the yo-yo; it moves only from side to side as it unwinds from one side and winds up on the other.

If you run the animation in RAM Preview at this point, it will look pretty silly because the string moves just horizontally. We need to cover up the excess string that appears at the bottom of the yo-yo while it's traveling up and down, because we will not move the string with the yo-yo.

8. To do this, we'll need to create a new solid layer that can follow the yo-yo's motion path. Select Layer > New > Solid, set the width at 30 pixels and the height at 400, and set the solid color to black. The dimensions of the layer should be only large enough to move around and cover up the string where needed, so a full-frame size is not necessary.

9. With the Indicator at 0 on the Timeline, move the new black solid layer in position to cover up the string layer, and click the Stopwatch for the position settings. Move the Indicator down to the bottom of the yo-yo's motion path, and move the black solid layer to match the position of the bottom of the yo-yo at that point. Apply the Easy Ease In Keyframe Assistant to this point so the rate will match that of the yo-yo layer.

10. Adjust the marker back in the Timeline so the motion paths match (Figure 4.15). Continue following the string layer path with the solid, keeping the string covered up underneath the yo-yo. This is not a precision motion path, so don't worry about exact tracking with the other layers. Run the RAM Preview to make sure that every frame has coverage over the string below the yo-yo.

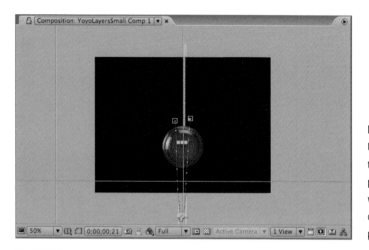

Figure 4.15

Using a solid color layer to follow the motion path of the yo-yo, you will reveal the string only above the upper portion of the yo-yo.

11. Finally, add a motion blur to smooth out the animation and give it more visual realism. Select both the yo-yo and highlight layers, and apply a Directional Blur (Effect > Blur & Sharpen > Directional Blur). Press the E key on both layers in the Timeline, and click the Stopwatch for the Blur Length. At Frame 1, set the Blur Length to 25, and then move the Indicator to the 1-second mark and click the Add Keyframe icon in the Timeline. This will produce a constant blur that needs to be modified to more closely match the motion of the yo-yo.

12. Move the Indicator to the Frame 9 mark and set the Blur Length to 0. Move the Indicator to the Frame 22 mark and set the Blur Length to 0 again (Figure 4.16). Run the RAM Preview and notice how the blur effect is visible only during the fastest motion of the yo-yo's motion path.

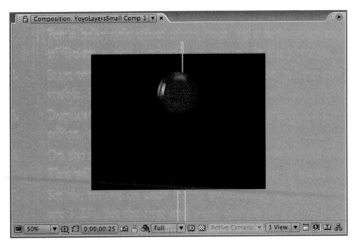

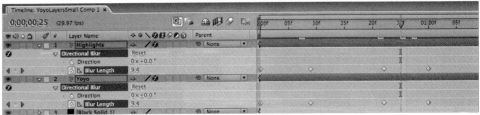

Figure 4.16
Adding a motion blur will give the animation a realistic appearance.

Inertia and Friction: What a Drag!

Simulating friction and drag in an animation is all about the timing. Think about some simple practical situations you may encounter in everyday life, such as rolling a chair across different floor surfaces or the difference between running on land and running in a swimming pool. Not only does friction increase the force needed for movement, it also slows down the speed at which the motion is made.

This project is a simple exercise in creating motion drag—a principle that can be easily applied to your animations and adjusted for different types of surfaces and conditions. We will look at variations in floor texture and their effects on a rolling chair with the same momentum and starting speed.

The office chair is pushed into the frame from the left on a smooth floor finish, and the energy of the momentum is absorbed by the wheels on the chair and is affected by the weight of the chair. The chair eventually comes to rest in a smooth motion. If it were to be pushed with the same amount of thrust on hard, slick ice, it would most likely go right through the frame without slowing down, because it would then be sliding on the surface instead of rolling on its wheels.

 Note: You can review this project file, ChairDrag.aep, on the DVD.

Import the single-layer Photoshop image of the office chair (ChairwShadow-Small.psd) into After Effects as a composition, and place it into an existing comp scaled to 640 × 480 NTSC with a white background. Position the chair layer outside the Comp 1 window frame, and set the Position Stopwatch at Frame 0. Drag the image across the Comp window and stop before reaching the other side—at approximately the 01:15 mark. This will be our stopping point for the chair's motion path (Figure 4.17). Select the Easy Ease In Keyframe Assistant, and set the Keyframe Velocity to 85%.

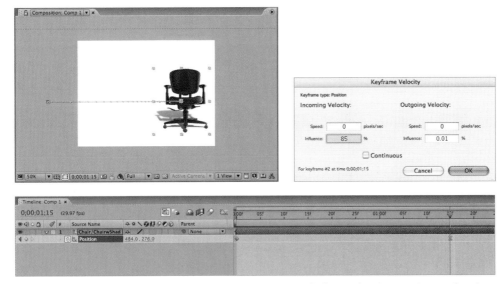

Figure 4.17 The chair will glide on a smooth surface almost all the way across the frame and come to a rest in a smooth motion.

Apply a motion blur for improved visual realism by selecting the Directional Blur filter (Effect > Blur & Sharpen > Directional Blur) and adding a 15-pixel blur at a 90° angle. Set the Blur Length to 15, and click the Stopwatch at the beginning of the Timeline. It's important now to find just the right placement for the next marker in order to end the motion blur before the chair slows down too much. Locate the motion path dots, and look for the area of the path where the dots get closer together (Figure 4.18). Run the RAM Preview to test the motion and blur effects, and make adjustments as necessary.

Contrary to the chair's motion on the smooth surface, a course surface will cause more friction and expel the energy from the initial thrust much more quickly. How gritty or bumpy the surface is (hard-packed dirt, sandy concrete, carpet, etc.) will determine how you will need to adjust the chair's animation.

Duplicate the chair layer in the Timeline window (⌘/Ctrl+D), and hide the original chair layer. Activate the gritty surface layer, placed beneath it. Move the Indicator in the Timeline to about Frame 7, and drag the chair back to the far-left side of the frame so it's barely touching the edge.

Move the old end marker to Frame 20. Set the Easy Ease In Keyframe Velocity to 100%. Drag the chair back to just right of the last marker, about 30 pixels (Figure 4.19). This will give the chair the appearance that it is being thrust into the frame at the same rate as the smooth floor example but is quickly brought to a stop due to the friction caused by the gritty floor surface.

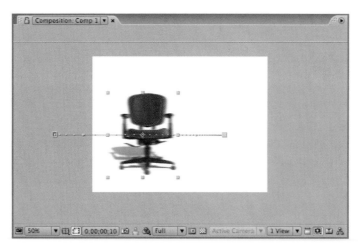

Figure 4.18
Adding a Directional Blur to the faster portion of the motion path will greatly aid in the animation's realism.

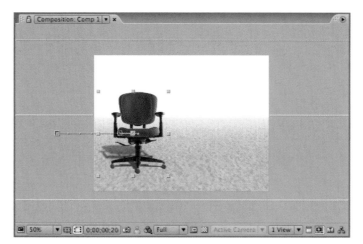

Figure 4.19
A gritty floor surface causes more friction and stops the chair abruptly.

Apply the Directional Blur filter to the chair layer as directed in the smooth floor example, setting the Frame 0 Blur Length at 15 pixels and the end of the blur just short of the Frame 20 mark to 0. This will provide the motion blur to the chair in motion.

Complex Animations: Combining the Techniques

You'll often encounter a project that requires you to refer to the application of several techniques. Animated subjects always have to go somewhere or do something that will require obedience to at least one or two of the basic physical laws described in this chapter.

This project uses several of the physical motion techniques. It's a bowl of popcorn sliding across a surface before it grabs quickly and tips slightly, spilling out some of the popcorn onto the surface. The sliding bowl speeds in and starts to slow down (friction and drag) before it catches a small bump at the end and tips slightly while popcorn continues to fly in motion (inertia). Some of the popcorn falls and lands on the surface, bounces, and comes to rest (gravity, collision, and drag), while a few pieces roll back into the bowl without escaping (recoil).

Note: For more detailed examples of character animation, see Chapter 5, "Exaggeration Equals Characterization."

The original image was a flat TIFF file that had an existing alpha channel of the outline of the bowl of popcorn against a white background. It was cut into smaller pieces, including the bowl and about half of the popcorn, while about 20 pieces of popcorn were extracted from the top half of the bowl (Figure 4.20).

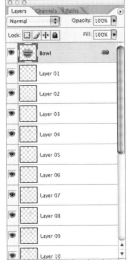

Figure 4.20 Cutting out individual pieces that will later be animated

Each piece of popcorn had to be cleaned up and its missing parts cloned back in (Figure 4.21). Most of the pieces fell back into place where they were first extracted, but it didn't matter too much because they were all realigned in After Effects later.

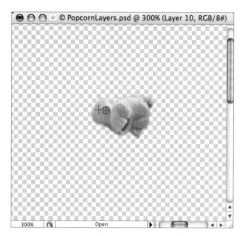
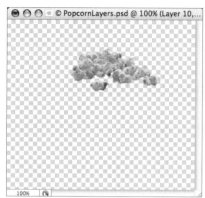

Figure 4.21 Great care is necessary to re-create each piece of popcorn in Photoshop.

Import the finished Photoshop file, PopcornLayers.psd on the DVD, into a new project in After Effects as a composition. Double-click the composition in the Project window. Because it's cropped down to the bowl, it will appear quite small in the Comp window. Change the Composition Settings to increase the comp size to 640 × 480 NTSC. This won't affect the actual layers, only the background and frame size of the composition.

Now we'll set things in motion:

1. In the Timeline window, select all the layers; then drag them in the Comp window off the left side of the frame, out of sight.

2. Press the P key, and all of the layer's Position settings will pop down. Select the Position Stopwatches on all layers. Move the Indicator to the Frame 15 mark, and drag the selected layers straight out near the halfway point.

3. Apply an Easy Ease In Keyframe Assistant, and set the Keyframe Velocity to 10% (Figure 4.22). Run the RAM Preview to see that all of the layers move exactly the same all the way through to the half-second mark. They should appear as one moving image.

4. Deselect all of the layers except the bowl layer, and press the R key to show the Rotation settings and click the Stopwatch. This will set the rotation of the bowl to 0 degrees during its slide. Move the Indicator down a few frames and slightly rotate the bowl up (clockwise) a degree or two. Move two frames down and rotate back (counter-clockwise). Add a couple of "wobbles" by repeating the added frames and slight rotations in small increments until the bowl comes to rest back at 0 degrees.

5. Select all the layers again and apply the Directional Blur filter, with the Rotation set at –90° and the Blur Length at 12 pixels. Click the Effects Stopwatches for each layer. Move the Indicator to Frame 10 and set the Blur Length to 10 pixels. Move to Frame 15 and set the Blur Length to 1 pixel (Figure 4.23). Run a RAM Preview to make sure all of the layers' motion blur is in sync.

Figure 4.22 For the first half-second of the animation, all of the layers move in unison before the bowl tips.

Figure 4.23 Add motion blur globally for the 15 frames before the layers start to fly apart.

Now comes the fun part! You may want to open the existing After Effects project file, Complex_Popcorn.aep on the DVD, to see how the individual layers are positioned, rotated, and blurred. Each piece of popcorn that is separated onto its own layer is manually moved in a path that looks believable when played back in real time. You'll have to apply any or all of the techniques used in this chapter to decide how each piece will travel and bounce, rotate, and slide (Figure 4.24). Use the Indicator to scrub the animation paths as you create them. Make sure to keep each piece on its own random motion path and use your creativity!

Make sure a few pieces move in the bowl and roll back with the static kernels that are part of the bowl layer. This will add dimension and movement in the focal point of the animation subject (Figure 4.25).

Make Your Work Easier Visually

Take the complexity out of a large project: Hide the layers you're not currently working on by deselecting the eye icon on the Timeline. When there are several small pieces in motion in a group, as there are in this project, concentrate on only one layer of animation at a time in the Comp window. Things can be a bit confusing if you see too many paths crossing all at once.

Figure 4.24
Apply the techniques in this chapter to each individual piece, using random paths.

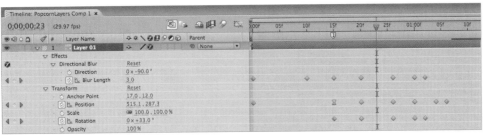

Figure 4.25
To help disguise the largest static layer, keep a few kernels in motion in the bowl.

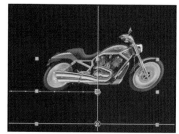
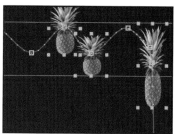
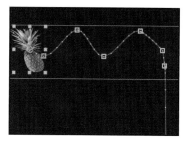

Exaggeration Equals Characterization

Have you ever noticed how classic cartoon characters are so exaggerated in their actions? Everything seems like it's made out of rubber! Cars bend around corners and spring forward when they stop. Characters don't just drop off a cliff but hang suspended in air and stretch out in length before finally disappearing out of sight. How do you make a simple object that has no facial features come to life? It's all a matter of exaggerating the timing of motion, scale, and distortion of the object or character you're animating.

5

Chapter Contents

The Classic Sudden Stop

What's the visual difference between a normal stop and a classic stop of an object? In the natural world, something with mass that's moving rapidly either rolls to a stop or needs a great deal of friction to bring it to a complete stop. If it's a solid object, a car for instance, it will most likely roll or skid to a stop. The only effect that inertia will have on it will be transferred through the tires, wheels, and suspension and to the body, which may move up and forward slightly and then come to rest back in its normal position.

However, in the cartoon world, the car's tires will just stop suddenly and the whole vehicle will bend or lurch forward, as if it were made of Jell-O. Then it will spring back slightly beyond its normal position before resting. This effect isn't confined to just classic cartoons; you will notice it in TV commercials and movies.

Let's do a simple experiment with this effect, using an image of a motorcycle. Create a new project in After Effects and a new composition, 640 × 480 NTSC. Import the file HD_V-Rod.psd from the Chapter 5 folder on the DVD as footage, and drag the PSD file into the Comp window (Figure 5.1).

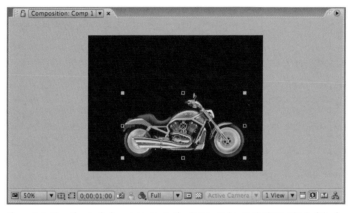

Figure 5.1 Place the single-layer image onto the Comp window in the lower third of the frame.

Note: As always, you can see the final effect we're after here by viewing the finished Inertia-Stop movie on the DVD.

1. We need to first move the motorcycle across the screen, setting the start and stop points on the Timeline. Move the Indicator on the Timeline down to the Frame 17 mark, press the P key, and click the Stopwatch to set the stop point key frame.

2. Move the Indicator back to the Frame 6 mark, and drag the motorcycle layer out of the frame off to the left so it's out of view (Figure 5.2).

3. Move the Indicator down to approximately a half second so the motorcycle is visible in the Comp window. Apply the Transform effect to the motorcycle layer (Effect > Distort > Transform) and set the Skew to 20 at a +90° angle. Move the Indicator to Frame 21 and click the Skew stopwatch to set the key frame with the current amount of skew. Move the Indicator back to Frame 14 and set the amount of skew to 0.0, so the motorcycle isn't leaning all the way into the frame.

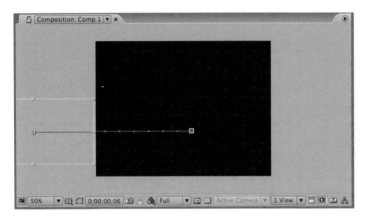

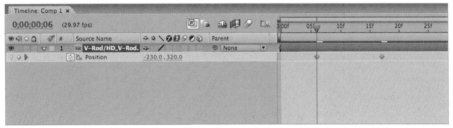

Figure 5.2
Create the start and stop points for the motion path of the motorcycle layer.

4. The entire motorcycle skews from the center of the image, so we need to reposition the Anchor Point to the base of the motorcycle to make it lean forward at the tires (the center of rotation is at the ground level). Click the Anchor Point crosshair button in the Effects palette, and set the position manually in the Comp window (Figure 5.3). Because the effect is applied to the layer, it will make the motorcycle jump up to the layer's Anchor Point to match.

To make the motorcycle appear to lean forward under the force of inertia, the timing of the skew placement is important. The longer it takes for the effect to move forward before the recoil, the more energy appears to be applied to the motorcycle. If it's a short "snap back," then either the vehicle wasn't traveling very fast or the mass of the object is not that great.

5. After the skew forward is applied, move the Indicator down a few frames and reverse the skew at a lesser degree, and then move back to the upright unskewed position at rest (Figure 5.4). Apply the settings for the position and the applied Skew effect from Table 5.1; then use RAM Preview to see the timing of the effect.

Figure 5.3
Apply a Skew effect to the layer to make the motorcycle lean forward, and reposition the Anchor Point to raise the bike into the frame so that the skew rotation is anchored at the ground level.

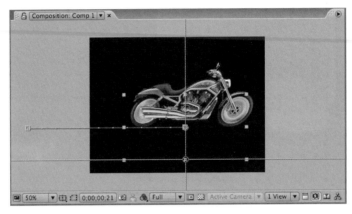

6. To enhance the effect of the motorcycle's speed, let's add some motion blur. Select Effect > Blur & Sharpen > Directional Blur. Set the Direction to +90.0° and the Blur Length to 20.

7. Move the Indicator to Frame 17 in the Timeline, and click the Blur Length Stopwatch to set the key frame (Figure 5.5). Move the Indicator to Frame 20, and set the Blur Length to 0.0.

Figure 5.4 A reverse skew of a smaller degree provides the "snap back" of the effect.

▶ **Table 5.1** Position and Skew Effect

Effects: Transform	00;00	00;14	00;17	00;20	00;24	00;28	01;02
Anchor Point	223, 228.5						
Skew		0.0		20.0	20.0	−5.0	0.0
Skew Axis		+90.0°					
Transform							
Position	−230, 320		350, 320				

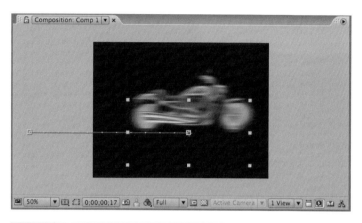

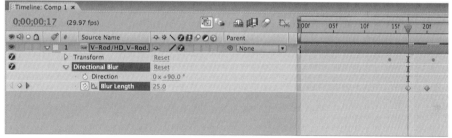

Figure 5.5

Adding motion blur to the motorcycle will enhance the illusion of speed.

Bouncing and Falling: Defying the Rules of Gravity

You can give life to simple, inanimate objects by animating their movements. Merely falling off a ledge is easy, and the expected result is to just disappear quickly (like the orange slice in Chapter 4, "Cause and Effect"). However, if you give the object an expression of "Oh noooooooooo!" before the final fall, it will take on a whole new meaning!

We're going to animate a single image of a pineapple that bounces across the frame and right off the edge. The slight delay before the stretch and then the fall will add to the characterization of this simple object.

Create a new project in After Effects and a new composition, 640 × 480 NTSC, 3 seconds in length. Make the Rulers visible and drag down a guide horizontally approximately halfway. Import the image Pineapple.psd from the DVD and drag it to the Comp 1 window. Scale it to 50% and move it on top of the guide (Figure 5.6).

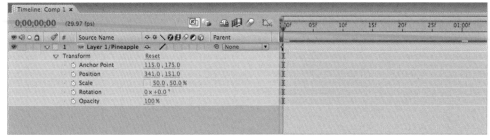

Figure 5.6

Import and scale the pineapple layer to fit on top of the guide.

Note: When you need to stretch, zoom, or scale up an image layer, make sure the original is at least as big as the largest scaled size or length of the stretch, so there won't be any loss of image quality. If you bring an image layer in at 100% and need to stretch it or scale it larger, you will experience image degradation and pixelation.

To make the pineapple appear to "bounce" across the frame, we will move not only its position but also the vertical scale at the bottom of each bounce. We also need to adjust the angle of the pineapple on the approach and take-off of each bounce to move it forward.

Let's first create the position and scale path. Start with the Indicator on the Timeline at zero and drag the pineapple off the left side of the frame. Click both the Position and Scale Stopwatches and apply the settings in Table 5.2. This will set the key frames for the basic motion path of the animation (Figure 5.7).

Note: When inserting variable settings on only one axis, make sure you deselect the link icon on the Timeline, or you will change all of the linked axis settings as well.

To give the effect of hang time, as we discussed in Chapter 3, "3-D Layers from Photoshop Layers," let's slow down the upper key frames of the bounces by applying the Easy Ease Keyframe Assistant to both the Position and Scale key frames. The default setting of 33.33% will be sufficient ease in and out of these points, occurring on each bounce.

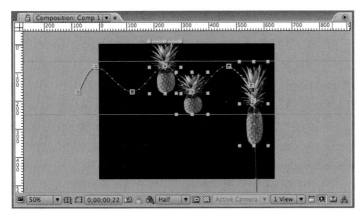

Figure 5.7
Set the key frames for scale and position in the bounce and fall of the pineapple.

▶ **Table 5.2** Position and Scale Keyframes

Transform	00;00	00;08	00;15	00;23	01;00	01;07	01;15	01;22	02;00
Position	−75.0, 172.0	−9.0, 82.0	123.0, 172.0	243.0, 79.0	341.0, 172.0	475.0, 82.0	558.0, 150.0	567.0, 205.0	574.0, 652.0
Scale (%)	50.0, 40.0	50.0, 50.0	50.0, 40.0	50.0, 50.0	50.0, 40.0	50.0, 50.0	50.0, 50.0	45.0, 80.0	

Next, we need to create the slight delay before the pineapple falls off the ledge on the right side of the frame, and we need to apply the Easy Ease Keyframe Assistant to both the Position and Scale key frames. Select the Keyframe Velocity for the Position key frame only, and set it to 100% for both Incoming and Outgoing settings. Leave the Scale Keyframe Velocity settings at the default 33.33% (Figure 5.8).

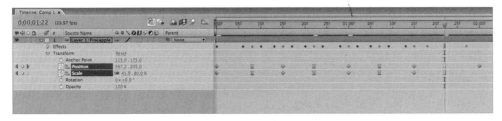

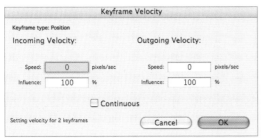

Figure 5.8
Set the Position Keyframe Velocity higher than Scale Velocity to produce the delay just before falling.

Now let's create the angles to the pineapple's motion that will give the illusion of it being propelled forward under its own power, similar to the animated vegetables in *Veggie Tales*. Move the Indicator to zero in the Timeline, and apply the Transform effect to the pineapple layer. Click the Skew Stopwatch in the Timeline, and apply the settings in Table 5.3 (Figure 5.09).

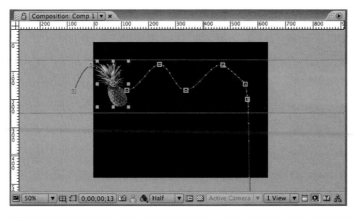

Figure 5.09

Apply the Skew effect to create the illusion of forward motion on the bounces.

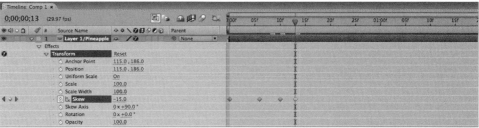

▶ **Table 5.3** Effects: Transform: Skew Keyframes

Skew	Keyframes
15.0	00;00, 00;06, 00;17, 00;20, 01;02, and 01;05
−15.0	00;10, 00;13, 00;24, 00;28, 01;09, and 01;13

Run a RAM Preview to make sure the animation settings are correct and make corrections if necessary. You can compare the timing of your animation to the Quick-Time movie PineappleJump-320.mov, in the Chapter 5 folder on the DVD.

To give a more realistic look to the animation, we will apply some motion blur to the faster sections of the motion path. Apply the Directional Blur filter (Effect > Blur & Sharpen > Directional Blur), move the Indicator to the zero position on the Timeline, and click the Blur Length Stopwatch. Leave the Direction set at 0.0°.

In the sections where the pineapple is moving up or down in the bounce, apply a Blur Length of 7.0, but apply a setting of 0.0 in the compressed bounce and "hang time" sections (as shown in Table 5.4).

▷ **Table 5.4** Effects: Directional Blur: Blur Length Keyframes

Blur Length	Keyframes
7.0	00;00–00;06, 00;10–00;13, 00;17–00;20, 00;24–00;28, 01;02–01;05, and 01;09–01;13
0.0	00;08, 00;15, 00;22, 01;00, 01;07, and 01;18–01;22
25.0	01:27

The final fall of the animation gets a much larger amount of blur applied to it (25.0) because it's an exaggerated free-fall (Figure 5.10).

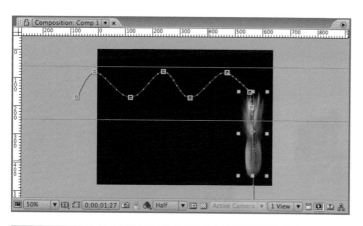

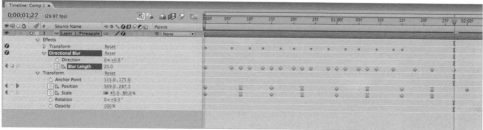

Figure 5.10 Applying a motion blur to the faster sections of the motion path will enhance the realism of the animation.

Rubber Planets: 3-D Animation Effects

If you've ever watched *Third Rock from the Sun* on television, you're familiar with the bouncing, dashing, crazy 3-D planet animations they ran during segment breaks. We can create very similar effects with two-dimensional animations of actual planet photos against a starry background. For this project, we'll use several animation tricks, such as exaggerated bounces, stops, falls, swings, and pop-ups. It's all about adjusting the motion paths, timing, speed, scale, and skew.

Because this will be a complex project with several animations all happening simultaneously, I'll concentrate on only one at a time. If you want, you can open the After Effects project file, PlanetProject.aep, from the DVD and turn individual layers off and on to see the motion and effects paths.

Planet 1: Earth Stop

Create a new project in After Effects and a new composition, 640 × 480 NTSC, 6 seconds in length. Import the Photoshop image files (Earth.psd, Moon.psd, Mars.psd, Saturn.psd, and Stars.psd) from the Chapter 5 folder on the DVD and drag them to the Comp 1 window. Hide all of the planet layers except Earth. Press A to reveal the Anchor Point, and set the X-axis to 0.0 so the Anchor Point will center on the left side of the planet layer (Figure 5.11). This will make the Earth jump over toward the right side of the frame.

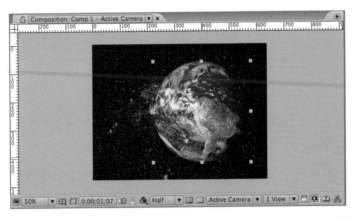

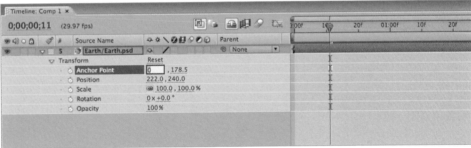

Figure 5.11 Hide all of the planet layers except Earth and reposition the Anchor Point.

With the Earth layer still in this position, move the Indicator to Frame 11 on the Timeline, and click the Position Stopwatch to set the current key frame location. Move the Indicator to Frame 5 and set the X-axis position to –384.0 to move the Earth layer off the left side of the frame. This will be the extent of the motion path for this planet layer. The abrupt stop effect will be the focus of this animation.

Similar to the motorcycle project earlier in this chapter, we will be skewing this layer, but we will also be adjusting the horizontal scale—like a sideways bounce. This will give the stop animation a flapping, rubberized effect.

Starting at Frame 11, click the Scale Stopwatch on the Timeline to set the first key frame (press S to bring up the Scale mode in the Timeline). Move the Indicator down to Frame 13, set the X-axis scale per Table 5.5, and continue for every other key frame until the animation ends at 100% at Frame 01;07 (Figure 5.12). The motion will regress as the Timeline continues.

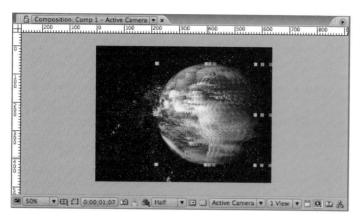

Figure 5.12 Set horizontal key frames for the stop bounce animation.

Apply the Transform effect to the layer (Effect > Distort > Transform), and set the Skew Axis angle to +90.0°. Click the Anchor Point crosshair button (called the Pan Behind tool in the toolbar), and set the crosshairs on the bottom-left corner of the layer in the Comp window (Figure 5.13). The Anchor Point circle will appear in the middle of the Earth layer, so drag it down to the bottom-left corner to set it.

▶ **Table 5.5** Earth Scale Keyframes

Keyframe	Scale (X-Axis)	Keyframe	Scale (X-Axis)	Keyframe	Scale (X-Axis)
00;11	100	00;21	105	01;01	98
00;13	110	00;23	95	01;03	100
00;15	90	00;25	103	01;05	99
00;17	107	00;27	97	01;07	100
00;19	93	00;29	101		

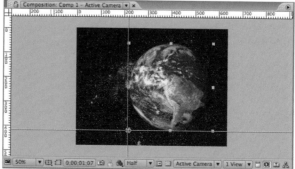

Figure 5.13 Set the Skew Anchor Point on the Earth layer to the bottom-left corner.

The Skew settings will match the Scale settings, so they will work together to create the rubberized effect. Apply the Skew settings in the regressive order shown in Table 5.6 until they return to the at-rest position at Frame 01;07 (Figure 5.14).

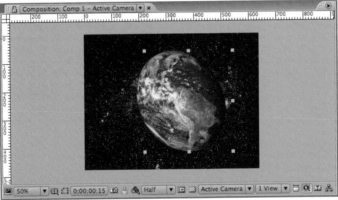

Figure 5.14 Apply the Skew effect to "rubberize" the Earth's movement.

▶ **Table 5.6** Effects: Transform: Skew Keyframes

Keyframe	Skew	Keyframe	Skew	Keyframe	Skew
00;10	0.0	00;21	10.0	01;01	−4.0
00;13	20.0	00;23	−6.0	01;03	3.0
00;15	−10.0	00;25	8.0	01;05	−3.0
00;17	12.0	00;27	−5.0	01;07	0.0
00;19	−8.0	00;29	5.0		

We'll now add some motion blur to the animation to smooth out the fastest sections. Move the Indicator to Frame 10 on the Timeline and apply the Directional Blur filter. Set the Direction to +90.0°, and click the Blur Length Stopwatch to set the key frame, with a Blur Length of 15.0 (Figure 5.15). Move the Indicator to Frame 11 and set the Blur Length to 5.0; then move on to Frame 01;07 and set it to zero. Run a RAM Preview to check that all of the key frames are placed correctly in the Earth animation.

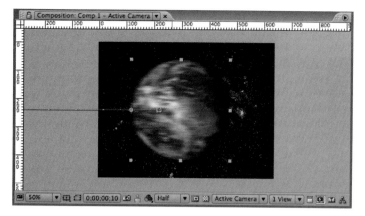

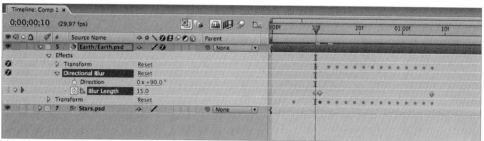

Figure 5.15 Applying motion blur to the faster sections of the motion path will enhance the realism of the animation.

> **Note:** Because we will be moving the planets around in 3-D space, convert all of the planet layers to 3-D layers. Select all the planet layers in the Timeline, Right-click/Ctrl+click on a layer, and select 3-D Layer from the selection. Another way is to just click on the 3-D Layer box in the Timeline for each layer you want to convert. However, don't convert the stars background layer, because we won't be moving it or casting shadows on it.

Planet 2: Mars Bounce

We will animate Mars to fly in from the lower-left side of the frame and move back behind the Earth, bouncing off the right side, top, and then bottom of the frame before finally bouncing out into space and resting. This will require position and scale moves and manual adjustments of the Bezier curve handles on the key frame points to control the motion path of the Mars layer. This will also require us to build this project as 3-D layers so the planets will appear to move around each other.

Select the 3-D Box for each planet layer (not including the stars layer). Hide the Earth layer, and make the Mars layer visible. Start with the Indicator set at Frame 25, and assign the Position and Scale key frames first, from Table 5.7. This will create our initial path where we can then adjust the Bezier curve handles (Figure 5.16).

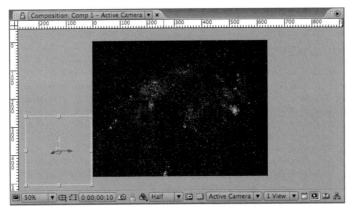

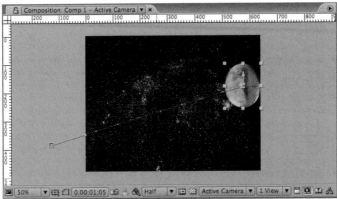

Figure 5.16
Set the Position and Scale key frames for the Mars layer.

▶ **Table 5.7** Mars Position and Scale Keyframes

Transform	00;25	01;05	01;11	01;19	01;26	02;03	02;10	02;15
Position	−128.0, 386.0, 0.0	597.4, 174.8, 74.0	410.0, 45.0, 73.0	232.0, 441.0, 56.0	174.4, 339.3, 92.2	98.8, 184.3, 138.3	56.9, 109.8, 162.6	21.1, 58.6, 182.0
Scale (%)	85.0, 85.0, 100.0	50.0, 60.0, 100.0	55.0, 45.0, 100.0	50.0, 40.0, 100.0	48.0, 43.0, 100.0	43.0, 40.0, 100.0	38.0, 35.0, 100.0	35.0, 35.0, 100.0

Once the key frames are set, eliminate or contract the Bezier curve handles on the long bounce passes. Click the handles and drag them up to the key frame Anchor Point, or use the Convert Vertex tool from the Tools palette to create straight motion paths, up to Frame 01;19 (Figure 5.17). You'll have to adjust the Bezier curve handles to create the "bounce" effect, as described in the next few paragraphs.

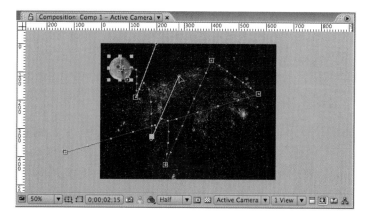

Figure 5.17
Minimize, accentuate, or eliminate the Bezier curves on the straight bounce paths.

Note: Because the process of adjusting the Bezier curve handles is subjective—not absolute—you may want to run several RAM Previews of your animation and make slight adjustments until it looks "just right."

Now that the general key frames are set, we need to accentuate the bounce effects by forcing the scale from symmetrical to asymmetrical at the point of impact. We do this by checking the Scale dimensions at each key frame and adding a new key frame on either side, making the Scale dimensions symmetrical. For instance, at Frame 01;05, the Scale is 50.0, 60.0, 100.0. By adding a key frame on either side and scaling the Mars layer to 60.0, 60.0, 100.0, the planet looks as if it is being compressed against the wall briefly (Figure 5.18).

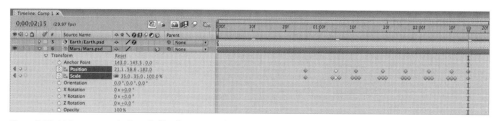

Figure 5.18 Adding symmetrically scaled key frames on either side of the compressed key frames will give the effect greater impact.

We want the ball to now bounce from key frame 01;19 out into space. Right now, it merely slides out there. Selecting the key frames out to the end of the motion path, one at a time, grab the right-side Bezier curve handle and pull it up to about the 1 o'clock position. Pull it out far enough to create a large arc with a rapid drop toward the top of the key frame mark below. Repeat this process with the remaining few key frames, progressively decreasing the amount of arc on each key frame. For these detailed steps, I hid the background stars layer so I could see the path dots and handles more clearly.

To smooth out the animation and give it pleasing realism, let's add some motion blur to the faster moving segments. This animation is going to require a more complicated Directional Blur for all the directions the planet layer is traveling in the frame. For instance, the first path segment requires a longer blur length and angle than the rest of the segments, because it's traveling at the fastest rate of speed and the farthest distance (Figure 5.19). We'll set the Directional Blur to zero on the bounce key frames to accentuate the effect and ensure that the viewer will see the compressed sphere. Then, we'll apply the Motion Blur again when the compressed sphere takes off in the next direction. Follow the Directional Blur settings in Table 5.8 to complete the Mars layer animation.

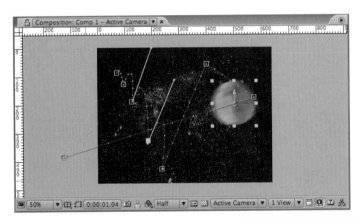

Figure 5.19

Apply motion blur in the direction the object is traveling and change it for each direction.

► **Table 5.8** Mars Directional Blur Keyframes

Effects: Transform	00;26–01;04	01;05	01;06–01;10	01;11	01;12–01;18	01;19	01;20	01;25
Direction	0 x –110.0°		0 x +135.0°		0 x +35.0°		0 x +155.0°	
Blur Length	35.0	0.0	33.0	0.0	30.0	0.0	18.0	0.0

Planet 3: Moon Pop-Up

The moon will take a wide sweep around and behind the Earth layer and pop up in front of it. To keep the motion fluid, we will use only a couple of key frames with large Bezier curve arcs. We will end with a series of short position and scale movements—similar to the rubberized effect we gave the Earth layer.

We'll start with the moon off the left side of the frame at the 2-second mark and scaled down to 50%. We will then give it two more key frames in order to create the curve and position we need for it to move behind and in front of the Earth. Using Table 5.9, apply the first three Position and Scale key frames, stopping at Frame 02;19. Then drag the Bezier curve handles on the first two key frames to create a smooth arc (Figure 5.20).

▶ **Table 5.9** Moon Position and Scale Keyframes

Transform	02;00	02;15	02;19	02;22	02;25	02;27	02;29	03;01	03;03
Position	−170.0, 326.0, −166.0	801.0, 234.0, 308.0	635.3, 352.2, −10.9	455.0, 300.0, −120.0	480.0, 320.0, −120.0	460.0, 305.0, −120.0	477.0, 317.0, −120.0	465.0, 310.0, −120.0	475.0, 315.0, −120.0
Scale (X and Y, %)	35.0	50.0	70.0	85.0	70.0	83.0	73.0	80.0	76.0

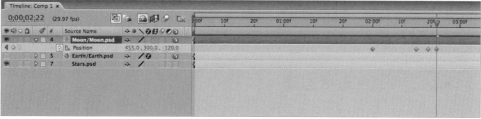

Figure 5.20 Drag the Bezier curve handles to create an arc in the motion path.

Continue adding the key frames for the rest of the animation per Table 5.9, and run a RAM Preview to make sure your numbers are entered correctly. Keep in mind that the exact numbers aren't as important as how good the animation looks to you. It's a subjective process, and your eyes will be your best judge. These numbers are only a guideline.

We'll add motion blur to the moon layer animation, changing the angle at key frames to follow the direction of travel (Figure 5.21). The Directional Blur effect decreases toward the end of the motion path but overlaps for the first big pop-up. Follow Table 5.10 for the Directional Blur key frame settings.

▷ **Table 5.10** Moon Directional Blur Keyframes

Effects: Transform	02;00	02;10	02;13	02;22	02;25	02;29
Direction	0 x +76.0°	0 x +105.0°		0 x +184.0°	0 x +220.0°	
Blur Length	35.0		35.0		10.0	0.0

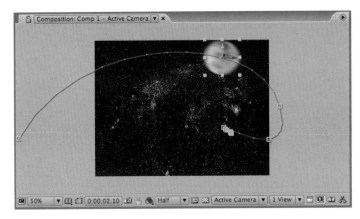

Figure 5.21
Add a Directional Blur to the moon layer animation.

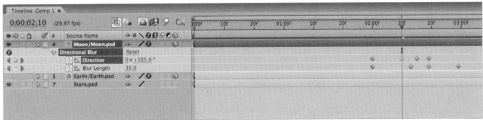

Planet 4: Saturn Drop

We will have Saturn drop straight down as if it's on an imaginary string and suddenly reaches the end of the line with a jerk. The layer moves in only one direction, so we only need to apply position and scale key frames and add a single-direction motion blur.

Because we want to give the illusion that the Saturn layer is suspended from an imaginary string by the center of its sphere, we will move the Anchor Point up the center to 50.0 in the Y-axis. This will allow the scale to "tilt" the planet slightly when it bounces at the end of the string. Starting at the 3-second mark, add Position and Scale key frames per Table 5.11 (Figure 5.22).

▷ **Table 5.11** Saturn Position and Scale Key Frames

Transform	03;00	03;08	03;10	03;14	03;17	03;20	03;23	03;26	03;28	04;00	04;02	04;04
Position	170.0, −159.0, −73.0	170.0, 340.0, −73.0		170.0, 250.0, −73.0	170.0, 275.0, −73.0	170.0, 253.0, −73.0	170.0, 270.0, −73.0	170.0, 255.0, −73.0	170.0, 265.0, −73.0	170.0, 258.0, −73.0	170.0, 263.0, −73.0	170.0, 260.0, −73.0
Scale (Y-axis, %)		100.0	130.0	90.0	115.0	93.0	105.0	96.0	103.0	98.0	102.0	100.0

Of course, now we need to add motion blur to this animation—and where would we be without it! Apply the Directional Blur filter in the default direction of 0.0°. Move the Indicator to Frame 03;08, click the Blur Length Stopwatch, and set it to 35.0 (Figure 5.23). Then at Frame 03;10, set the Blur Length to 0.0. This will let the planet layer fall straight down smoothly and then come into focus right at the snap-up. Move the Indicator down two frames to 03:12 and set the Blur Length to 5.0; then set it back to 0.0 at 03;14. This will give the initial snap-up a brief motion blur before the final bounces.

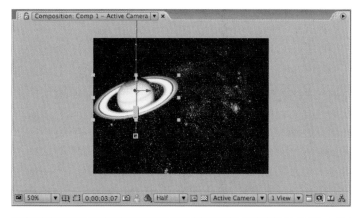

Figure 5.22
In addition to animating the Saturn layer's scale, slightly offsetting the Anchor Point up from the center will give the animation a more 3-D illusion.

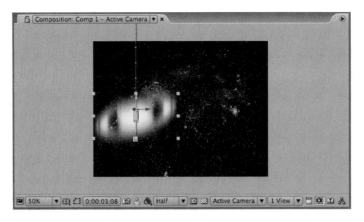

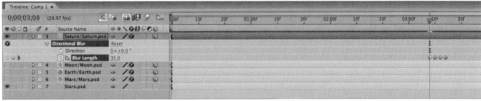

Figure 5.23 Directional Blur is applied to the Saturn layer for the main drop, plus a little is added on the initial snap-up motion.

Completing the Scene: Adding Lights

To give the 3-D layer effect its depth and richness, we need to add lights to the scene. Start by adding an ambient light (Layer > New > Light) and selecting the Ambient Light Type. Set the Intensity to 35% and select a warm yellow color (Figure 5.24). This light does not cast shadows but only warms up the scene after we add the spotlight, so the scene will appear fairly dark at this point.

Figure 5.24

Add an ambient light that will warm up the shadow areas in the final scene.

Add a spotlight to the scene (again, Layer > New > Light) and choose the Spot Light Type. Set the Intensity to 80, and select a lighter hue of the yellow you used for the ambient light. Set the Shadow Darkness to 85 and the Diffusion to 20 (Figure 5.25).

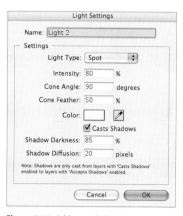

Figure 5.25 Add a spotlight to the scene—this will become the Sun's light source.

Select the Left side view window, and reduce the scale of the frame viewing area to better access the Spot. Click the Spot wireframe (without selecting the X-, Y-, or Z-axis handles), and then drag the light down and out to under the 3 o'clock position. Drag the Point Of Interest handle down to the Earth layer's center (Figure 5.26). Switch to the Front side view window, and drag the Spot wireframe over to the left side, just above the 8 o'clock position. This angle should light up the entire scene well and cast shadows in the right places.

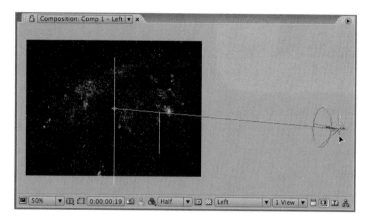

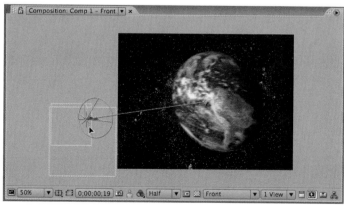

Figure 5.26

Move the spotlight into position to closely match the original position of the Sun to the planet image layers.

Select each planet layer in the Timeline, and open Material Options and turn on the Casts Shadows option (Figure 5.27). Move the Indicator to a point where two planets intersect, and notice the shadow that is cast on the planet layer in the background.

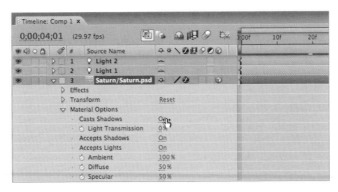

Figure 5.27
Turn on the Casts Shadows option for all of the planet layers.

When all of the planets are in the frame toward the end of the animation, you'll have a collection of planets casting shadows on one another in a fantasy scene. What's more, you've just applied several concepts of animation in a 3-D environment that you can apply to your motion graphics and titling projects.

Kinematics: Human Figure Character Animation

Kinematics, in computer graphics language, is motion created by the force of another material body in motion—usually something that's attached, as a hand is to an arm. If the arm is moved, then the hand must go with it, even though the hand is still free to move on its own.

This is something usually practiced by 3-D character modelers who create video games and animated motion pictures. Fortunately, After Effects gives us some pretty powerful tools to accomplish kinematic motion on two-dimensional characters that can really fool the eye!

For these examples, I've taken a single stock image of a skeleton that had an alpha channel already created, and I tore it to bits! You'll find the Photoshop image,

SkeletonSmall.psd, on the DVD, so you can see the many layers that were created out of this original image (Figure 5.28).

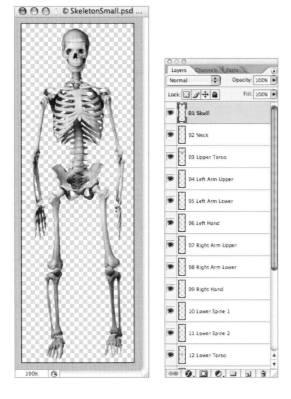

Figure 5.28

Open the skeleton Photoshop file to examine how the layers are created and how they go together.

Create a new project file in After Effects, and import the file SkeletonSmall.psd as a composition to retain the layer information. Open the composition from the Project window, and edit the Composition Settings to resize it and allow more side-to-side motion when animating the layers.

Determine a central point of the body, which all the other parts can link to and move naturally. I've chosen the upper torso layer, where the arms, neck, and spine can connect to it. From this point, we will work out from the upper torso through all of the extremities. You may want to at least peek at the After Effects project file, Skeleton_Practice.aep, on the DVD, to follow along until you get the hang of what we're doing.

The Knee Bone's Connected to the Leg Bone

Connecting the layered pieces will require important techniques: proper positioning of the Anchor Points and parenting the layers. The Anchor Points need to be located on each layer where the swivel point of the joint would naturally move. This is where it will be "connected" to the layer to which it is parented.

Moving the Anchor Point on each layer requires you to open each layer in its own window and zoom in so you can really see what you're doing! Drag the Anchor Point to the joint or nearest connector point where it can swivel around (Figure 5.29).

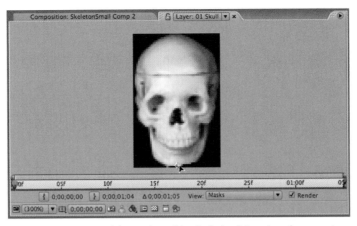

Figure 5.29 Zoom in on each layer and reposition the Anchor Points where they connect with other pieces.

To "connect" the layers, we use the Parent option on the Timeline. This doesn't really completely connect the layers, but it does allow you to move the parented layer and have those layers attached to it move with it. Parenting also allows you to rotate layers, and they will rotate around the Anchor Point that you positioned at the joint, so they will appear to be attached to the parented layer.

Let's look at a smaller segment to further understand how this works. Hide all of the layers except for the two left arm layers and the left hand layer. With the Anchor Points at the joints connecting to the preceding layer, select the preceding layer as a parent layer using the Parent Layer Selector on the Timeline (Figure 5.30). Rotate the lower arm layer and see how it moves at the elbow. Rotate the hand layer, and it should bend at the wrist. Move or rotate the upper arm layer, and both the lower arm and hand will move with it.

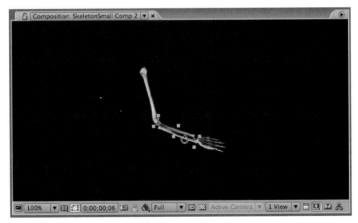

Figure 5.30 Experimenting with a small section of the skeleton will help you understand the physics of the motion and how the layers work together.

With everything parented in all the way to the upper torso layer, you should be able to move the layer, and the whole skeleton will move with it. If you rotate the upper torso slightly, you will need to rotate the spine segments, lower torso, and legs to bring the feet back down to the ground (Figure 5.31).

Figure 5.31 Rotate the upper torso layer, spine segments, and lower torso layer to see how twisting the body makes the rest of the limbs react.

Making adjustments to all of the limbs from this position, you can start to emulate graceful movements (Figure 5.32). It's like combining a stop-motion wire figure animator with a puppeteer. With a little creativity and finesse, you can really have fun animating your skeleton character!

In some cases, you will need to adjust the length of a foot, arm, or leg segment to give the appearance of upward or downward motion in the Z-axis—even though there is no Z-axis present in a two-dimensional animation (Figure 5.33).

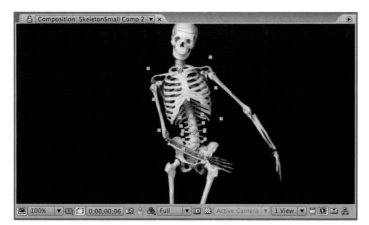

Figure 5.32
Some experimentation and practice will help you get the feel for putting your character in motion.

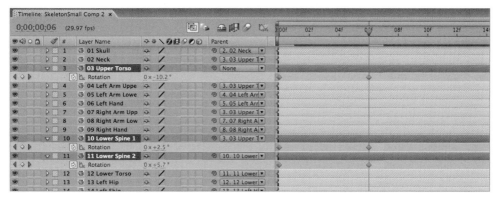

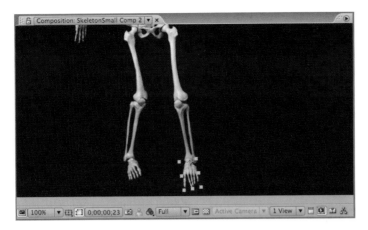

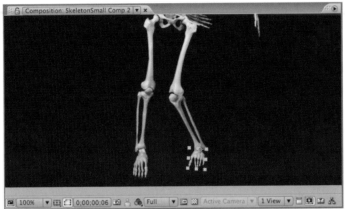

Figure 5.33
Scale the length of a segment to adjust for the lack of a Z-axis in a two-dimensional animation.

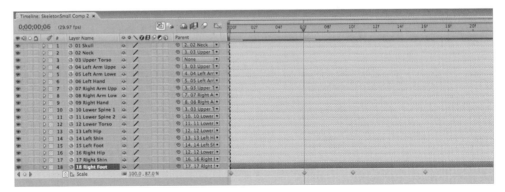

Kinematic Animation Example

Let's make a simple animation that moves every layer in our skeleton, simply by rotating layers with kinematic motion. Using the principles previously covered, we'll build this animation key frame by key frame, instead of layer by layer.

Because of the possible variations in building your model, it would be best to use the file Skeleton_Practice.aep from the DVD. The parent layers have already been applied, so all you have to do is follow the settings in Table 5.12 and study what is happening in each layer's rotation.

▶ **Table 5.12** Simple Kinematic Skeleton Key Frames (All in Degrees)

Layer Transform Rotation	00;00	00;06	00;08	00;10	00;16	00;23	00;25	00;26	01;04
01 Skull	−0.8	+11.1			+0.5	−14.3			−1.9
02 Neck	−0.3	+11.7			−3.1	−16.5			+0.8
03 Upper Torso	+1.1	−10.2			+4.7	+17.5			+1.0
04 Left Arm Upper	+0.0	−13.9	−17.5	−4.6	−0.3	+23.3		+15.5	−1.1
05 Left Arm Lower	+6.2	−35.5	−58.0		−3.3	−14.6	+5.2	−7.1	+8.6
06 Left Hand	−7.4					−16.9			−9.7
07 Right Arm Upper	−0.9	−22.9	−29.2	−23.7	−6.6		+11.5	+3.5	+0.2
08 Right Arm Lower	−5.0	−4.0	−10.0	+10.0	−1.4	+39.6	+48.4		−8.2
09 Right Hand	+5.2	+27.8					+41.2	+24.5	+12.7
10 Lower Spine 1	+1.1	+2.5			−3.7	−5.7			−1.3
11 Lower Spine 2	+0.0	+5.7			−4.1	−5.0			−1.3
12 Lower Torso	+1.4	+13.0			+5.9	−1.6			+5.2
13 Left Hip	−5.6	−8.7	−9.4		−8.1	−15.2	−20.7	−15.8	−4.2
14 Left Shin	+2.8	+6.5		+7.5	+9.9	+23.1	+48.7	+35.5	+0.1
15 Left Foot	−6.1	−15.0		−9.2	−18.6	−45.2	−52.8	−43.1	−4.7
16 Right Hip	+2.2	+10.5	+16.2	+9.7	+2.6	−5.1		−0.5	+4.7
17 Right Shin	+0.0	−43.6	−55.8	−35.1	−3.2	−6.4			
18 Right Foot	−11.0	+26.9		+25.3	−3.5		−3.6	−8.9	−5.1

Note: If you would like to see the completed After Effects files in their entirety, open Skeleton-Project1.aep and SkeletonProject2.aep on the DVD and compare them to the projects in this section. You can also view the completed QuickTime movies of the completed animations.

Details in Kinematic Animations

Subtle movements and fine details are what give realism to figure animation. Although this skeleton doesn't have individual moving fingers and toes, you can still apply movement that emulates a real figure, just by keeping constant motion present in small amounts.

The effects of kinematic motion are most noticeable when you are applying them to shoulders or hips, where there are many intersecting points. The tilt of a shoulder will cause necessary adjustments of the head and neck, as well as of the arms and the lower spine. Something as simple as crossing the arms or shifting to one foot causes a ripple effect throughout the entire body—as in SkeletonProject2.aep, the sample animation located in the Chapter 5 project folder on the DVD.

When creating animations that require precision in movement, you will need to use rulers and guides to keep track of where your character is moving. While you are concentrating on the upper body, the legs may shift out from under you, and before you know it, you could end up with a floating ghost with dangling legs!

While shifting the weight of the figure to one foot, you can see how much the rest of the body is influenced by this move (Figure 5.34). When the leg crosses over, the hips swivel upward, the spine adjusts to keep the head and upper body level, and the body comes to rest centered over the standing leg.

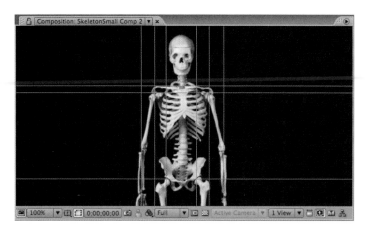

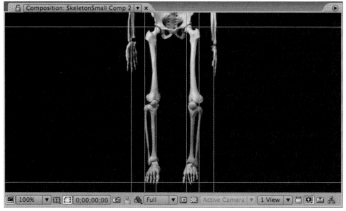

Figure 5.34
Using guides is very important to track your motion and make sure everything lines up correctly.

Clean-Up, Mattes, and Objects

In the early days of filmmaking, characters were shot against a white background, and then animations were drawn and superimposed onto the footage to make a composite. Then came the art of matte painting—where a scene is shot, the film is partially developed, and a piece of glass is painted with the scene that couldn't have been created realistically in any other way. The rest of the film is exposed to this painting—creating a seamless composition. Today, the animations, mattes, and composites are all done digitally, and we're going to explore some of those processes in this section.

III

  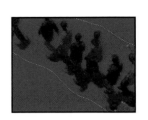 

02:01:56:17

Blue-Screen Garbage Mattes

Blue-screen and green-screen compositing have become more and more popular, with higher-quality prosumer DV cameras and video editing software becoming more accessible. But sometimes stuff gets in the way; you want to edit out something that falls in front of or next to your blue screen. A simple crop or mask of the scene might eliminate the majority of the unwanted materials. If the shot has too much movement in an asymmetrical pattern or was shot at an angle in the frame, then a combination of techniques, such as garbage mattes and rotoscoping, may be necessary.

Chapter Contents

What Is a Garbage Matte?

Unfortunately, locations and chroma backgrounds aren't always the best suited for a shot, but you have to work with what you have. For instance, if you have a distant shot of subjects in front of a chroma tarp, you may be limited to the available size for the scene. This would leave edges of the frame, hardware, lights, or cables exposed in the shot around the subject. All of these items and edges have to be removed before you can use the blue-screen footage in a composite.

A garbage matte is a solid-layer mask that covers up the majority of "garbage" around the blue-screened subject—staying clear of any motion paths that may get covered up. This helps to minimize the amount of rotoscoping necessary to remove the remaining unwanted material.

A *garbage matte* is usually a single, static layer that overlays the blue-screen footage in an After Effects composite. Placed in combination with solid-colored layers that track the movement in the frame, a garbage matte can help you cover up a great deal.

The project used in this chapter is a blue-screen shot from a crane above the actors walking across a chroma tarp. The lighting was natural daylight with a few large reflectors to soften any hard shadows on the actors. The problem was that the chroma tarp was too small for the entire required scene, so a garbage matte and rotoscoping were required to fill in the gaps and outlying areas beyond the tarp in the frame.

A Blue-Screen/Green-Screen Primer

Proper lighting for blue/green screens varies for the location and shoot. If it is an outdoor shot that doesn't require capturing the actors' shadows, then the screen is placed well behind the actors with reflectors flooding it with light. Most blue/green screen shots are done in a controlled studio environment that virtually emulates optimum natural lighting conditions. Keeping the chroma background evenly and brightly lit is important so that you can eliminate as many shadows, wrinkles, or imperfections as possible and give an even space for proper removal. The actors are usually placed at least 10 to 15 feet in front of a well-lit chroma background to keep the background evenly lit and have the minimum amount of spill onto the back and edges of the actors.

Why use blue rather than green—or vice versa? Green has an obvious advantage over blue for complete and separate keying from a background, because this shade of green doesn't exist in nature. However, the blue is much more tolerant to spill onto the actor, because the light does exist in nature and is less discernable in a composite. This is why blue has been preferred for close-range keying, where the shadows and close proximity of the actors mean that they come in physical contact with the chroma background.

Today's software matte and keying plug-ins (commonly referred to as "keyers") are more capable of accurately blending edge tolerances and background-to-foreground color correction than their predecessors of only a few years ago. You can learn more about these software plug-ins for After Effects and Photoshop in Chapter 9, "Matte and Keying Plug-ins."

The Static Garbage Matte: Defining the Matte's Boundaries

Defining precisely where the boundaries of the garbage matte need to be placed depends on the extreme motion path of your actors in the frame. You will need to define the beginning and end of their path, as well as how far outside of a straight line in that path that they venture—including any extremities or props used in the scene.

Note: The work in this chapter requires the upgrade to QuickTime Pro, not QuickTime Player. Pro is available from Apple for less than $30.

1. For this project, we'll start with the QuickTime movie file, WalkingBluescreen.mov, located on the DVD in the Chapter 6 folder. Open this movie file in QuickTime Pro (Figure 6.1).

Figure 6.1 Open the movie file in QuickTime Pro to set up the edge definition process.

2. Start from Frame 1 and copy the frame to the clipboard (⌘/Ctrl+C), and then create a new file in Photoshop, using the dimensions from the clipboard.

3. Paste the image into the Photoshop file, which will become Layer 1 in the Layers palette.

4. Return to the QuickTime movie and drag the playback Indicator to the position where the actors stop briefly, bend over, and look off to the lower-left side of the frame. This will be the extreme lower-left position defined in our garbage matte. Make sure to scrub the Indicator back and forth to locate the exact frame that moves into the extreme position, and copy it to the clipboard.

5. Return to Photoshop and paste the frame into the file we've created, as Layer 2 in the Layers palette. Set the Blending Mode for Layer 2 to Darken (Figure 6.2). This will allow the placement of the actors from the previous frame to show through so both will be visible to trace.

Figure 6.2 Paste the new layer over the old and set the Blending Mode to Darken to expose the layer below.

6. Continue this process with a few more frames that take the actors outside a direct path from beginning to end, including the last frame—giving you several reference layers.

7. Create a new layer on the top. Use the Lasso tool with a 10-pixel feather to roughly draw an area around the entire path of your characters, creating a large, oblong selection. Invert the selection (⌘+Shift+I/Ctrl+Shift+I) and fill with a solid color that matches the existing blue-screen background, using the Eyedropper to select the color as necessary (Figure 6.3).

8. Save the PSD file with the layers intact, because this is the static garbage matte that will be imported into After Effects.

9. Create a new project in After Effects, as a composition 640 × 480 NTSC, 11 seconds in length. Import the movie file, WalkingBluescreen.mov, and only the top garbage matte layer of the PSD file you just created (or use the file BluescreenMatte.psd, also found on the DVD).

10. Drag both files from the Project window to the Comp 1 window, with the garbage matte layer on top (Figure 6.4).

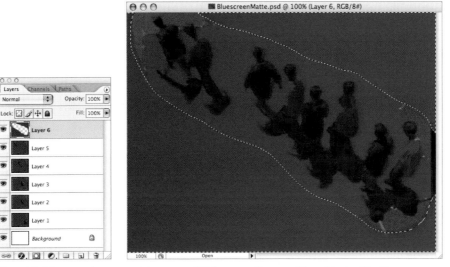

Figure 6.3 Select a rough area around the actors and fill the surrounding area with a solid color of the blue-screen background.

This completes the static portion of the garbage matte. Scrub the Indicator in the Timeline window to verify that the garbage matte layer doesn't interfere with the motion path of the characters in the movie. If there is an error in your matte, then simply edit the original file (Edit > Edit Original, or ⌘/Ctrl+E) to make corrections.

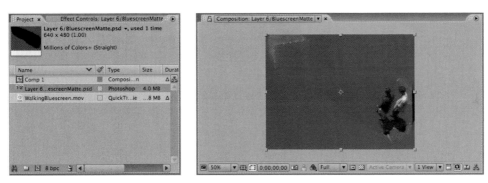

Figure 6.4 Import the blue-screen movie file and the garbage matte layer into a new After Effects composition.

The Garbage Matte in Motion

Sometimes the static garbage matte is sufficient to cover up the bulk of unwanted material, leaving only a small portion of the footage to be retouched. In this example, sections of the footage where the actors are off the edge of the blue screen are at both the beginning and the end of the motion path. We will add some solid blocks of color that can be moved to fill in the largest gaps, so only the first and last few frames will need to be rotoscoped.

1. Add a solid layer (Layer > New > Solid, or ⌘/Ctrl+Y), and set the dimensions small enough to quickly resize and position where needed. Set the color of the layer to match the garbage matte, using the Eyedropper in the dialog box. Resize and position the solid layer as close to the right side of the actors as possible.

2. Duplicate the solid layer three more times (Edit > Duplicate, or ⌘/Ctrl+D). Move and resize each layer to fit over the largest area of background to cover it up without getting too close to the characters. Position one layer on the bottom side of the actors and two in the top-left corner, completely covering up the exposed area (Figure 6.5).

3. Select all of the solid layers in the Timeline, press the P key to open the Position settings, and select the Stopwatch on each layer to set the initial position of the layers.

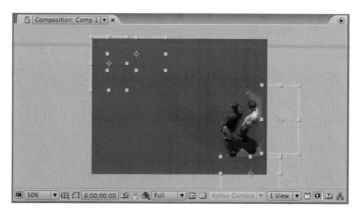

Figure 6.5
Create solid layers that can be animated to follow the characters' motion path and fill in the exposed areas off the blue-screen tarp.

4. Select just the two bottom-right layers, move the Indicator on the Timeline down a few frames, and drag the solid layers to follow the actors' motion path to close up the exposed area. Continue a few frames at a time, trying to cover as much unwanted material as possible until the gap is completely filled (Figure 6.6).

5. Move the Indicator toward the end of the actors' motion path, just until they touch the edges of the upper-left solid layers, and then back off one frame so they don't touch. Click the Set Marker box for both layers in the Timeline. Move the layers just ahead of the actors every few frames—just the opposite of the movements made in the lower-right solid layers (Figure 6.7).

6. Save the After Effects project file.

Note that the main middle section of the blue-screen footage has a clean and clear background and needs no further retouching or roto work—the garbage mattes have done the bulk of the work. However, the first one or two seconds of footage, as well as the last, need to have work done on them.

Move the Work Area slider from start and finish to capture just the last couple of frames that need to be exported and worked on. Render out a noncompressed full-size QuickTime movie of the Work Area, and repeat the process for the opening sequence of the footage. View the rendered movies in QuickTime Pro (Figure 6.8).

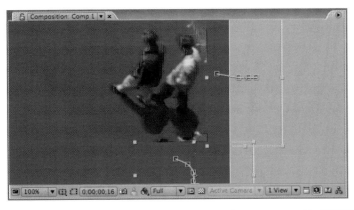

Figure 6.6
Move the solid layers to follow the actors' motion path to close up the exposed area off the edge of the chroma tarp.

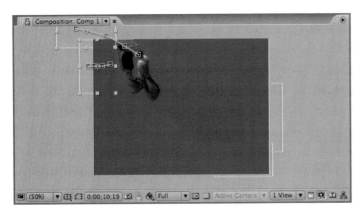

Figure 6.7
Repeat the process with the solid layers on the actors' exit path, but in reverse motion.

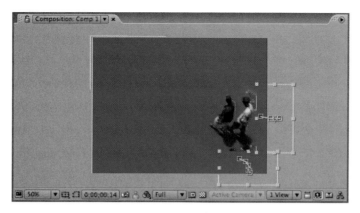

Figure 6.8
Render only the Work Area of the section of footage that needs roto work to a QuickTime movie.

Preparing Frames for Rotoscoping

To do frame-by-frame rotoscoping in Photoshop, you need to convert the movie to separate editable frames. By opening the movie in ImageReady, single layers and frames will be automatically created from the QuickTime movie footage.

In ImageReady, open the QuickTime movie clip you rendered out of After Effects (File > Open). You'll see a dialog box asking you to select some options (Figure 6.9). In this case, because we rendered only the portion we need to rotoscope, we'll select the From Beginning To End option. You may also select a range within a QuickTime movie to import.

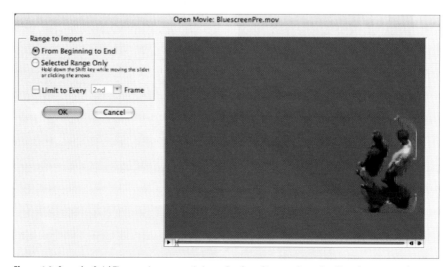

Figure 6.9 Open the QuickTime movie sequence in ImageReady and import the entire clip to be rotoscoped.

ImageReady turns the image frames into individual layers that can be rotoscoped in Photoshop. Jump to Photoshop so that you can start the frame rotoscoping work (Figure 6.10), and save the new file as a Photoshop document.

Figure 6.10 ImageReady converts the frames to individual layers that you can edit in Photoshop.

Your File Really Isn't Too Big

When jumping back to ImageReady from Photoshop with a rather large multilayer file, you may encounter a recommended file size warning (40 MB maximum). Don't be alarmed—though you might be taken aback by the warning message, you can continue the process without interruption. (You may also choose to disable the warning message in the future).

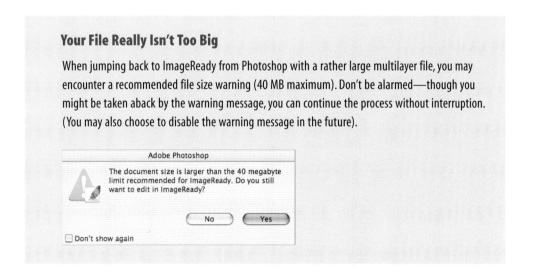

Jump to Photoshop and perform the rotoscoping edits to each layer as necessary (Figure 6.11). See Chapter 7, "Rotoscoping Techniques with Photoshop," for more information on how to tackle this task. Once the editing is completed on all of the affected layers, save the Photoshop file and jump back to ImageReady.

Figure 6.11 Rotoscope the individual layers and jump back to ImageReady to export the rotoscoped movie.

You can now export the file as a QuickTime movie by selecting File > Export > Original Document and choosing the QuickTime Movie format. Once you click the OK button, a dialog box will appear to allow you to set the compression and color depth of the QuickTime movie. Because this movie needs to remain as pure and unadulterated as the original blue-screen frames, you will want to select None for the compression and choose the maximum color space.

Note: Alternatively, you may want to export single frames from ImageReady instead of a QuickTime movie. Select File > Export > Layers As Files or Animation Frames As Files. These sequenced image files can be opened in QuickTime Pro by selecting File > Open > Image Sequence. A dialog will appear, asking you to set the Frame Rate in frames per second. Because the original footage was 30 fps, you will want to match that exactly. Save the new movie as a noncompressed QuickTime movie file.

Check the QuickTime movie in real time to see if any frames require additional editing. Sometimes it's hard to tell if you are rotoscoping too close to the actors, which may cause some frame flickering. More on controlling this effect is found in Chapter 7.

Bringing Matte Techniques Together

Once you have rotoscoped both of the sequences and converted them back into QuickTime movies, you can import them back into After Effects to complete the blue-screen footage.

Open the After Effects project with the garbage mattes (you can select the file BluescreenMatte.aep on the DVD), and import the two rotoscoped QuickTime movies (also on the DVD, titled BluescreenPreRoto.mov and BluescreenPostRoto.mov).

Place the beginning rotoscoped movie at the beginning of the Timeline, and position it to match the frames of the existing blue-screen footage. Do the same with the ending rotoscoped movie (Figure 6.12). The entire footage sequence should now be entirely clean and free of all unwanted background materials, leaving only the blue-screen background in the full frame behind the actors. Render out this movie in full scale with no compression to use in a composite movie. (We'll refer to this blue-screen movie later in the book; see Chapter 11, " Motion Matte Painting in Photoshop.") Figure 6.13 shows a sample frame.

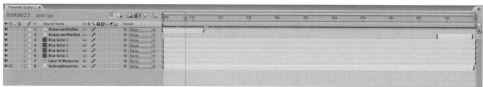

Figure 6.12
Position the rotoscoped movies with the garbage mattes and the original blue-screen footage to create a complete full-frame blue-screen movie.

Figure 6.13
Now you can use this rendered, cleaned-up blue-screen movie in your composite, with no interference or loss of image quality.

Rotoscoping Techniques with Photoshop

7

Rotoscoping is the process of animating, compositing, or editing individual frames of a video or film. Before computers were used in special effects, films were projected onto special animation stands, called rotoscopes, where animated characters could be traced or drawn to match the footage step-by-step. This process is now completed digitally, using software that can manipulate layers on each frame to be modified, such as After Effects and Photoshop.

Chapter Contents

Roto Sequences: Getting In and Out

In order to edit frames of running footage, you need to capture the individual frames and put them back when you've finished working on them. ImageReady will automatically divide a movie into sequenced frames and layers so they can be edited and exported again as a lossless QuickTime movie. Being able to edit the frames as layers allows you to work with transparency, so you can see the details in this section. Another way to divide a movie file into sequenced frame files is to use QuickTime Pro to export them and then open the entire folder in ImageReady as animation frames and layers. The layers can then be edited in Photoshop and exported as a QuickTime movie from ImageReady.

Open the QuickTime movie file, LoungeGuy_MED.MOV, located on the DVD in the Chapter 7 folder, with ImageReady, and import the entire movie sequence (Figure 7.1). The sequence will be imported as individual frames and layers, ready to jump to Photoshop for editing.

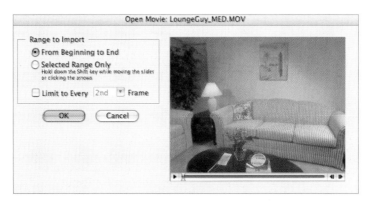

Figure 7.1 Open the movie file in ImageReady as an Image Sequence and layers.

Simple Roto Removal

As we continue with this project, we'll remove the jacket the guy tosses on the arm of the sofa before he plops down. This is an easy video clip in which to do this because it's a locked-off camera shot and we have excellent resource material from Frame 1, before he enters the scene.

Jump to Photoshop and select Layer 1 (Frame 1 of the video sequence). Using the Clone Stamp tool and a 5-pixel hard-edge brush, clone out the tip of the jacket that is coming into the frame in the lower right (Figure 7.2). Be sure that the stripes on the sofa line up correctly as you apply the tool.

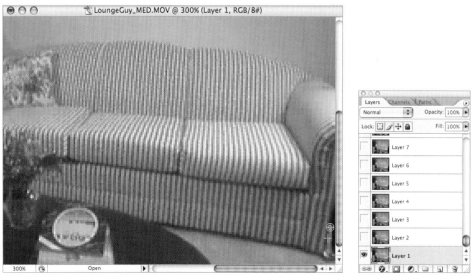

Figure 7.2 Clone out the small portion of the jacket against the bottom right edge of the sofa.

Note: When rotoscoping details, zoom into the area you're working on so you can be sure that each layer (or frame) lines up perfectly. If you don't carefully pay attention to detail, you will create a pattern that will skip and jump frantically when the video is played back.

Select All and copy Layer 1 to the clipboard. Go to Layer 2 and paste. Link Layer 2 and the pasted Layer 1 together, and choose Merge Linked from the Layers palette menu, or you can choose Layer > Merge Down (⌘/Ctrl+E). Continue until you reach Layer 10. At this point, the guy's foot and leg start to show and will need to be revealed in the frame. Set the pasted Layer 1 Opacity to 35% so you see a ghosted image over the sofa pattern, and then use the Eraser tool with a 5-pixel hard-edge brush to remove only the area where the leg and foot are visible (Figure 7.3). Set the pasted Layer 1 Opacity to 100%, and make sure you have a clean edge on the pant leg, without any of the jacket showing.

Figure 7.3
Use the Eraser tool to remove only the areas where the guy's leg and foot are visible.

Since the guy is coming into frame in the room, his body will begin to cast shadows on the surrounding furniture, starting with the coffee table. Click the Layer Visibility icon on and off to see where the shadows lie. Use the Eraser tool with a large soft-edge brush (at least 65 pixels in diameter) to remove material on the pasted Layer 1 to expose those shadows (Figure 7.4).

Figure 7.4
Use a large soft-edge brush with the Eraser tool to remove the areas covering the shadows in the foreground.

Once you are satisfied with the edited layer, link it with the layer below and choose Merge Linked. Repeat this process for a few more layers until the guy is completely into frame and has already tossed the jacket onto the sofa.

We are now at a place where we no longer need to paste such a large area, because our edits will be concentrated around the jacket and the guy as he moves in front of it. Use a large 65-pixel soft-edge brush with the Eraser tool to remove all but a general area around the jacket (Figure 7.5). This will leave a soft area that will cover the jacket without affecting the rest of the image—requiring only smaller edits around the guy's legs and feet through the end of the video clip.

Figure 7.5

Use a large soft-edge brush with the Eraser tool to remove all material except for a general area covering the jacket.

Before continuing to edit this layer, we want to copy it to use in additional layer edits, but, if we just copy and paste it, the pasted layers will now center the small amount of material in the frame instead of placing it exactly in the proper location. To remedy this, we will replace a very small portion of the layer in all four corners, using the History Brush.

In the History palette, go back to the point where you pasted Layer 1, and click the check box next to it, identifying this as the reference point for the History Brush to get its information from. Return to the current state in the History palette and hide the subsequent layer, leaving the background transparent. Use a 9-pixel soft-edge brush to replace a small portion of the pasted Layer 1 image into the four corners (Figure 7.6). Select All and copy this layer to the clipboard. This will allow proper placement of the copied layer, aligned correctly from this point forward.

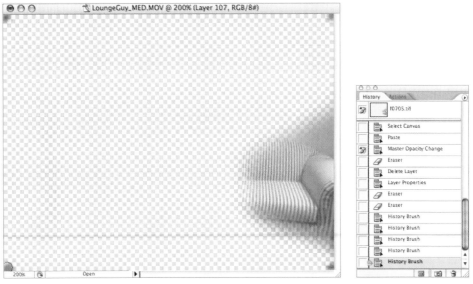

Figure 7.6 Use the History Brush to replace the four corners of the pasted layer to assure proper alignment.

Continue editing the pasted layers with the Eraser tool brushes and merging the remaining layers accordingly. Once you have completed the entire sequence, start from the first layer and duplicate it (⌘/Ctrl+J). Repeat for all remaining layers until each layer has a duplicate above it in the Layers palette, save the file, and then jump to ImageReady.

From the Animation palette menu, choose Delete Animation and then Make Frames From Layers. This will give us the correct playback rate from the duplicated frames, giving us 30 fps from the original 15 fps video clip (Figure 7.7).

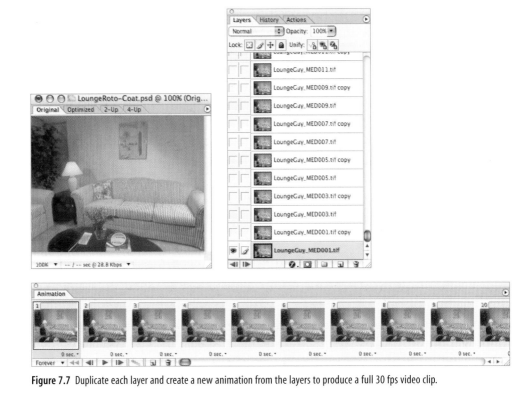

Figure 7.7 Duplicate each layer and create a new animation from the layers to produce a full 30 fps video clip.

Save your work, and then export the movie (Export > Original Document) and choose QuickTime Movie from the Format selector (Figure 7.8). Save the movie uncompressed for the best possible quality, and play it back in QuickTime Pro for review.

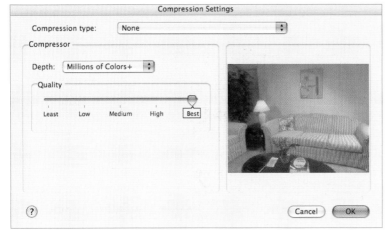

Figure 7.8
Export the roto-scoped sequence as a QuickTime movie from ImageReady.

Blue-Screen Matte Rotoscoping

As we covered the process of making garbage mattes in Chapter 6, "Blue-Screen Garbage Mattes," several frames required rotoscoping where the actors walked off the edge of the blue-screen tarp. From the After Effects file, we rendered out two QuickTime movies—a "pre" and "post." Those edited-out movies contain about 1 second of video that needs to be roto edited.

1. Open the movie file, BSMattePre.mov, in ImageReady and jump to Photoshop. Start with the first layer (Frame 1), and use the Paintbrush tool with a small hard-edge brush to paint in the missing blue background (Figure 7.9). You must

take great care in selecting brush sizes and edge hardness/softness to blend in with the edges of the characters and around their shadows. You will notice some natural video noise along the edges of the characters; try not to remove too much of it, or it will show in the final composite.

Figure 7.9 Carefully paint in the blue background around the characters and their shadows.

2. Use the Clone Stamp tool to fill inside the shadow area that's off the matte, being careful not to create duplicate patterns or banding, because these will show up in the final video (Figure 7.10). Do not clone more area than is necessary to help minimize the changes from frame to frame.

3. Continue with each layer, checking your progress against the preceding layers and taking care not to paint in too close to the character edges.

4. When you have finished, save the file and jump to ImageReady. Export the original as a QuickTime movie with no compression so it will match the garbage matte original movie.

5. Repeat the entire process for the "post" blue-screen matte sequence, and export it as a QuickTime movie.

6. Open After Effects. Import the original garbage matte composite movie as described in Chapter 6, along with the two new QuickTime movies. Align the rotoscoped movie sequences to both ends, and render them as one complete movie to be used in composite projects (Figure 7.11).

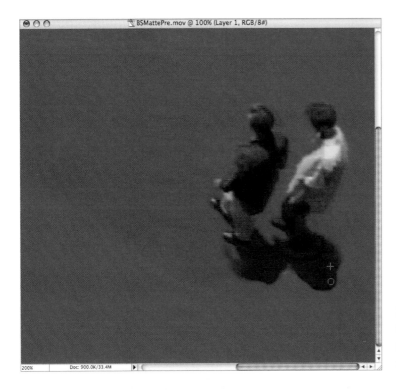

Figure 7.10
Use the Clone Stamp tool to fill in the missing details of the shadow areas.

Figure 7.11
Export the edited sequence as a QuickTime movie from ImageReady, and import them into After Effects to be aligned with the original garbage matte movie.

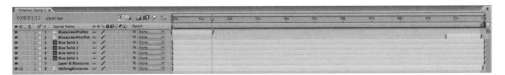

Stabilizing and Rotoscoping Old Movies

Before they are digitized, many old movies require a lot of restoration work because of deteriorating film and the crude photographic equipment that was used in the early twentieth century. During film exposure, early moviemakers used hand-cranked cameras with loose mechanisms. This loose quality was usually compounded by equally crude-fitting projection equipment, making for a pretty jumpy viewing experience.

Restoration of old movie footage requires many techniques, depending on the amount of deterioration or affected motion. In this project, we will stabilize the footage, reframe it, and rotoscope the worst dirt particles and scratches. Stabilization is performed in After Effects, which will give us a steady palette on which to do our roto work. Unfortunately, with hand-cranked cameras, the exposure on each individual frame varies too much to make the proper adjustments, because too much information is lost in overexposed frames.

1. Create a new project file in After Effects and import the movie file HorseStabilize-.mov; create a new composition 640 × 480 NTSC, 7 seconds in length.

2. Scale the movie up to 102%. This will hide the rough edges in the original movie file.

3. Apply a stabilizing tracker to the movie (Animation > Stabilize Motion). This will create Tracker 1 and will place a square Track Point 1 in the middle of the Comp window. Locate a stationary object in an area of the movie that has contrast—such as the lettering on the sign—and drag the box out and around some of the smaller details (Figure 7.12).

Figure 7.12

Apply and align stabilizing trackers to detailed contrast areas in your movie.

4. Click the forward Analyze button on the Tracker Controls palette and let it run all the way through the movie. Watch the Track Point box in the Comp window as it passes to make sure it doesn't jump far from its original position. If the tracker looks okay after the movie is analyzed, then click the Apply button.

5. Add a second tracker by clicking the Stabilize Motion button and repeating the process on another section of the sign.

6. Render the project as a QuickTime movie, at full resolution and with no compression. Open the rendered movie in QuickTime Pro and export it as an Image Sequence so that you can roto out the dirt and scratches. Because this movie is already 30 fps, make sure to export the Image Sequence at 30 fps as well.

7. Import the folder of sequence files into ImageReady, and then jump to Photoshop to begin the roto process.

Note: For this example, I rotoscope edited only 1 second of the movie. The before and after example movies can be found in the Chapter 7 folder on the DVD.

8. On each layer, use the Clone Stamp tool with various size brushes to carefully remove dirt, dust, and scratches in the frame (Figure 7.13). Compare each layer with the preceding and following frames to be sure that the "spot" you remove really should be removed! Take care to not disturb contrasting edges of clouds, buildings, and other objects in the movie.

Figure 7.13
Rotoscope out the dirt, dust, and scratches from each frame with the Clone Stamp tool.

Once you've completed the rotoscope edits on all layers, save the file and jump back to ImageReady. Export the sequence to a QuickTime movie file and review it in QuickTime Pro.

Colorizing Old Movies with Photoshop Layers

Once you've stabilized and rotoscoped an old movie, you may want to give it a little character and modernization by tint colorizing. Instead of perfect colorizing in fine detail, this stylized process will result in something you may have seen in the fifties or sixties with tinted black-and-white movies. This process can be done easily by creating a few layers in Photoshop and animating them in AfterEffects on top of the black-and-white QuickTime movie.

In this project, we'll use an old Los Angeles street scene, featuring a few classic cars in motion. Open the movie file CarsRoto.mov in QuickTime Pro. Find a few frames of the movie that show the best view of each of the cars. This might be a bit more difficult for the faster moving cars, but we don't have to be too precise in this process.

Copy each frame where a car is in view to the clipboard, and paste it into a new Photoshop file of the same dimensions (Figure 7.14). Keep adding the layers, one on top of another.

Figure 7.14 Locate the frames that best show the cars, and copy and paste them into a Photoshop file as layers.

Start with the background cars and buildings, hiding the other car layers. Create a new layer above the street-level layer, and set the Blending Mode to Color. Use the Paintbrush tool with hard-edge brushes to paint color around all of the objects in the frame, using colors that may be somewhat natural, but don't try for perfect shading (Figure 7.15). Change the Blending Mode to Normal occasionally, and check to see that you have total coverage on the buildings, the street, and the two cars in the background.

Figure 7.15 Paint in colored areas in a layer above the street-level layer.

On the remaining layers, select and remove all of the image material around the cars you want to colorize. This does not need to be an accurate selection, because the colorization will be very generalized in the areas of motion in the final movie composite.

Similarly to the street-level layer, create a new layer above each car layer and set it to Color Blending Mode. Paint the colored layers completely on this layer, switching back and forth between the Color and Normal Blending Modes, to make sure there aren't any "holes" in the colors (Figure 7.16). If an area is to be left with no color, such as around the wheels or chrome, then use white or gray, so they do not become transparent. It is fine to leave some transparency in the windows so the background colors will pass through.

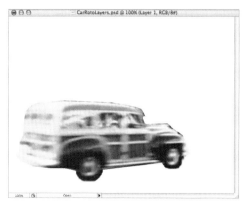 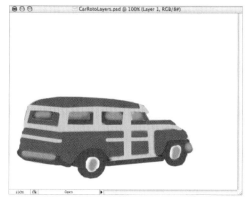

Figure 7.16

Isolate the cars on their own layers and paint on color layers above each of them, and don't leave any gaps in the painted areas.

Once you have created color layers for each separate car and the street-level layers, save the PSD file and create a new project file in AfterEffects. Import the CarsRoto.mov QuickTime movie file and the color-layered PSD file as a Composition to retain the layers.

Create a new composition, 640 × 480 NTSC, 3 seconds in length, and drag both imported files to the Comp window. Delete the still black-and-white and background layers from the PSD file in the Timeline window. Change the Blending Mode on all of the color layers for the individual cars and the street-level layer to Color (Layer > Blending Mode > Color). Arrange them in order on the Timeline so the street-level layer is on the bottom, just over the movie layer, and then proceed with Layers 2, 3, and 4 in order on top of that (Figure 7.17). At Frame 1 on the Timeline, hide Layers 3 and 4, because those cars are not in the frame yet.

Starting with Layer 2 at Frame 1, the beige car is in the center of the frame. You may need to drag the layer into position over the car if it isn't already aligned. Because the car will be moving at an angle off the left side of the screen, the color layer will need to be scaled and moved along to follow the car beneath. Open the Transform option on Layer 2 in the Timeline, and click the Stopwatches for both Position and Scale. This will set the key frames for Frame 1.

Figure 7.17 Arrange the layers in order on the Timeline so that the street-level layer is just above the movie layer, followed by Layers 2, 3, and 4.

Move the Indicator down to the point where you see the yellow car start to go off the screen, and then drag the color layer to the left to match up with it (Figure 7.18). You will need to adjust both the Scale and Position as the car approaches, and try to align it as close as possible to the car in the movie layer. When you click on and drag a color layer, it will temporarily turn opaque. This is normal behavior, and the layer will return to the colorized mode as soon as you let go.

Figure 7.18 Reposition and scale the color layer of the yellow car to match the motion as close as possible with the movie.

 Note: Layers that have the Blending Mode set to Color in After Effects will override the colors of the layer beneath as they pass over the top of one another. This makes it easy to colorize using only the color layers without having to set each colorized object on its own layer.

Continue with the remaining color layers, repositioning and scaling them to match the car's motion on the movie layer beneath them. Notice how the colors of the cars and background show through the transparent portions of the windows (Figure 7.19).

Figure 7.19 Move and scale the other two color layers for the cars.

Shooting a Clean Blue/Green Screen

8

Perhaps the most problematic shooting condition for most amateur or intermediate videographers and cinematographers is blue/green screen chroma-keying production. This technique has been around for decades. It has been used for projects ranging from special effects in motion pictures and television to the meteorological graphics on the evening news. It is now possible for even the smallest budget production to have good results with a minimal setup in either a studio or outside. The key (no pun intended) is to light the blue or green screen behind the subject evenly, without creating "spill" onto the subject or creating too much of a difference in background/foreground exposures.

Chapter Contents

Blue versus Green Screen
Green Screen Materials
Lighting the Green Screen and Subjects
Matching the Subject Lighting to the Composition Environment

Blue versus Green Screen

There are no hard and fast rules regarding screen color choice, but there are some known issues and guidelines you need to consider before choosing between a blue or green screen. Obviously, you don't want to put a person with a blue shirt in front of a blue screen unless you are purposely trying to key out the shirt and allow their head and hands to float freely!

Blue is normally reserved for film and high-end professional HD cameras (not the prosumer models that have compression in the DV codec) and can handle dimly lit scenes. On rare occasions, red or even magenta can be used in filming effects scenes that might require a great deal of foreground blue in the subjects. For most DV compositions, however, green is the key color of choice. DV stores luma information (the brightness and contrast) at up to four times the color information, so you want as much contrast between the background and foreground exposures as possible. Plus, the green channel in DV (the "G" in RGB) is where the luma values come from, and it is sampled more than the blue channel, which maintains less color information. This is the same reason why you will find less noise in the green channel compared to either the red or blue channels when they are viewed separately. In addition, a green background requires less light to illuminate it.

Although green is used most often by far, there is an exception to using green. If the subject(s) in an outdoor scene must get close to the screen, casting shadows on it or coming in direct contact with it, you should use blue because the color spill of the blue background is more naturally occurring in an outdoor setting (especially at night, or out of direct sunlight) than that of a green light spill. However, several keying plug-ins for After Effects handle any kind of spill quite nicely, especially Ultimatte. Chapter 9, "Matte and Keying Plug-ins," contains several comparisons that show you how different keying plug-ins work in various situations.

Green Screen Materials

Several types of screen materials, from cloth to special paint and assorted papers, are available. If you need portability, a cloth screen on a stand might meet your needs. This will give you the flexibility to position the background anywhere that's convenient, and many pro lighting equipment and supply houses will rent them to you by the day. With a little research online at regional supplier sites, or on eBay, you'll be able to find backdrop starter kits complete with stands and lights. Backgrounds made from foam-backed material will lay flat, are easier to light evenly, and are not as translucent as green screens made of muslin cloth. Whichever screen material you choose, be very careful when handling and storing your backdrops so that you do not crease them or tear them.

When you are using a cloth backdrop, make sure there isn't any strong lighting from the back side, which would change the overall hue of the cloth surface and could show shadows and objects through the cloth itself. It's also best to use some kind of clamps on the sides of the hanging cloth to stretch it out flat across the surface, providing a tight, wrinkle-free background. I've also found that using a simple hand steamer will remove most wrinkles or creases from a quality muslin backdrop, if needed.

For more professional (and somewhat permanent) studios, you can create complete sets with pro cycs (cycloramas) that blend the floor into to the background wall for smooth, seamless results. These are then painted with a special formula paint (about $60 a gallon from Rosco) for either DigiComp or Ultimatte color specs. Some resourceful producers utilize painted skateboard ramps on location when portability is an issue.

For talking-head shots and shots of small objects, double-sided blue/green "pop-up" backdrops can be used on location for ultimate portability (Figure 8.1).

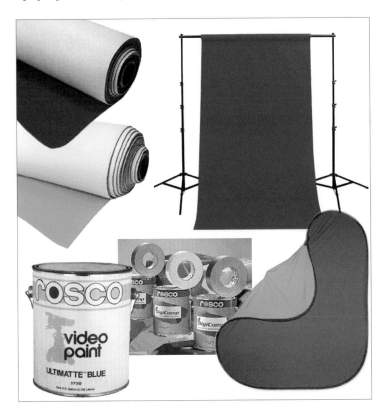

Figure 8.1
Many materials for blue/green screen backgrounds are available from pro suppliers for rent or purchase.

If you're on a budget (who isn't these days?) and can't afford a $60 gallon of paint, you can substitute a poor man's version of a blue/green screen. Using PMS colors that very closely match the DigiComp colors (Figure 8.2), your local home supply or paint center can mix it for about a third of the cost. Keep in mind that house paint won't have the same pigment-to-base ratio, and you will most likely need several coats to cover your wall or background materials. Also be sure to get a completely flat paint, as you won't want any gloss or hot spots to show up on the background surface.

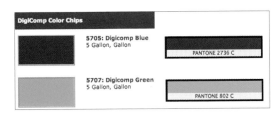

Figure 8.2
Standard PMS colors that come very close to the DigiComp colors can be mixed.

If you're really desperate and just don't have the time or resources to obtain the best materials for the job, a few other materials may just work in a pinch—but expect to spend a great deal more time getting the lighting even and tweaking during the compositing process! For example, a solid dark-blue bed sheet might work if you have plenty of contrast in your foreground subject. Although it might be harder to find, a lime green bed sheet or tablecloth (cloth, not vinyl) could be substituted. Papers are usually the last resort; solid-color papers are usually too pale and dull, and they wash out horribly under most lighting conditions. If you're fortunate enough to find large pieces (or rolls) of matte-finish coated paper that come close to the PMS colors previously described, then they might work. Just make sure to handle/store the paper carefully because any creases or footprints will show up in your composite and create more work for you!

Lighting the Green Screen and Subjects

Lighting is probably the most important part of proper blue/green screen production. If either the screen background or the subject isn't properly lit, then the composite will be a disaster. Following a few simple guidelines will save you hours of frustration in compositing or possibly prevent you from scrapping your footage and starting all over. Even as forgiving as several keying plug-ins can be, you want to eliminate as many potential problems *before* you shoot to get the optimum results and save time in compositing.

You must make sure that you evenly light your background screen. If there are hot spots or shadows or even heavy wrinkles in the cloth, they will create problems in your composite. Unless you are shooting outdoors with natural light, you should always use separate lights to illuminate your background from those used on your subjects. On professional sound stages, banks of special fluorescent light fixtures (usually Kino Flos) are placed all around the edge of a large wall, providing a soft, even, true-color illumination of the background. In smaller sets and on location, a couple of wide halogen lights can be used to light the background, with the subject well in front of the lights to avoid any light spill or edge glow (Figure 8.3). A separate light is used to illuminate the subject, usually with an additional fill light through a soft box or a reflective umbrella to eliminate shadows on the subject's face. If you need additional contrast, as in the case of a subject with flowing blonde hair, you can use a small back light aimed at the subject's head to provide a soft glow and create more contrast from the background.

If you're working with a cyc wall or have a long length of fabric for shooting full-length subjects, you'll need additional lights to light the back wall and floor behind the subjects (Figure 8.4). The best way to do this is to use a bank of fluorescent fixtures along the top edge of the cyc wall and two side lights shining against the wall. This will light the background evenly and "hide" the transition of the wall to the floor. The subject's shadows on the floor should come only from their light source and not have multiple shadows from back light spill.

 Note: You can learn more about professional lighting methods and lighting blue/green screens by visiting the Kino Flo website at http://kinoflo.com. Make sure to visit the FAQ list and the product catalog.

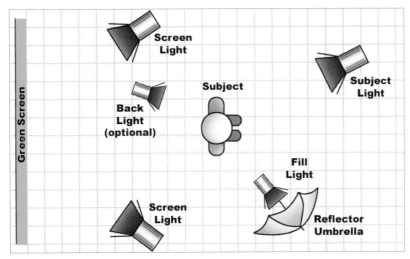

Figure 8.3 Positioning your studio lights correctly will provide the cleanest background key.

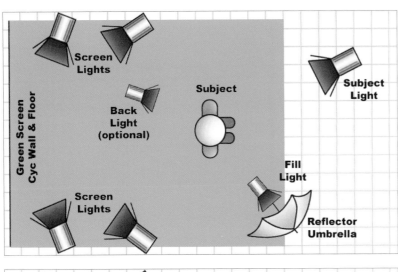

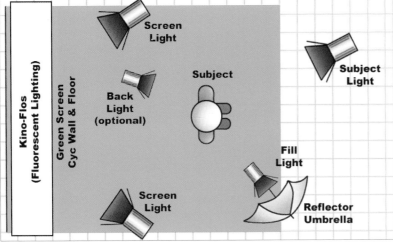

Figure 8.4 When using a cyc wall, light the floor for a seamless background.

To better demonstrate this kind of simple studio setup, I created a virtual environment in After Effects, using 3-D layers and a mock green screen stage. I placed one subject, the guy in the straitjacket, back in the green screen light (Figure 8.5). Notice how the green spill and oversaturation is washing him out. This is what happens when your subjects are too close to the background screen.

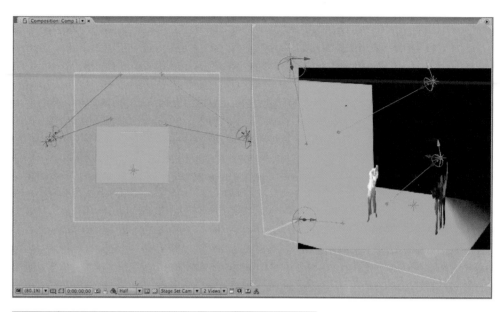

Figure 8.5
Positioning subjects too close to the background screen and in the path of the screen lights will wash them out and cause green light spill.

The other subjects are positioned well in front of the screen lights—at least 10 to 15 feet from the screen. They have their own lighting source that correctly illuminates them for the composite scene (Figure 8.6). Notice their shadows on the ground in natural positions that softly fade back.

I rendered the scene (without the background character) with a composited background environment and put it together in another 3-D composition in After Effects (Figure 8.7). You can also view the virtual stage and the composited movies in the Chapter 8 folder on the DVD.

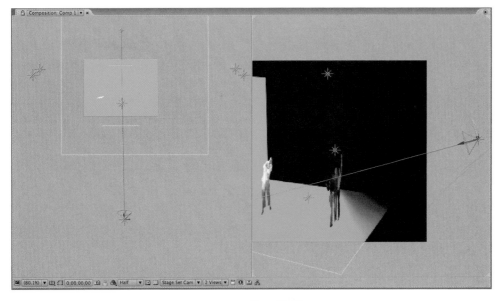

Figure 8.6
The correct positioning of the subjects is far enough away from the screen so there is control of their lighting exposure without spill or hot spots.

Figure 8.7
The composited scene with the foreground subjects and a background environment.

Matching the Subject Lighting to the Composition Environment

Regardless of what background materials you choose or your studio or location, it's very important to pay close attention to the lighting of the scene in which your subjects will eventually be composited when you are shooting your subjects for composition. You'd be amazed at how frequently scene lighting is overlooked in production, and how often scene lighting requires a complete reshoot or fixing in the composite.

Color temperature of the lighting, direction of the original light sources, and shadows are your primary concerns when properly lighting your subject for a scene. For instance, you won't want a brightly lit subject with a strong back light if the subject will appear deep in the woods in the final composite. You must be sure that you are shooting your subjects for the environment into which they will be eventually composited. If they will be placed into a virtual environment, you must provide the director of the shoot with the appropriate lighting information; otherwise, the environment director will have to match his scene to the subject's lighting in production. Low-budget TV programs and video games frequently break these rules. Today's viewers are smarter and more visually tuned to quality composites and effects, so your challenge to provide a convincing composite starts with the initial shoot.

In the scene shown in Figure 8.8, the actors were filmed from a crane in an outdoor parking lot. The final composite was to be outside with a single light source, the sun. The actors were composited onto a virtual environment that was re-created to match the light source of the subjects shot on the blue screen.

Figure 8.8 The use of the sun as a single light source provided all the lighting and shadows needed for this scene.

I created a more complicated composite involving a puppet composited into a scene with shadows and diffused lighting (Figure 8.9). Rotoscoping the puppeteer's hands and rods out of the shot required extra care, so as to not interfere with the natural shadows from the light source in the studio.

 Note: I keep updated technical information and links to related blue/green screen production articles available for downloading from my website: http://pixelpainter.com.

Figure 8.9 The composited scene with the foreground subjects and a background environment

Matte and Keying Plug-Ins

9

If you have the Standard version of After Effects, your blue-screen keying choices are pretty limited. You can manage to get a decent outline of your subjects, but forget about fine details such as hair, transparency, or shadows. The Professional Bundle version of After Effects 7 ships with a very powerful professional chroma keying plug-in called Keylight. Other professional keying plug-ins, as well as specialized plug-ins specifically for DV, have been available from third-party developers for several years.

Chapter Contents
Keylight
Ultimatte AdvantEdge
zMatte
dvMatte Pro
Side-by-Side Plug-In Comparisons

Keylight

This is the plug-in that currently ships with After Effects 7 Professional. This new version of Keylight is derived from the version originally created for high-end software-editing systems for the professional film industry and is simple and easy to use. If you have this plug-in installed, you probably won't need anything else for your general keying needs. It does an overall great job and retains the texture and subtle nuances of the keyed material's highlights and shadows. You may have to install it separately if you purchased the Professional version of After Effects 7.

In most cases, a single click of the Eyedropper from within the plug-in will give you great results with either green-screen or blue-screen shots. With the background layer and blue-screen or green-screen layer (also known as the chroma key layer) placed on top in the Comp window, select the Keylight plug-in from the Effects menu (Effects > Keying > Keylight). Use the Eyedropper tool in the Effects window and select the blue or green chroma background (Figure 9.1). If you have a clean shot of the chroma key layer, then even details such as fine hair will be nicely composited with the background layer at this point.

Figure 9.1

One simple click with the Eyedropper tool in the Keylight effect plug-in will give you good results most of the time without the need for further adjustments.

Removing Chroma Spill from Details

When you have a chroma key shot that has a lot of background color bleed or "spill" into the details and edges of the subject, the shot will require a bit more than just the simple click to remove it. Keylight can remove spill from fine hair or separate reflections from glass with only a few adjustments.

In this first example, the figure was lit very lightly against a dark blue-screen background, which was composited against a scenic background (Figure 9.2). The problem was that her fine, wavy blonde hair was picking up too much of the surrounding chroma hue, so when the initial key was made, there was still a great deal of blue-magenta color in her hair that needed to be removed (Figure 9.3).

Figure 9.2 The image to be composited had fine details with a lot of color spill in the hair.

Figure 9.3
The initial keying still left a lot of residual color in the hair details.

For this example, just increasing the Despill Bias from 0.0 to 25.0 seemed to eliminate most of the unwanted color spill, without taking away the natural colors of the figure's skin and hair color. The default plug-in setting has the Lock Biases Together check box selected, which changes the Alpha Bias along with the Despill Bias when adjusted. I also increased the Clip Black and decreased the Clip White Screen Matte settings to get the cleanest edges. Finally, I moved the edge Color Saturation down to 0.0, eliminating the majority of the color bleed in the hair (Figure 9.4).

Figure 9.4 Increasing the Despill Bias and decreasing the Edge Color Saturation helped to eliminate the color spill in the hair details.

This next example had a very dark, poorly lit, green-screen background in the chroma key image (Figure 9.5). The fighter pilot was to be composited over the background with the two trailing jets in flight against the sky.

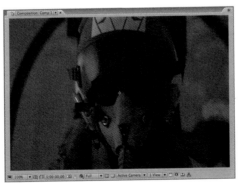

Figure 9.5 This was a more complicated composite, where the chroma key image had a very dark background with which to deal.

When the initial key was applied by using the Eyedropper tool in the most neutral green background area, most of the image was adversely affected by not providing a clean matte (Figure 9.6). The resulting effect was more of a double exposure than a keyed matte.

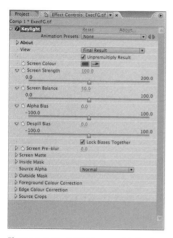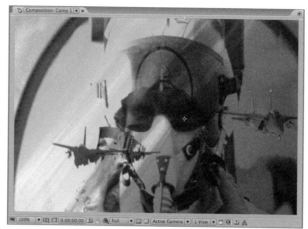

Figure 9.6 The initial key provided only a very crude beginning to our composite matte, requiring some major adjustments to the matte.

At this point, adjusting the Screen Strength and Screen Balance sliders helped bring back the matte details. By changing the view selector to Screen Matte, I could preview the density and edges of the matte being generated (Figure 9.7). Once I evened out the matte's density and edges, I returned to the Final Result view and adjusted the Despill Bias down to eliminate any bleed or "holes" in the subject.

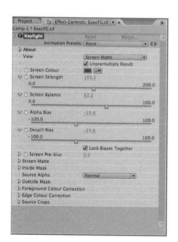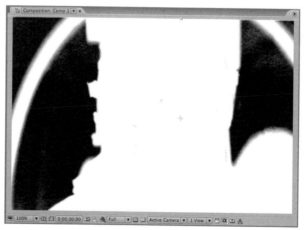

Figure 9.7
Making a few adjustments to the density of the matte provided the desired results.

Ultimatte AdvantEdge

Ultimatte is the true pioneer of chroma keying technology and has won several awards for advances in compositing hardware and software. Ultimatte AdvantEdge is the most sophisticated keying plug-in available for After Effects and Photoshop, and it actually operates as a separate application when the effect is applied.

With an easy-to-navigate interface and live previews of any phase of the composition, Ultimatte has made AdvantEdge user friendly for beginners and powerful enough for the top professional. You can save color corrections, color matching, and matte settings for repeated application in your projects—and it offers advanced controls and a navigable histogram for each session for multiple Undos (Figure 9.8).

 Note: To try a demo of Ultimatte AdvantEdge, visit their website at www.ultimatte.com. The User Guide for Ultimatte AdvantEdge is included on the DVD.

Applying a Chroma Clean Plate

Ultimatte allows you to use a "clean plate" with your chroma key shots, which works similarly to a difference matte of sorts. An exact locked-off shot of the blue-screen background and environment is taken without objects or actors. More often, this is used with blue or green painted environmental objects that shadows will be cast on or that the actors will interact with in the final composite. This Clean Plate layer is then used in Ultimatte to produce a more accurate matte.

The three sources are imported into After Effects and placed in the Comp or on the Timeline, with the foreground chroma layer on the top and the Clean Plate layer hidden or beneath the background layer. You must first select the preview and Clean Plate layers before launching the Ultimatte AdvantEdge application by choosing Effects > Ultimatte > AdvantEdge (Figure 9.9). When the Ultimatte effect is applied, the Effects palette appears.

 Note: Ultimatte will *not* allow you to mix resolutions or sizes of background and foreground layers for preview. The background and foreground layers must be the same size and resolution to allow previewing the composite in the application. If they aren't the same size, a warning dialog pops up telling you so.

You reset crop lines by dragging them from the outside edges of the image window in to where you want to crop the matte (Figure 9.10). Make sure you don't crop into the live action areas of a moving subject.

Use the Sample Backing Eyedropper in the Screen mode to select the initial background chroma color from the chroma foreground layer. When looking at the matte, you'll notice that not all of the blue is selected at the first pass. If you use the Add Overlay tool and select those areas that have holes in the mask, then the keyer will include that range of pixels in the creation of the matte (Figure 9.11). If too many pixels are selected too close to the objects in the scene, you'll need to use the Remove Overlay tool and select the areas that bleed over onto the image.

Figure 9.8 Ultimatte AdvantEdge has advanced controls for handling details, shadows, transparency, and color matching.

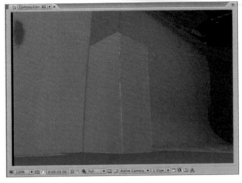

Figure 9.9

Using a Clean Plate layer in Ultimatte AdvantEdge, you can retain many of the chroma keyed background's shape and shading.

Figure 9.10

Set the outer edge crop to create a large garbage matte reference.

If you click the More button, advanced settings will pop up from the bottom of the screen; select the Inputs tab and make the Clean Plate layer visible (Figure 9.12) to see your preview. In my example, the details and shadows on the building now show up, and there's a clean composite around the young woman.

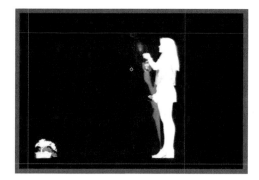

Figure 9.11 Select the background color with the Sample Backing Eyedropper, and fill in the missing areas with the Add Overlay tool.

Figure 9.12 Turn on the Clean Plate layer to complete the composite.

You can do a comparison between the final composite and the original foreground layer or mattes at any time, either by selecting the dual-screen button on the bottom left of the user interface or by selecting the split-screen button and dragging the handle back and forth on the screen to see the preview (Figure 9.13).

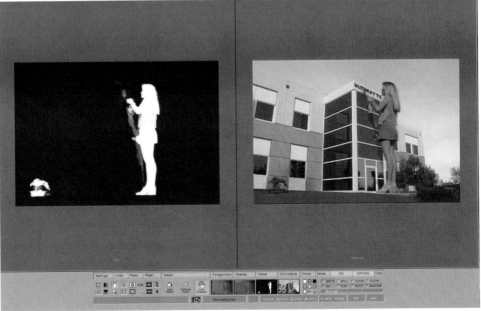

Figure 9.13 Two different previews are available: dual-screen and split-screen modes.

Using Ultimatte in a Production Composition

Let's look at the blue screen that we cleaned up with a garbage matte and rotoscoping in Chapter 6, "Blue-Screen Garbage Mattes." This footage is going to be composited over a motion matte painting (which is created in Chapter 12, "Making Movies from Stills"). The blue-screen footage has been scaled down to the appropriate size for this composition and positioned where the actors will walk across the catwalk in the scene (Figure 9.14).

I applied the Ultimatte AdvantEdge plug-in to the foreground chroma key layer and then clicked the AdvantEdge logo in the Effects palette to launch the application. Because the resolution of both foreground and background layers did not match, they could not be used as a background preview.

To set the source color to mask, I used the Sample Backing Eyedropper and dragged a selection of the blue background (Figure 9.15).

Figure 9.14
The blue-screen footage was scaled and positioned over the matte painting footage in After Effects.

Figure 9.15
I selected the blue background with the Eyedropper.

Because the background wasn't completely clean and free of defects, I needed to apply the Add Overlay tool to the noisy areas (Figure 9.16). This actually covered up the shadows under the actors, so I used the Remove Overlay tool in just those areas.

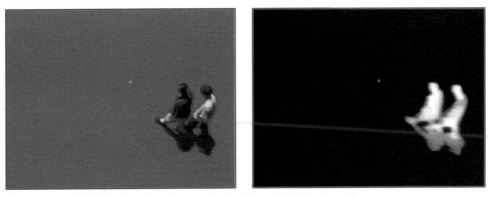

Figure 9.16 I used the Add Overlay tool to clean up and mask out the noise in the background.

I then clicked the Composite button to see the preview against a gray background. Then I clicked the Screen button and selected Spill. I used the Remove Spill tool to get rid of any blue or magenta on the edges of the backs of the actors (Figure 9.17).

Figure 9.17 I used the Remove Spill tool to eliminate spill color on the edges of objects.

Once I was satisfied with a composition in Ultimatte AdvantEdge, I clicked the OK button and ran a RAM preview to see the composite in motion (Figure 9.18).

Figure 9.18
The final composite revealed subtle shadows and smooth edges against the background matte.

zMatte

Digital Film Tools has created a very easy-to-use plug-in—not to mention a more affordable solution for most chroma keying purposes. As with other more-expensive keying plug-ins, you can use it to key out most blue and green backgrounds, including a blue sky. zMatte has tools to quickly adjust the matte to eliminate uneven backgrounds. This example combines a scenic city image and a freeway sign against a blue sky (Figure 9.19).

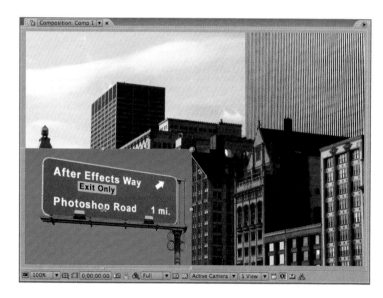

Figure 9.19
Even a blue sky can be keyed out easily with the zMatte plug-in.

Note: To try a demo of zMatte, visit the Digital Film Tools website at http://www.digitalfilm-tools.com/html/zmatte_download.html.

When I applied the zMatte plug-in to the sign layer by choosing Effects > DFT zMatte > zMatte and changed the View selection from Output to Matte on the Effect Controls palette (Figure 9.20), the layer turned to a reversed black-and-white matte in the Comp window.

Figure 9.20 I selected View Matte to see how much the matte needed to be adjusted to get a clean key from the sky.

I then spun down the Primary Matte arrow and opened the Background and Foreground sliders and dragged the sliders to fill in the background and foreground areas in the matte (Figure 9.21). I adjusted the Background to 30.0 and the Foreground to 20.0, which looked like a fair balance between the two.

Figure 9.21 I adjusted the Background and Foreground to get a clean key but a solid mask.

I set the View back to Output and checked that the composite was nice and clean. However, there was still a bluish hue to the metal on the signpost that looked out of place against the city. If it had been actually photographed as a freeway off ramp in the scene, it would have had a warmer tone to match the background colors of the city.

I was able to adjust the color without affecting the matte in the foreground layer. I spun down the Color Correct arrow, opened the Red and Blue settings (Figure 9.22), and used the sliders to reduce the amount of blue while increasing the amount of red in the layer. Because the green level was already where I wanted it, I left that alone. The final composite shared a balance between the two light sources.

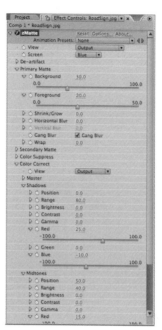

Figure 9.22 I was able to make color corrections with the plug-in without affecting the matte.

Primatte Keyer

This plug-in, from Red Giant Software, is a simple and easy-to-use keyer with plenty of additional control when needed. The sample image they provide to test it with shows that it handles transparency and spill quite well with little fuss.

Note: A demo copy of the Primatte Keyer plug-in is available on the companion DVD.

I used one of Red Giant's provided sample blue-screen images of a fountain with water pouring over a statue's head (Figure 9.23) This is usually a pretty tricky combination for the less-sophisticated keying plug-ins, but Primatte appeared to handle it with a broad sampling of the blue-screen background.

To get rid of the slight blue spill in the water edges, I selected the Spill Sponge and click-dragged over the area with the spill (Figure 9.24). It amazingly removed just the blue and not the subtleties of the water flow and highlights.

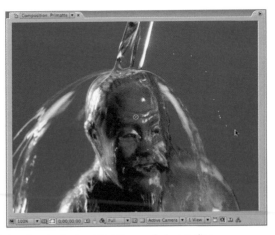

Figure 9.23 Primatte allows you to click-drag the selection to get its full range of color sampling.

Figure 9.24 Using the Spill Sponge, I removed the blue cast from the flowing water.

Changing the view to Matte, I then cleaned up the matte by click-dragging the Matte Sponge along the light gray areas inside the white part of the matte (Figure 9.25). This helped the plug-in to distinguish the opaque areas of the matte from those that should be transparent.

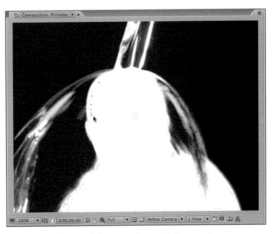

Figure 9.25 The Matte Sponge cleaned up and removed areas of the matte that needed to remain opaque.

dvMatte Pro

Everybody shooting chroma key shots using DV, mini-DV, Digital Beta, and HD already knows it's nearly impossible to get a decent key through the DV compression jaggies on the edges of the matte characters. The development group at the DV Garage has created dvMatte Pro, a plug-in keyer specifically designed for DV footage. This very affordable keyer is extremely easy to use and does everything it promises to do—give you professional chroma keys with digital video footage.

Note: A demo copy of dvMatte Pro is available on the companion DVD.

Using the footage files I downloaded from the DV Garage website, I completed a nice keyed composite with just a few steps. This footage was not well lit and had a lot of detail in the person's hair—the worst combination you can have with DV chroma footage.

I started by cropping as much of the outside of the motion area on the green-screen layer as possible, using an adjustable mask to create a garbage matte. I then feathered the mask (Layer > Mask > Feather) 30 pixels horizontally and vertically to create a softer edged mask (Figure 9.26).

Figure 9.26
I created a garbage matte by adjusting the handles on the rectangular mask and feathering the edges.

I applied the dvMatte Pro plug-in to the chroma footage layer (Effects > DV Garage > dvMatte Pro) and selected the two extreme ranges of the color key—lightest and darkest—with the Eyedropper tools (Figure 9.27). I changed the view to Base Matte and adjusted the Black Point slider under the Base Matte settings to darken the background until it was solid black. To lessen the effect of the jaggies visible in my example on the edges of the jacket and hair, I applied about 5 pixels of the Softness Black Point setting.

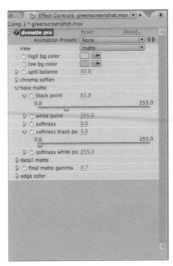 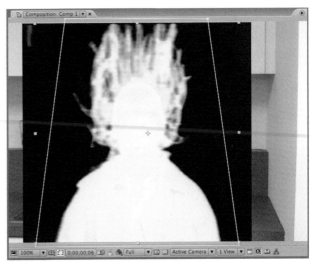

Figure 9.27 Next I adjusted the Base Matte Black Point slider until the background in the Base Matte was solid black.

I changed the view back to Composite to see if I needed to increase the softness around the edges without making it blurry. Because the original green screen was not lit well, there were dark corners at the top, so I cropped out most of it with the feathered mask. Some of the black was still showing through, so I increased the Final Matte Gamma to 0.7 to eliminate it from the final composite (Figure 9.28).

Figure 9.28 I was able to make color corrections with the plug-in without affecting the matte.

Side-by-Side Plug-In Comparisons

So, how do all of these plug-ins compare with one another? How do they perform in different production situations? They all do a great job in specific areas, and I'd recommend every one of them if you need those specific requirements. But which one will serve you well for all of your general needs?

I've created a few examples of different situations you may encounter in the real world with chroma key compositing. Of course, the more expensive products do extremely well, as expected, but the others may surprise you!

The "One-Click Wonder" Test

I took a professionally shot blue-screen composite, provided courtesy of The Foundry's website sample gallery (Figure 9.29). I then applied the different plug-ins and used only the initial color key selector—the "one click" in our "one-click wonder" test.

Figure 9.29 Here's the original chroma key shot and background for the composite test.

To avoid confusion, I'm listing these in the order in which they appeared earlier in the chapter—starting with Keylight (Figure 9.30). Notice the matte screen with the pointer showing the subtle areas that are masked out, allowing the light reflections from inside the car to show up on the window. As I stated before, if you have the After Effects 7 Pro version with Keylight, you may not need anything else for all-around general keying. The only exception may be dvMatte Pro for those DV clips that cause us so much grief.

Figure 9.30 Keylight does a great job with just a single keying.

Next, I tried Ultimatte AdvantEdge. It provides excellent keying as well, but the matte shows extensive image graininess from the original shot (Figure 9.31). This matte would probably require some refinement to soften the lighter areas a bit before making the final composite.

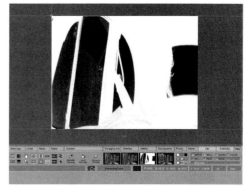

Figure 9.31 Ultimatte AdvantEdge does an equally excellent job of keying out the blue and leaving the details of the reflections in the matte.

With the first application, zMatte does a basic key, removing all the blue and the highlights as well (Figure 9.32). It would take some adjustments on the mattes to bring back the reflections in the window.

Figure 9.32 zMatte has a hard time distinguishing the subtleties of the matte right off the bat and needs further tweaking of the matte.

dvMatte Pro does a surprisingly decent job on the chroma shot from just the straight keying (Figure 9.33). Because it looks at two keys, I had to actually give it the "two-click" test, but I sampled the same spot in the back window, so as not to lose the reflections on the side window. dvMatte Pro created a somewhat greenish cast over the chroma layer that would need some color correction.

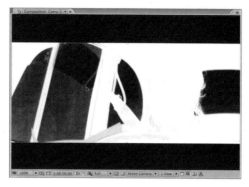

Figure 9.33 dvMatte Pro steps up to the plate and hits a double.

Primatte Keyer seemed to eliminate the reflections in the window, even with a 1-pixel sampling (which I tried in several areas of the window just to see if I could get a better sample). But looking at the matte, it appears that a coarse shading of the reflections remains in the matte (Figure 9.34).

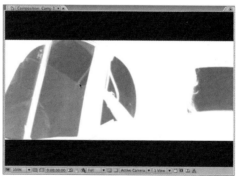

Figure 9.34 Primatte Keyer has a hard time retaining the subtle reflections in the window.

Blue Skies

This was a test to see if any or all of these plug-ins would provide a believable composite of two images using only the blue sky behind autumn leaves (Figure 9.35). Because the sky is gradated from bottom to top, I had to push the settings in all plug-ins until a clean matte could be generated. In addition, I placed a 10-pixel feathered mask around the live area of the trees to avoid any hard edges showing in the composite. All of the plug-ins performed well in this test.

Figure 9.35 The blue sky behind the trees was used as the chroma key source for this composite.

In this test, Keylight needed only to have the Screen Balance turned all the way down to 0.0 to clean up the background matte (Figure 9.36). The edges of the leaves were clean and the color was retained from the original.

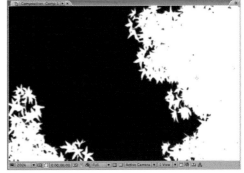

Figure 9.36 Keylight required only one adjustment in addition to the key sample.

Ultimatte performed similarly; with only a click of the Clean button, the matte was clear (Figure 9.37). The color was retained from the original, and there was no noticeable difference from the Keylight matte.

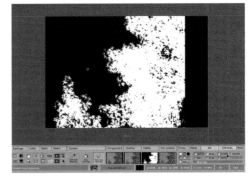

Figure 9.37 Ultimatte AdvantEdge worked equally well with minimum adjustments.

zMatte is a straight keyer, so this is the type of image with which it works best. Because there was no real key sampler—just a selection of Blue or Green applied to the entire image—it's amazing that it handled this so well (Figure 9.38). Only the Primary Matte needed adjustments for a clean matte; those adjustments were made by setting both the Background and Foreground to 15.0.

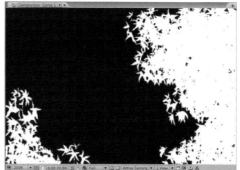

Figure 9.38

zMatte keyed this image quite well with only a couple of adjustments to the matte.

dvMatte Pro performed well as expected. Because this keyer allows you to select the lightest and darkest areas of the background to be keyed, it needed only to have the Base Matte Black Point set down to 65.0 (Figure 9.39).

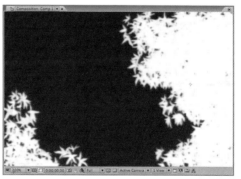

Figure 9.39

dvMatte Pro required only one adjustment.

Primatte Keyer does a quick key, but even after a lot of adjustments, I couldn't seem to get rid of the dark cast in the sky (Figure 9.40).

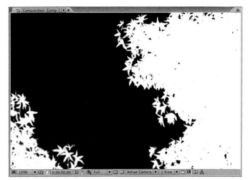

Figure 9.40 Primatte left a dark cast in the sky that was difficult to correct through the plug-in.

Blue-Screen Textures: Shadows and Highlights

This test was a bit different, in that the chroma layer not only covered the image that it was being keyed over, but it also became the displacement map for the background image. The only thing being keyed here was the color—not the shadows or highlights or the texture of the cloth (Figure 9.41).

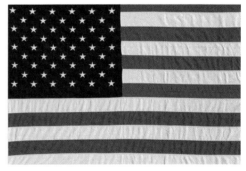

Figure 9.41 The foreground chroma layer also served as the displacement map for the flag layer in the background.

I selected the flag layer in the background and applied the displacement map (Effects > Distort > Displacement Map). Then I selected the blue cloth layer for the Displacement Map layer and set both the Max Vertical Displacement and Max Horizontal Displacement settings to 35.0 pixels (Figure 9.42). This created waves and wrinkles in the flag that follow the contour of the highlights and shadows in the chroma layer.

Keylight did a great job of taking the blue out, but it left the highlights of the chroma layer a bit strong (Figure 9.43). The details of the cloth texture showed up, but the overall composite seemed a little bit washed out.

Ultimatte AdvantEdge was the hands-down winner in this comparison (Figure 9.44). Not only was it a simple, one-click key, but it retained all the texture, shadows, and highlights in their normal levels, creating the best final composite.

Figure 9.42 The displacement map was applied to the flag layer to create wrinkles that match the chroma-keyed layer above.

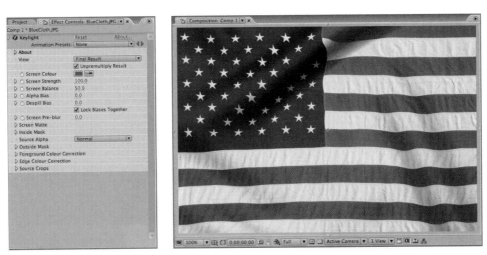

Figure 9.43 Keylight did a nice job of creating a believable composite.

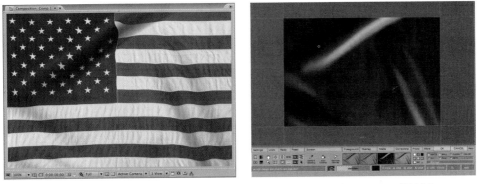

Figure 9.44 Ultimatte AdvantEdge did a fantastic job of creating the best composite, retaining textures and highlights.

zMatte did a decent job with the keying but left a light blue haze over the composite. Adjusting the Saturation to –100.0 in the Color Correction settings took out the blue, but it still left the composite overall a little washed out (Figure 9.45).

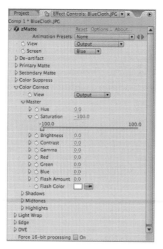
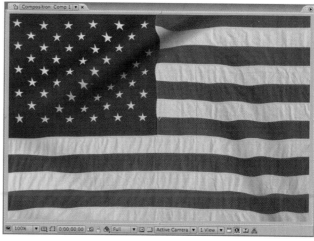

Figure 9.45 zMatte made a decent composite, although it remained a bit washed out and the texture of the cloth wasn't prominent.

Unfortunately, dvMatte Pro didn't give the results hoped for—not that it promises that it can be used in this way. Creating a detailed matte without turning the mid-to-dark areas of the chroma layer to green was difficult. With a few attempts at sampling the right color range with the Eyedroppers and adjusting the Detail Matte In Point to 75.0 and setting the Detail Channel to Color Difference, I was able to create a barely acceptable matte (Figure 9.46). Texture is pretty much nonexistent, but that's really what the plug-in is supposed to do with noisy DV footage.

Figure 9.46 dvMatte Pro was barely able to provide a detailed matte, because it wanted to remove too much material and texture—just what it was designed to do.

Primatte Keyer did a remarkably nice job of removing just the blue, with a broad range selection of the sampling tool (Figure 9.47). No other adjustments were necessary after the initial click-drag sampling of the varied blues in the foreground image.

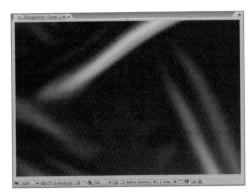 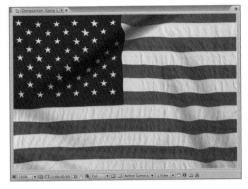

Figure 9.47 Primatte Keyer did a great job of removing the blues from the foreground image in only one step.

Static Matte "Painting" in Photoshop

10

Matte paintings have been part of the motion picture industry for decades. Traditionally, background scenes were painted on vertically mounted sheets of glass and were either mounted in front of the camera while shooting a scene or exposed to masked portions of the original film. Today, with computer technology, matte "painting" is a composite of several photographic and artistic elements overlaying the original footage. This allows for more control in post-production and makes it easier to match the degree of perspective and detail to the original footage.

Chapter Contents
Embellishing on a Location
Relocating the Location

Embellishing on a Location

Location matte painting is often done in motion pictures and major television movies. Often, a location may have excellent characteristics and "feel" for the ground-level shot, but it may not have the entire scene that is desired. Sometimes additional buildings and objects need to be added or existing buildings need to be modified to fill out the scene's frame. Through the use of computer-generated compositing, only some portions of the matte painting are actually "painted"—the bulk of the elements come from source photos or 3-D design elements and animation.

Still, creating some elements from scratch is a major part of this process and requires an eye for details and good digital painting skills. Every project you encounter will be different from the last and will have very specific requirements, so a broad generalization of matte painting is nearly impossible to cover in one chapter. I have, however, selected a couple of example projects that will cover some of the biggest hurdles you may encounter in a composite with a matte painting.

This first project is an example of adding taller buildings and a water tower to an existing piece of footage. It has all the elements of possible problems that might occur when creating a matte painting that has to coexist with elements in motion, such as moving trees that will slightly overlap some of the painted buildings. I'll use a combination of source photos, cloning, masking, and painting techniques to demonstrate.

I started by opening a locked-off clip of DV footage (on location in our small historic downtown Fullerton, California) in QuickTime Pro and exporting a single frame as a PICT file that I could use as a base for my matte painting in Photoshop (Figure 10.1). You can follow along with this project with the files located in the Chapter 10 folder on the DVD. Due to the "suggestive" nature of this production process—the highly individual and creative choices to make, such as painting elements—the complete Photoshop file FullertonMaster.psd, with all of its layers intact, is provided.

Figure 10.1
Open the movie file in QuickTime Pro and export a single frame as a PICT file.

I opened the PICT file in Photoshop and began working on the big building in the center of the frame. The traffic signal in the foreground was blocking part of the building and distracted from the scale of the building.

Photoshop CS2 has a feature called Vanishing Point, where you can create grids in perspective and clone or paste items in a layer that will automatically keep the scale and perspective in line. I selected Vanishing Point (Filter > Vanishing Point) and created my left side perspective grid, using four visible points on the side of the building (Figure 10.2).

Figure 10.2
Create a perspective grid on the side of the building in Vanishing Point.

Then I expanded the grid to the outside edges of my composition for the sides of the structure, grabbing the handles on the outer edges of the grid. I created a second grid for the right side of the buildings and expanded it as well (Figure 10.3).

Using the Clone Stamp tool inside of Vanishing Point, I selected a source point in the corner of a window that would match up with another window to the left. Vanishing Point works differently than the regular Clone Stamp tool in Photoshop, as it actually gives you a "preview" of the area you're cloning over before you click the mouse to apply it. The Clone Stamp will show you the cloned region as it is scaled and put into perspective (Figure 10.4).

Figure 10.3 Vanishing Point grids can be stretched and expanded to match the buildings in this movie.

Figure 10.4 Cloning over the unwanted area in Vanishing Point will automatically rescale and keep the cloned area in the perspective plane.

Note: You can only apply changes to the selected layer in Vanishing Point. If you clone or paste anything inside Vanishing Point, it will not create a new layer that you can edit later. Once you've applied and accepted the changes in Vanishing Point, all of the changes will be on the layer you had selected when you opened it.

The building needed to be taller, and I tiered a second level to enhance the perspective of height. Simply adding a couple stories straight up to the existing building wouldn't have had the same visual scale or architectural interest as adding a second tier—especially since the building would be the closest in the group of buildings being matte painted.

Because I wanted the second tier of the building to resemble the rest of it, I selected the top two floors of the building with the Lasso tool, copied them, and pasted the selection to a new layer. I then set the Opacity of the pasted layer to approximately 65% so that it was ghosted over the original building, and I used the Transform options to scale it down so that it matched the original building in the perspective scale toward the top of the building. The perspective angles of the roofline needed to be adjusted for the new height, so I selected one half of the addition, divided at the corner, and skewed it down—Edit > Transform > Skew (Figure 10.5). Refer to the perspective grid in Vanishing Point for reference. You only have to open Vanishing Point. Don't make any changes while you have it open, though.

Figure 10.5 Rescale and skew each half of the building top addition to account for the change in perspective.

I then needed to remove the vertical sign from the lower part of the building that I sampled to create the top tier using the Clone Stamp tool (Figure 10.6). I increased the Opacity of the layer to better see what I was working on. It also helped to hide the bottom layer while I was working on it. Then I carefully aligned the perspective angles along the building's horizontal lines and window ledges.

Figure 10.6
Clone out the sign and any other unwanted objects repeated from the original source image.

After making the bottom layer visible again and setting the top layer's Opacity down to 65%, I used the Eraser tool with a hard-edge brush to carefully remove the overlapping material from the top layer (Figure 10.7).

I created a railing that ran across the top edge of the lower part of the building, as if there were a terrace level, to give the building a little more character. (A couple of historic buildings in the area feature similar architectural elements.) I created a new layer and used a 1-pixel Paintbrush with the Shift key; I "snapped" lines to create a straight railing. The colors I chose were sampled from light and dark areas on the original photo to create the top of the railing (lighter colors) and the bottom of the railing (darker colors). I simply cut a single vertical rail, pasted it to a new layer, rotated it 100°, and then duplicated it several times to create a length of railing (Figure 10.8). Zooming in about 300% allowed me to work on the details, pixel by pixel.

Figure 10.7
Use the Eraser tool to eliminate the overlapping material from the top layer.

Figure 10.8
Create lengths of railing by starting with just two 1-pixel lines painted on top of each other and duplicating the vertical rails.

Note: A quick way to create lengths of railing is to duplicate several layers and then link them and merge the linked layers. Duplicate the groups and repeat the process until you have longer and longer lengths with which to work.

After I created a length of the railing that would fit the long side of the building top, I used the Perspective Transform option to shrink the far-left railing to match the building's perspective. (I could also have used the Perspective Transform option to skew the left side down to follow contour of the building top.) I then trimmed the railing at both ends, selected a section of the railing, and pasted it to a new layer. I duplicated the layer and trim-adjusted the sections for the opposite angle on the roof's top on the right (Figure 10.9).

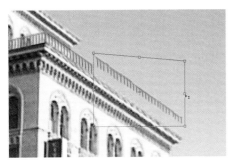

Figure 10.9 Use the Perspective Transform option to size and align the railing sections to the rooftop line.

The next three additions to the scene—a tall building in the back, a taller building next door, and a water tower—were all derived from source images, or the source images were used as references for painting (Figure 10.10). In all cases, a great deal of image manipulation and painting or cloning was needed to make up the right combination for our scene.

Figure 10.10 Use these source images as guidelines for creating new buildings and objects in the new scene.

The back building started off as only the front-facing wall with the windows, which I had to severely clone to remove the light pole and wires, as well as brighten and properly highlight to match the direction of the light source on the scene (late afternoon sun). I extracted the crown from the original image and reshaded it to look like it was on the building (Figure 10.11). Then I placed a solid block of neutral color on the adjacent wall, which would have tile covering it. Then I checked the perspectives with Vanishing Point, as I did with the front building.

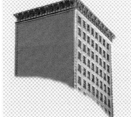

Figure 10.11 Use cloning, along with copying and pasting selections, to create this building from scratch.

I wanted to add an aged brick side to the building, with some old painted advertising from days gone by. I found an old Coca Cola sign and modified it a bit. I added some chunky noise on a gray solid layer above the sign and used my Eraser tool with a soft-edge brush to remove a lot of the material, exposing only a small portion of the noise in a random order over the top of the sign. Then I made a duplicate of the layer, inverted the Mode, and changed the Blending Mode to Screen (Figure 10.12). This gave the illusion of peeling paint and created more of a 3-D effect on the side of the building.

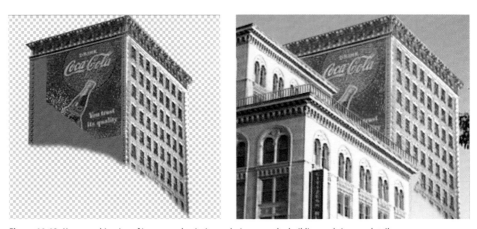

Figure 10.12 Use a combination of images and painting techniques on the building and signage details.

Because I didn't have an exact photographic match for the building addition on the right, I made it primarily from painting layers in Photoshop, with some reference from an architectural photo. I did use the crown of the building from source image material, because it was lit correctly for the scene and I was able to utilize the details. The first painted section was the front wall face itself, complete with the shadows of the trees across the street (Figure 10.13). I added the windows to the blank wall next, by painting a larger block and using a hard-edge Eraser tool brush to eliminate the in-between sections and create a grid for the windows.

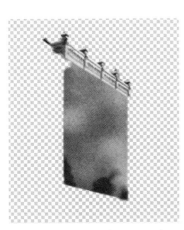

Figure 10.13 Other than the crown on the top of the third building, I needed to paint all of the sections and elements in Photoshop.

I added the rest of the building's face details by brushing lines on several layers and enhancing shadows and light features that showed the direction of the light source (Figure 10.14). I checked to see that I stayed in the proper perspective with Vanishing Point.

Figure 10.14
Add the details in the architectural design of the building with a paintbrush.

The final element I added was the water tower, which I recolored, and I added a graphic to it for realism (Figure 10.15). Notice how the water tower and additional buildings covered up trees along the edges. This was intentional because I was going to add a masked section of trees in After Effects, which was going to be in motion to match the rest of the scene.

Figure 10.15

I added the water tower to the scene, and partially covered it up again in After Effects with a masked section of trees in motion.

Masking Motion Layers

What really tied in the static matte elements was the incorporation of motion layers, masked or keyed on top of the static layers. In this case, the new buildings and water tower covered up some of the trees. I could have just pasted a layer of static trees there, but they wouldn't have looked natural in the scene. What I did instead was to duplicate the movie layer, mask just the overlapping tree area, and key out the blue sky to let the matte painting show through.

In a new After Effects project, I imported the Fullerton PSD file as a composition to retain the layers and the movie of the original background. I opened the PSD file by double-clicking it in the Projects window, which revealed that all of the layers were in their proper placement and hierarchy in the Timeline, eliminating the Background layer. Then I created a new comp and dragged the PSD comp as well as the original movie clip into it, placing the movie on the bottom layer in the Timeline (Figure 10.16).

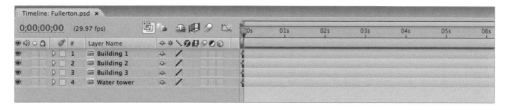

Figure 10.16 Import the PSD and original movie files and place them in the project comp.

Next, I created a new composition and dragged a copy of the original movie into it. I used the freeform Mask tool to draw a selection around the water tower and the front of the building. Then I added a 15-pixel feather to the selection to create a smooth vignette in which the moving leaves would appear (Figure 10.17).

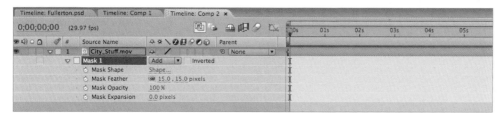

Figure 10.17
Use a feathered mask on the duplicated original movie comp to help blend it into the scene.

The only portion of the masked footage that was not needed was the blue sky, because this was going to be a layer on top of the matte painted buildings and the original background layer. I used the Keylight plug-in to key out the blue sky (Figure 10.18). I also boosted the Screen Strength to 110.0 and the Despill Bias to 60.0.

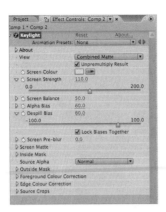 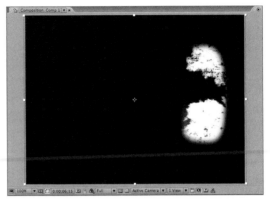

Figure 10.18
Key the blue sky out of the masked tree layer, allowing it to move above the matte painting and background layers.

Because the original movie footage and the masked tree layers were both in full motion, they generated a natural DV movie noise that was visible even in the still areas with no motion. The same problem appeared on film, where the film grain was in constant motion across the screen. If I had left the new matte painting in the shot as it was, it might have been noticeable as not part of the original footage because of the absence of this DV noise or film grain.

To rectify this, I added a motion noise movie to the mix, changed the Blend Mode to Multiply, and masked it to affect only the matte painted areas (Figure 10.19). Using the freeform Mask Pen tool, I made a rough selection around the buildings in one mask and then again around the water tower. This selection didn't need to be precise, because the noise layer effect was very subtle and the edges couldn't be easily noticed.

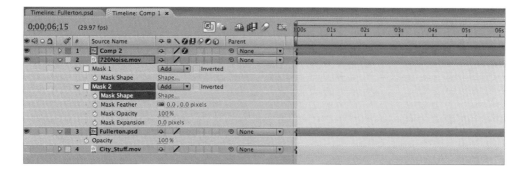

Figure 10.19 Mask a noise layer to the boundaries of the matte painted areas to blend in the motion effect.

> **Note:** Chapter 15, "Atmosphere, Film, and Noise Effects," describes how to create the noise movie used in this project, 720Noise.mov. The file can also be found on the DVD in the Chapter 10 folder.

Relocating the Location

Sometimes a scene can't be realistically shot on location—or the location simply doesn't exist. So directors may choose to shoot at a location that can be digitally transformed into the final scene they're looking for. You may also encounter a project that requires several subjects in motion on the same location shot, which requires compositing many different pieces of footage over the top of one another.

This project used several pieces of footage, locked off in one location to gather a number of moving vehicles on the road that would be combined and composited into one shot. It also used additional sky footage, still images, cloning, and painting, along with small masked trees and bushes in motion from the original footage. To fill the riverbed with water, I used a remarkable third-party plug-in called Psunami.

> **Note:** You can follow along with this After Effects project by opening the file BreaMatteProject.aep in the Chapter 10 folder on the DVD.

From the original location, I shot several minutes of running footage to capture several vehicles in motion (Figure 10.20). I edited out the best portions of footage and composited them to make it appear that several cars were traveling on the road at the same time.

Figure 10.20
Shoot the original location footage over a period of several minutes to capture enough activity to composite in the final movie.

I ran the base footage in the background on the bottom layer with the first car in motion, while running three separate footage clips in upper layers, which were masked to reveal only the cars so they could be added to the road in sequence (Figure 10.21). I had to be careful to select only footage where the cars were traveling at the same rate of speed, or else they would "run into" each other in the composite.

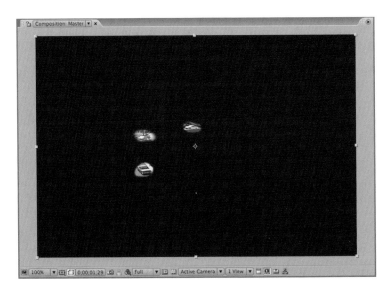

Figure 10.21
Mask out individual cars from additional layers of footage.

I used the layer Track Matte method of masking the cars on the layers, adjusting the matte size and shape on solid layers above each of the car footage layers (Figure 10.22). Since the footage was shot in a locked-off position, the mask did not need to be precise around each car because the surrounding ground would not move or change in color or exposure.

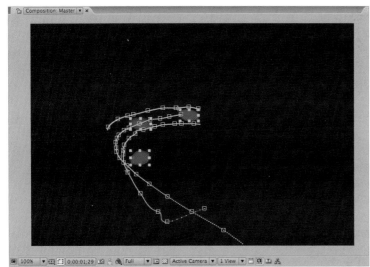

Figure 10.22
Track the solid layer masks to the cars on the movie layers below. They'll act as movable masks.

Each solid layer had a fairly simple mask with a 10-pixel feather on it, so it could be easily scaled and moved along a path to follow each car (Figure 10.23). With the car footage layer selected and the mask layer above it in the Timeline, I applied the Track Matte mask (Layer > Track Matte > Alpha to allow the mask to become transparent so I could move and adjust it over time.

Adding a New Sky and Horizon

The final location depicts a lush green valley with the city barely visible over the hills. I added a more interesting sky that wasn't overexposed, as the original footage sky appeared to be.

I duplicated the original footage layer, placed it directly above in the Timeline, and scaled it down, stretched horizontally. I was interested only in the horizon line of buildings in the center of the frame, so I drew a mask with the Mask Pen tool to isolate the area (Figure 10.24). I then applied a 10-pixel feather to the mask to let it blend in better.

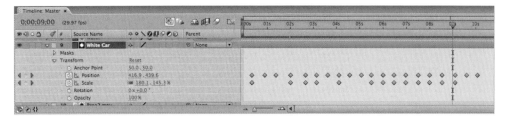

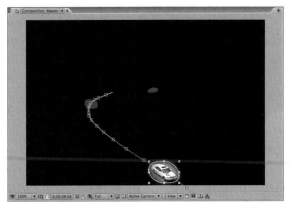

Figure 10.23
Use the Track Matte masking on the solid layers to allow the mask to be positioned and scaled to match the cars on the footage layers below.

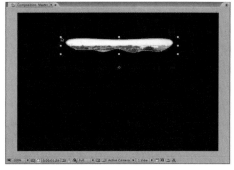

Figure 10.24 Scale the central focus of the horizon and stretch it to fit where the valley meets on both sides.

The new sky came from a piece of footage of only clouds moving in the sky. I first positioned and scaled the clouds vertically to the upper one-third of the frame, where they were compressed and positioned to match the angle of the location shot. By adjusting the Time Stretch of the cloud layer (Layer > Time > Time Stretch) to 50%, I sped up the cloud footage slightly to make the clouds move across the sky more dramatically (Figure 10.25). To make the new sky footage blend in with the horizon, I created a mask with the Mask Pen tool and applied a 25-pixel feather to it.

The hills on the sides of the valley leading into the city horizon were created in Photoshop from source photos and painting techniques and imported into After Effects (Figure 10.26). I placed this layer well above the sky and horizon layers in the Timeline so that they would fall behind the tops of the hills.

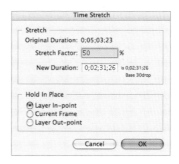

Figure 10.25 Speed up the cloud footage and mask it to fit the scene.

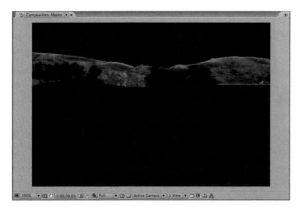

Figure 10.26
Create the hills in Photoshop, and place them
above the horizon in After Effects.

Note: Because this was a large static image area of the project, it needed to have noise applied to it. Instead of using the noise layer method previously described in this chapter, I opted for a third-party plug-in, from Digital Film Tools (www.digitalfilmtools.com), called 55mm Faux Film. I used this plug-in instead of the noise layer because I could control and adjust the size and density of the noise until it matched that of the running video footage. A demo version of the 55mm Faux Film plug-in is available on the DVD.

Just Add Water

To fill up the spillway with running water that matched the mass and scale of the location, I used a third-party plug-in called Psunami from Digital Anarchy. A demo version of Psunami is included on the DVD for you to try out and use on this project if you wish (or just play with it—you won't be disappointed in the results!).

I started by painting a mask in Photoshop up to the top water level in the spillway, and then I imported the file as a composition to retain its exact placement. I then placed the masked water layer in the Timeline to use it as a mask for the layer to which I would apply the Psunami plug-in effect (Figure 10.27). I hid the mask layer by clicking the eye icon in the Timeline.

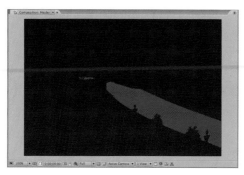

Figure 10.27 Paint a mask for the water level in Photoshop and import it into After Effects.

I created a new solid layer and placed it underneath the water mask layer in the Timeline, and I applied the Track Matte Alpha option. I then applied the Psunami effect plug-in to the solid layer, which brought up the Effects palette, where I started creating my water effect (Figure 10.28). Because I was starting from scratch, I had to first select my camera angle and wave scale. I then adjusted the water color and set the light angle to match the sun on the day the original footage was shot. This gave a realistic reflection on the water surface as well.

Figure 10.28 Apply the Psunami effect plug-in to a solid layer that's masked by the Photoshop mask layer.

There are many options for creating water in Psunami—more than in an ordinary 3-D application in some aspects. Waves and swells are all controllable as well, so that Psunami gives an incredibly realistic result.

To create the shadow of the bridge on the water, I created a small gray solid layer above the water mask layer and used the Mask Pen tool to draw a shadow that matched the curve of the bridge (Figure 10.29). I changed the Blend Mode to Multiply and reduced the layer Opacity to 85%.

Figure 10.29
Add a simulated bridge shadow to the water surface with a masked solid color layer.

Collecting the Details

Many of the detailed areas, such as sidewalks, railings, simple trees, and grassy spaces, were all painted in Photoshop layers. A snapshot of the project in After Effects served as the background for the painted detail layers (Figure 10.30). I used the same principles of painting the railings in the first project earlier in this chapter. Remember that it's important to pay as much attention to light and shadow as it is to scale when creating elements from scratch.

Figure 10.30 Paint the details in Photoshop on layers.

I imported the Photoshop file as a composition to retain all the layers in their proper position (Figure 10.31). Then I added the entire comp to the Timeline above the water layers, because the static detailed layers needed to overlay the layers in motion. Next, I applied the DFT 55mm Faux Film effect plug-in to the composition, which affected all of the layers in the composition.

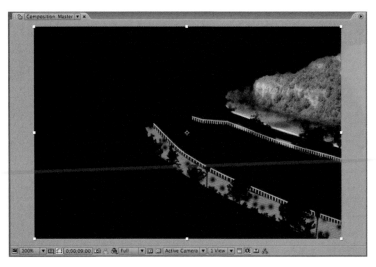

Figure 10.31
Import the Photoshop file as a composition to retain all of the layer transparency and proper placement.

There were still a few areas where some camouflage was needed to get rid of some buildings, power stations, and holes and where there were missing trees and bushes. Instead of just adding more static layers, I duplicated the original footage layer about four more times and repositioned, scaled, flipped, and masked specific trees or shrubbery that I wanted to place in these areas (Figure 10.32). I replicated them in motion because there was a nice breeze on the original footage shot, and I wanted to use them to distract the viewer from much of the static painted areas.

Figure 10.32
Use masked areas of the duplicated original footage to fill in spaces with moving trees and bushes. (Compare with Figure 10.31).

You can view the final rendered QuickTime movie from the Chapter 10 folder on the DVD.

Motion Matte "Painting" in Photoshop

11

Motion mattes are those that move, pan, zoom, or track along with footage, or they are mattes where simulated motion is created in the background from a still photograph. Another popular technique used in film and television today is the layering of several still images that are cut out and set into motion to create a complete moving scene.

Chapter Contents
Background in Motion
Masks and Mattes in Motion
Simulated 3-D Mattes and Layers

Background in Motion

This process of creating a background matte that has elements in motion provides a realistic setting for a blue-screen composite. Oftentimes, an entire background matte does not lend enough detail and believability to a scene, especially if it's a setting that should show some activity.

In this example, I used a single frame from a digital video clip of a Manhattan cityscape that I shot from the observation deck in Tower 1 of the World Trade Center in 1998 (Figure 11.1). It seemed like a perfect angle for the blue-screen footage I had from another client's project—the blue-screen rotoscope project in Chapter 7, "Rotoscoping Techniques with Photoshop."

Figure 11.1
Use a single frame from a digital video clip for the background matte base.

 Note: If you would like to follow along with this project, you can find the Photoshop file (BSCompBG .psd) and the After Effects file (SkyWalker_Comp.aep) in the Chapter 11 folder on the DVD.

To turn this still image into a believable background, I had to put several small elements in motion. The obvious choices were the cars, trucks, and buses on the streets below. I chose the larger items such as trucks and buses first, selecting them with the Marquee tool and copying and pasting them to a new layer (Figure 11.2). I then moved the large vehicles to another unoccupied portion of the street for easy reference later in After Effects. I continued with some of the taxis and cars on the left side of the frame, producing several items that would be put in motion at various intervals, speeds, and directions.

Figure 11.2 Duplicate individual vehicles and place them in empty areas on the streets below, so they can be easily animated later in After Effects.

I used the composite frame of the actors walking on the blue screen from the garbage matte project in Chapter 6, "Blue-Screen Garbage Mattes," and centered them in the frame. I then created a new layer below them and painted a rough perspective guide for the path they would be walking on in the final composite (Figure 11.3).

Figure 11.3
Add a rough guide layer for the path on which the blue-screen actors will walk.

For the plank on which I wanted the actors to walk, I used digital image samples of rusted metals and applied several Transform functions to make them match the rough perspective layer created in the previous step (Figure 11.4). I used the Perspective, Skew, and Distort options to position the layer as close to the rough layer as possible.

Figure 11.4
Combine several building material images to create the plank base across which the actors will walk.

I then created another layer and painted in some steel poles and cable for safety railings in the foreground of the actors layer. Next, I duplicated this layer, positioned it behind the actors layer, and modified it to match the correct perspective and scale in the scene (Figure 11.5).

Figure 11.5
Add separate layers of rusted
steel poles and cable as a
safety railing.

Adding a Foreground Matte

Another moving matte technique commonly used is an atmosphere matte, where a still image of clouds, fog, or rain is often screened over a scene to produce a more realistic outdoor effect. For this project, I created a clouds layer in Photoshop, reduced it in opacity, and changed the Blend Mode to Screen to add a "haze" to the atmosphere overall.

I started by adding a new layer to the Photoshop file, and I filled it with the foreground color (though any solid color will do). I then applied the Clouds filter to the layer (Filter > Render > Clouds; Figure 11.6). This layer will be animated across the Timeline in After Effects to provide a thick "atmosphere" effect and create an illusion of depth in the final composition.

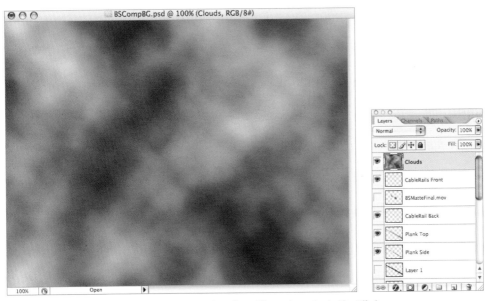

Figure 11.6 Add a clouds layer to create a hazy atmosphere that will be set in motion in After Effects.

Putting the Elements in Motion

All of the motion matte elements were contained in layers in the one Photoshop file. So using it in conjunction with the one blue-screen file with the actors on it, I could create a multilevel composite in After Effects.

I imported the Photoshop file into After Effects as a composition to retain all of the layer data, and then I dragged the entire folder from the Project window to the Timeline to ensure the proper alignment of the layers.

Starting with one vehicle at a time and the Indicator set at zero, I moved each vehicle along the streets and around the other cars and trucks as if they were in traffic. As with the truck in Figure 11.7, I played with the rate of speed and with the position and rotation of the layer elements to simulate realistic travel. I gave this truck a course to move forward and then pull over to the curb and park.

Figure 11.7

Move and rotate the truck layer to simulate parking alongside the curb.

I continued with all of the other vehicle layers, viewing RAM previews to test for speed; I did catch a few "exceeding the speed limit" quite a bit, so I had to adjust the keyframe markers. Some of the cars had "happy accidents," including the cab in Figure 11.8. I used the Rotate tool to make slight movements, but it had a mind of its own and ended up spinning out around the corner. I left it in the final project file and QuickTime movie, so you can see what's happening with it.

Figure 11.8

A cab lost control and spun out around a corner unintentionally, but I left it in for comedic effect.

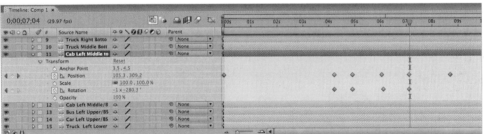

After completing all of the vehicle layers, I scaled down the imported blue-screen footage layer to fit the plank on which the actors were to walk. I used Keylight to provide the keying composite (Figure 11.9). Some additional foreground color adjustments were necessary to match the color hues of the background layers.

Using techniques covered in Chapter 15, I added a noise movie to create a simulated film grain over the static images below and animated the clouds layer. I placed the noise movie I used, Noise.mov, above all of the layers except the blue-screen video footage layer. I set the Opacity to 50% and the layer Blend Mode to Multiply (Figure 11.10).

Figure 11.9
Use Keylight to provide the chroma keying of the blue-screen layer.

Figure 11.10 Add a grainy effect to the static layers to provide a believable film grain to the static layers below.

To help provide an illusion of depth in the image, I placed the clouds layer directly under the plank layers. I stretched out the clouds layer to over 150% in width, while retaining its height at 100%. I could then place it at the extreme left side of the screen and move it horizontally across the frame during the length of the running footage (Figure 11.11). I set the Opacity to 25% and the Blend Mode to Screen, so only the lighter pixels will affect the layers below.

Figure 11.11 Stretch out the clouds layer and slowly move it horizontally across the screen.

Masks and Mattes in Motion

There will be times when you will have some footage that just needs some "pop" in the background—especially the sky shot on a hazy day. But how do you replace a sky in running footage when there's no defining color in the sky to key out? This is when painting a mask can help. Using a painted mask on a locked-off shot will allow you to replace a background with either a footage clip or still mattes in motion.

This project entailed many of the problems you may face with ordinary video footage, including stabilizing a handheld shot to lock it off and create a mask for it. In addition, I used two layers of clouds as background motion mattes for the sky effect.

 Note: To follow along with this project, you can find the QuickTime footage file, JF-NYC1.mov, and the After Effects file, NYC1-Stablz-Project.aep, in the Chapter 11 folder on the DVD.

Although this project is a "worst-case scenario," it's a perfect example of just how powerful the tracking and stabilization tools are in After Effects 6. The first step in stabilizing this clip was to lock the jumping motion of the camera (Figure 11.12). I simply found a point on the image I wanted to stabilize with the tracker and adjusted the box to fit tightly around that point.

Figure 11.12 Use the Motion Tracker in After Effects to stabilize the jumpy video clip.

The next requirement was to stabilize this clip to eliminate the rotation of the camera motion (Figure 11.13). I selected two definitive points on opposite sides of the frame so that the After Effects tracker could analyze the footage and correct the problem.

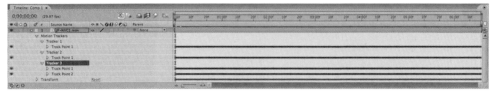

Figure 11.13 The Timeline shows all of the adjustment points the automated Tracker controls add to the clip.

Once the stabilization was applied, I increased the Scale to about 110% so the old edges would be cropped off.

Creating the Mask

If you open a movie in QuickTime Pro, you can go to any frame and copy that single frame to the clipboard. You can then paste that frame into a new file in Photoshop that will become the mask used in the project.

The pasted layer was "floating" in Photoshop, so I just deleted the background layer because I wouldn't need it later. Using the Magic Wand tool, I selected most of the sky to delete it. I then finished the detail areas with a small Eraser tool (Figure 11.14). When you try this procedure on your projects, make sure to remove all instances of the sky that are visible through the trees.

Figure 11.14 Edit a single frame of the video on a layer in Photoshop to use as a static mask for the video clip.

Once the mask was completed, I imported it into the After Effects file with transparency. I then aligned the mask layer with the stabilized video footage layer and increased the scale to 110% so it matched the resolution of the video layer. With the mask layer directly above the video footage layer in the Timeline, I selected the video footage layer and applied a track matte (Layer > Track Matte > Alpha Matte), which provided a clean mask of the sky (Figure 11.15).

Figure 11.15
Use a track matte of the video footage below the mask layer to create a clean void for a new sky.

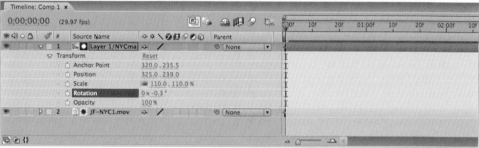

Creating Still Mattes in Motion

Instead of using stock video footage for a replacement sky, you can use a single still image and slowly "scoot" it along in the background. Or you can layer it, vary the motion between the two layers, and get very realistic results. This very simple method of creating mattes in motion is an effective replacement for video footage. By duplicating the sky layer, flipping it horizontally, and adjusting the Blend Mode, the clouds will look as if they intersect in three-dimensional space.

I started with an image file that was slightly larger than the 640 × 480 NTSC composition window, because it needed to be stretched, zoomed, and panned across the frame (Figure 11.16). I placed this layer just below the masked video layer.

To give the first clouds layer variable motion, I moved its position along the Timeline slightly, but I also zoomed in on the layer to give it the illusion that the clouds were traveling from left to right and toward the screen approximately 100 pixels. Over the duration of the 6-second Timeline, I moved the clouds layer and increased the scale from 100% to 103%.

Figure 11.16
Use an image file size slightly larger than the composition if you will be zooming or panning the background matte.

Next, I duplicated the clouds layer in the Timeline and flipped the image horizontally by adjusting the X-axis scale to a negative (–) amount. So as not to merely "mirror" the motion of these clouds with the previous clouds layer, I did not move the position. I applied only a small amount of scale, in reverse, starting with –92.0% and ending with –90.0% (Figure 11.17). Then I set the layer's Blend Mode to Lighten so the clouds would intersect between the layers. The final composite gives the illusion that there is a lot of cloud activity in the sky beyond the skyline (Figure 11.18).

Figure 11.17
In addition to panning the clouds layer, invert the duplicated clouds layer and very slightly zoom it to create a 3-D effect in the sky.

Figure 11.18
A lot of cloud activity and depth appears in the final composite.

Simulated 3-D Mattes and Layers

A popular effect in television commercials uses still images that are arranged and layered so that they appear to be all from the same image setting, but panned and zoomed to the camera to give the illusion of depth and realism. This effect appears to be three-dimensional not only because the layers pan and zoom against the background and other layers, but also because the focus of the individual layers is softened with a blur when each gets closer to the "camera."

This short 6-second animation project demonstrates how simple this effect is to produce for your own projects. I started with a very large Photoshop file, because it would be zoomed into very deeply (toward 100%). First, I needed to copy and paste foreground sections of the original image into layers; this would later allow for slight movement between the individual kids layers in the flower field (Figure 11.19). I used the Lasso tool to select sections of the floral image and copied and pasted them to create a new layer. I saved this as a Photoshop file with layers.

 Note: To follow along with this project, you can find the background Photoshop file, FieldBackground.psd, and the After Effects file, KidsZoom.aep, as well as the stock library TIFF images of the kids in the Chapter 11 folder on the DVD.

I used prematted images from PhotoSpin.com's library of kids' perspectives. These prematted TIFFs are extremely handy when you need just the subject and don't have time to manually create your own masks (Figure 11.20).

Figure 11.19
Start with a background scene
that is intentionally very large
so it can be zoomed into in the
composition.

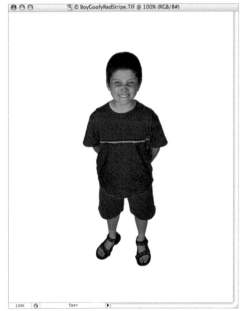

Figure 11.20
Use prematted objects in
this project so that importing them directly automatically sets their background
to transparent.

I then placed the individual images on the Timeline and positioned and scaled them to their initial size as they would appear at the start of the composition (Figure 11.21). I've provided a chart of the precise scale and positioning of the individual layers (Table 11.1).

Figure 11.21 Position and scale the object layers at the start of the Timeline.

▶ **Table 11.1** Initial Scale and Positioning of Object Layers at Frame 0;00

Transform	Scale %	Position X, Y
TwoGirlsPlaying...	85.0	196.0, 358.0
LittleBoyBlonde...	55.0	534.0, 399.0
Layer 1/Field...	25.0	324.0, 240.0
GirlPointingGlass...	55.0	429.0, 307.0
Layer 2/Field...	25.0	324.0, 240.0
LittleGirlBlonde...	40.0	281.0, 276.0
GoofyFaceBoy...	35.0	373.0, 240.0
Layer 3/Field...	25.0	324.0, 240.0
BoyGoofyRed...	25.0	301.0, 230.0
Layer 4/Field...	25.0	324.0, 240.0
LittleGirlHands...	15.0	343.0, 214.0
Background/Field...	25.0	324.0, 240.0

The characters and floral layers were individually "zoomed into" down the Timeline by changing their position, scaling them up, and applying a subtle Gaussian Blur that increases over time the closer they get to the "camera lens" (Figure 11.22 and Table 11.2). It's easiest to start with the farthest character and build up from there.

Figure 11.22 Reposition, scale, and blur each character layer as it appears to be passing up the "camera" or viewing plane.

▶ **Table 11.2** Scale and Positioning of the Layers at Frame 5;29

Transform	Scale %	Position X, Y
TwoGirlsPlaying...	375.0	−490.0, 886.0
LittleBoyBlonde...	260.0	1312.0, 1057.0
Layer 1/Field...	180.0	242.0, −62.0
GirlPointingGlass...	200.0	819.0, 599.0
Layer 2/Field...	100.0	234.0, 354.0
LittleGirlBlonde...	150.0	−9.0, 502.0
GoofyFaceBoy...	140.0	527.0, 404.0
Layer 3/Field...	90.0	224.0, 414.0
BoyGoofyRed...	110.0	171.0, 324.0
Layer 4/Field...	75.0	288.0, 35.0
LittleGirlHands...	65.0	359.0, 274.0
Background/Field...	75.0	278.0, 322.0

As the layers of a project start to stack up, you may experience a slower response from your animation if you are previewing at the highest resolution and full quality (Figure 11.23). If you turn the resolution to Quarter, your speed will be acceptable and you can then "scrub" the Timeline Indicator over periods of time to see how your animation is moving.

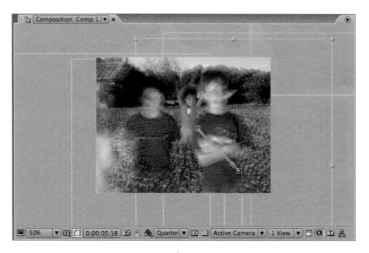

Figure 11.23
Lowering the resolution to Quarter will speed up the positioning and scaling process and will allow you to "scrub" preview the Timeline.

Next, I applied a Gaussian Blur over time in the Timeline for each layer to give the appearance of forced depth of field (Figure 11.24). I adjusted all the layers individually to control the effect (Table 11.3).

Figure 11.24 Increase the Gaussian Blur over time to help reinforce the 3-D effect of the zoom-in.

▶ **Table 11.3** Gaussian Blur Applied over the Timeline

Keyframe	0;00	3;00	3;22	4;08	4;21	5;29
TwoGirlsPlaying...	0.0				8.0	
LittleBoyBlonde...	0.0			8.0		
Layer 1/Field...	0.0		8.0			
GirlPointingGlass...		0.0				8.0
Layer 2/Field...		0.0				8.0
LittleGirlBlonde...			0.0			7.0
GoofyFaceBoy...				0.0		3.0
Layer 3/Field...				0.0		5.0
BoyGoofyRed...					0.0	2.0
Layer 4/Field...					0.0	2.0
LittleGirlHands...	N/A					
Background/Field...	N/A					

Because the zoom effect starts out with characters in the foreground, it will appear as if it zooms in very fast and then slows down. To help fool the eye in making a smoother zoom in animation, apply an Easy Ease Out on all of the keyframes for Scale, Position, and Gaussian Blur at the first frame (Figure 11.25). Adjust the Keyframe Velocity to 100% to make a longer Ease Out duration.

Figure 11.25 Adjust the Keyframe Velocity of the Ease Outs at frame 0;00.

Making Movies from Stills

Still images are great source material for motion graphics and video. You can bring an image to life by extracting foreground and subject elements onto layers that can be panned, zoomed, and moved in believable motion and perspective. You can create a quick animated clip for your DV project when there's no source footage available. You can create a 3-D stereo effect in a static scene.

This fantastic phenomenon is at the heart and soul of this book! Mastering the techniques in this chapter will differentiate your abilities as a motion graphics creator from those of just a DV editor or compositor.

12

Chapter Contents

Extracting the Subjects from an Image

Extracting subjects and layers of depth from your images requires a command of the Clone Stamp tool and some creative image compositing skills. Once you cut out your subjects from the original image, you need to fill the holes behind them (or at least the edges where motion will reveal the void).

In this first example, we'll be using the image Bird-n-BeachFlat.tif on the DVD in the Chapter 12 folder (Figure 12.1).

Figure 12.1 This image is a good example of clear foreground subjects and an easily editable background.

Because we want to be able to zoom into this image in After Effects, we want a large file with lots of image information in it so it will remain under 100% when we are fully zoomed in, to avoid pixelation. We will extract the seagull and the rocks in the foreground onto their own layer and patch up the background to fill in the missing image area. For the most precise method of accurately dividing the images, roughly copy and paste the subjects to a new layer and then carefully remove the unwanted material around the edges with the Eraser tool. This gives you great edge control, by changing brush sizes and edge hardness while editing.

1. Open the file and start by using the Lasso tool to quickly select the area well outside of the edges of the seagull and rocks; then press ⌘/Ctrl+J to copy and paste the selection to a new layer (Figure 12.2).

2. Use the Eraser tool to remove the excess material around the foreground subjects, changing brushes as needed to adapt to the edge softness and complexity.

With this image, you can start with a larger brush size along the edges of the rocks and switch to a smaller brush in the details, leaving the seagull for the next step (Figure 12.3). Select the seagull from the rocks layer, and use ⌘/Ctrl+J to copy and paste it to a new layer.

3. Return to the rocks layer and use the Eraser tool to remove the seagull and remaining background material from around the rocks.

4. Go back to the seagull layer and use smaller Eraser tool brushes to remove the background material around the edges.

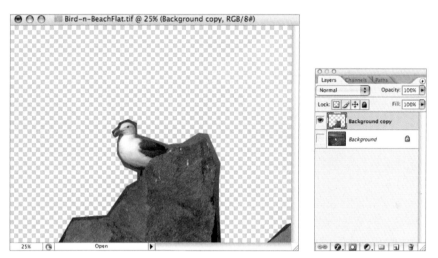

Figure 12.2 Select a rough area around the subjects in the image and copy and paste it to a new layer.

Figure 12.3 Remove the background from around the edges of the rocks with the Eraser tool brush.

5. Because the seagull will have some slight motion from behind the rocks, we need to add just a little more of the bird's image area. Use the Clone Stamp tool with a small soft-edge brush to carefully fill in toward the tail and legs of the seagull—adding about 1/4″ more of the image area (Figure 12.4).

Figure 12.4 Use the Clone Stamp tool to add some more feathers to our friend.

6. We now have three layers in our image: the background layer, the rocks layer, and the seagull layer. Select the background layer, hide the top two layers, and use a combination of techniques to fill in the area where the rocks and seagull were previously. A random application of the Clone Stamp tool with a large soft-edge brush works well in this case. Take care not to create a repeating pattern in the water and sand. If this occurs, you can use the Healing brush to touch up some of the repetitions (Figure 12.5).

Figure 12.5 Use the Clone Stamp tool and Healing brush to fill in the background image where the subjects have been removed.

Creating Zoom Effects with Moving Layers

Simply zooming in on a static image in After Effects provides expected but limited results—it still looks like a static image. By separating the elements of an image and putting them into motion during a zoom-in, you will create a dramatic and realistic effect that has dimension and interest. This effect requires files that are at least twice the size of your movie window, because we will be increasing the layer dimension to create the zoom in After Effects.

1. Using the layered image we created in the preceding section, or the file Beach-n-Bird.psd from the DVD, import the image into a new project in After Effects as a composition to retain all of the layers. For this project, set the project composition to standard NTSC 640 × 480 default, 3 seconds in length.

2. Drag the entire PSD file folder from the Project window, center it in the Comp 1 window, and scale down the group to slightly larger than the Comp 1 window area, as shown (Figure 12.6). This will be the position for Frame 1 of the zoom effect animation.

3. Hide the top two layers in the Timeline window, and move the Current Time Indicator to approximately 7 frames. Select the background layer, and press the S key to reveal the Scale settings for that layer in the Timeline window. Click the Time-Vary Stopwatch to set the current scale setting for this layer (Figure 12.7).

4. Move the Indicator down to the 2-second mark, and adjust the scale up to 71%. Right-click/Ctrl+click the scale marker, and select Keyframe Assistant > Easy Ease (Figure 12.7). This will automatically slow down the end of the zoom to give a more natural camera feel and not have an abrupt mechanical stop.

5. Repeat with the first scale marker at Frame 7, but select Easy Ease In.

6. Make the rock layer visible, and move the Current Time Indicator to the same Frame 7 marker to which the background layer is set. Press the S key to reveal the Scale settings in the Timeline window, and click the Time-Vary Stopwatch to set the current scale.

Figure 12.6 Import and place the Photoshop layers into your Comp window, and scale down to set the beginning of the zoom effect.

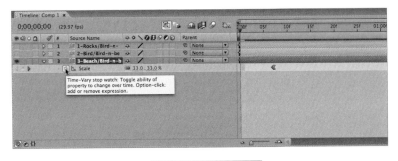

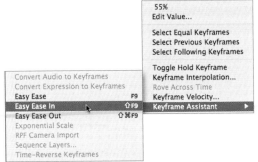

Figure 12.7

Begin the background zoom a few frames in from the beginning of the animation.

7. Repeat for the seagull layer, and apply the Easy Ease Out Keyframe Assistant to both markers (Figure 12.8).

8. Move the Indicator to the 2-second mark, increase the scale of both the rock and seagull layers to 55%, and apply the Easy Ease In Keyframe Assistant to both markers. We aren't increasing the scale of these layers (or "zooming in") as much as the background layer in order to give the effect of a camera lens that "pulls" the background and foreground together and decreases the depth of field. This technique simulates a zoom lens by effectively changing the focal length by compressing the shot.

   Because the different layers scale at separate center points, it's important to align them to keep the focus of the motion centered in the Comp 1 window frame and not move toward the bottom of the frame.

9. With the rock layer selected, return to the Frame 7 marker and press P for the Position settings in the Timeline window. Click the Time-Vary Stopwatch to set the current Position setting. Move the Indicator to the 2-second mark, and then drag the rock layer in the Comp 1 window to bring it up in the frame. Scrub the Indicator back and forth to see the motion of the rock layer. Be sure to move it in a matching vertical alignment with an object in the background layer, such as the birds along the water's surface, as shown in Figure 12.9. Set the marker in the Timeline and apply the Easy Ease In Keyframe Assistant.

10. Repeat the above process with the bird layer, keeping it in the same vertical path in relation to the rocks, but position it slightly lower (behind the rocks) to reinforce the motion zoom effect (Figure 12.10). After applying the Easy Ease In Keyframe Assistant to the marker, check that all of the markers at the 2-second mark have the same ease-in amount applied by right-clicking/Ctrl+clicking the marker and selecting Keyframe Velocity. Check the markers at the Frame 7 mark as well.

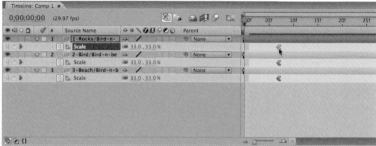

Figure 12.8

Set scale markers for both the rock and seagull layers.

Figure 12.9

Move the rock layer up in the frame to keep it centered in the motion zoom path.

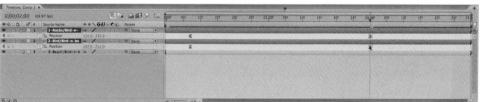

Figure 12.10 Move the bird layer in a vertical path to match the movement of the rock layer, and scrub the Indicator to view the motion path. Check the Keyframe Velocity of all the markers to make sure all the ease-ins and ease-outs match.

For variation, experiment with adding blur to the background layer over time, as shown in Figure 12.11. In reality, a zoom wouldn't necessarily take the background out of focus like that, but it does give a nice effect that puts the focus of the frame onto the foreground subjects.

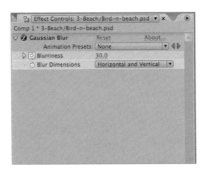

Figure 12.11
Try adding a blur over time in the background layer for an interesting effect.

Simulated Forward Motion with Zoom Effects

In addition to zooming in on an image as if you were using a camera lens, you can zoom right "into" the image—bringing it to life and actually creating the effect of moving through the image. You can do this by extracting not only the foreground objects but also predominant objects and landmarks, all the way to the farthest point in the background.

To make this effect realistic, you will need to start with an image that will allow many selections and transformations with a predominant perspective point. For this project, we'll use the image OR_HighwayFlat.tif found on the DVD (Figure 12.12).

Figure 12.12

Select an image with a predominant perspective and several layers going off into the background.

Start "peeling away" the layers of the image by selecting foreground objects first and working your way all the way back to the farthest point in the image. For every layer that you create, use the Eraser brush to remove excess material, and try to create as clean of an edge as possible but still blend in with the background elements (Figure 12.13).

Because the path of motion will be to zoom into the image, moving each layer farther to the outside and down into the frame, you will need to modify every layer and add an extra image area to the bottom edges with the Clone Stamp tool (Figure 12.14). Extra care is necessary to create believable textures and modifications to each layer, because repetitive textures will stand out and ruin your effect.

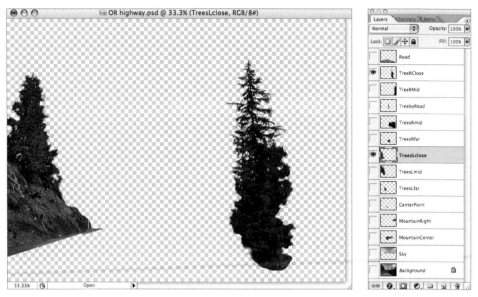

Figure 12.13 Separate the layers and clean up around all of the edges.

Figure 12.14 Use the Clone Stamp tool to add image area in the direction of motion where the foreground objects will pull away from the background.

Be sure to plan ahead. I want the clouds in the sky to move as well, so I have cloned and painted additional sky and clouds well beyond the boundaries of the original coverage area. The cloud layer will ultimately move from the right to the left in the animation, so you need to move the layer to the right, out of the frame window, and continue cloning and painting more sky and clouds to cover the open areas. You may want to adjust the scale and proportions of this layer as well (Figure 12.15).

Import the Photoshop file into a new After Effects project as a composition. Create a new composition, NTSC, 640 × 480, and 3 seconds in length. Drag the imported PSD file folder from the Project window, and center it in the Comp 1 window frame. The layers will be really huge in the frame, so make sure to select them all and scale them down to fit the frame. If you don't scale them all at the same time, they will not be aligned properly from the start of the animation.

Figure 12.15 By creating the sky and cloud layer larger than the active frame window, the layer will be movable horizontally in After Effects.

In this project, we want to create the illusion of traveling down the road, but when we scale the composition up at the 3-second mark, the road below disappears off the bottom of the screen. When we drag the layer in the Comp 1 window to bring it back up in the frame where we want it, it is not a straight vertical line; rather, it is a diagonal path that keeps the image on the layer in vertical alignment (Figure 12.16). This is similar to the motion path of the rocks layer in the previous Zoom project.

Each layer will have to move to the right or left to follow the edge of the road (except the background layer) to enhance the effect of forward motion. The trees on each side will have to move in the direction of their perspective motion path—just as if you were to draw perspective lines to the focal point at the end of the road. As you continue to make adjustments to the layers to create the correct amount of motion, scrub the Current Time Indicator back and forth to see the motion in low-res preview in the Comp 1 window (Figure 12.17). Use RAM Preview to view the animation in real time.

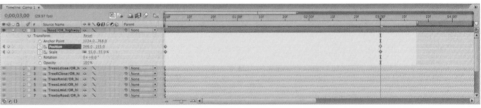

Figure 12.16
After scaling up the layers to the desired amount, move each layer in the screen to match the line of perspective along the motion path.

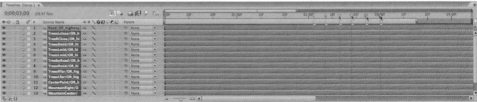

Figure 12.17
Scrub the Current Time Indicator back and forth to preview the motion of the layers.

If you discover that a layer needs some more editing, such as trimming a bit more closely to the subject or adding material to cover up a hole, select the layer name in the Project window and choose the Edit > Edit Original to open the PSD file in Photoshop (Figure 12.18). Once you've finished editing, save the PSD file and return to After Effects. Select the layer in the Project window again, and choose Reload Footage from the File menu. The edits will be automatically updated.

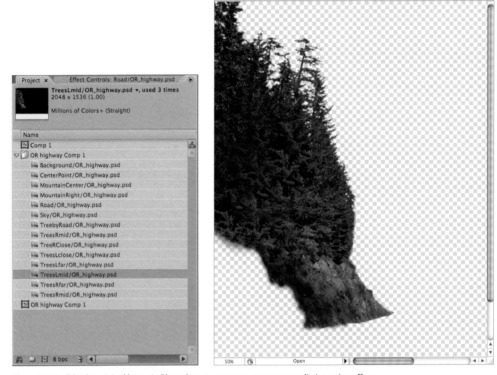

Figure 12.18 Edit the original layers in Photoshop as necessary to assure a realistic motion effect.

Three-Dimensional Moving Camera Pans

Panning a moving camera in a scene requires not just moving objects and scenery from one side to the other, but taking into consideration the three-dimensional angle that occurs in the foreground subjects. If your original static image is at an angle to start with, it may actually help you reconstruct the layers to allow a more believable moving camera pan. Keep in mind that this is a simulated motion effect with Photoshop layers and not a true rendered 3-D effect, and it does not use 3-D layers in After Effects.

The image I chose for this project is a small footbridge over a slow-moving stream (Figure 12.19). The problem I encountered at first was that the bridge was cut off on the left side and the format was Portrait instead of Landscape Mode. A lot of cloning and patching were needed to create the final Portrait Mode image, Footbridge.psd, found on the DVD.

Figure 12.19 (left) The original image in this project was in Portrait Mode, and some of the main subject on the left was cut off. (right) By carefully editing the image into layers, I centered the bridge and other elements within a Landscape Mode image.

I divided the bridge into three separate layers: front rail, boards, and rear rail (Figure 12.20). This not only allows the railings to be moved independently, but the floorboards can be moved and scaled to fit in After Effects. Because this is the subject of focus in this scene, it will actually appear to "rotate," as if the camera were moving around its center. Other elements in the image are separated by two foreground hills that move one over the other, some bushes right behind the left side of the bridge, the two trees, and the background trees and water.

Import the image into an After Effects project file, NTSC, 640 × 480, as a composition to retain the layers. Drag the composition file from the Project window to the Comp 1 window and center it. Adjust the scale of all layers simultaneously to maintain their positions.

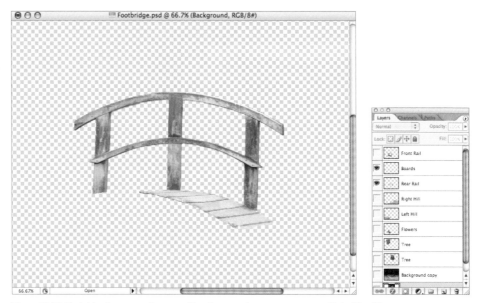

Figure 12.20 The bridge is cut up and separated into layers so that we can pan around it in After Effects.

Because this motion will be a camera pan from left to right (meaning the "camera" will "move" from left to right), the image layers will move from right to left. The background layer will move the least, while the closest hill on the right will move the most. While the front rail layer will move a bit more than the rear rail layer, the boards layer will need to stretch to match this movement, as well as change location (Figure 12.21). Open the After Effects file FootbridgePan.aep on the DVD for reference as needed.

Figure 12.21 Move the front and back rails of the bridge at different rates, and stretch the floorboards to scale with the alignment between the two side rails. Notice how all the layers move from right to left in the Composition window.

Note: When moving objects and elements in a panned animation, be sure to pay attention to how much or how little each layer moves; the effect may look fake or create a scaled-down scene in miniature when played back.

Still Camera with Moving Subjects

Take a still image and create a moving scene, one with no camera or lens motion but with subjects that pass by in front of you, with added atmospheric effects. This works well with multi-image composites too, as long as all of the images composited into one image match in perspective, lighting, and scale.

This is a fairly complicated sample project, so I won't get into too many details about all of the edits and cloning done in the Photoshop layers. You can follow along by opening the file CabsLayers.psd on the DVD, or you may want to skip ahead and open the After Effects project file, Cabs.aep, also found on the DVD.

Figure 12.22

The challenge of trying to pull contents out of this image was the large subject in the foreground with a heavy motion blur.

The original image was a Portrait Mode still shot with the foreground subject in a heavy motion blur (Figure 12.22). I decided that I would remove the front cab and the next cab in line to the left. This meant that I had to re-create the pavement surface and paint in the missing portions of the cabs in the background, as well as the markers and posts in the middle ground (Figure 12.23).

Figure 12.23

Removing the front and middle cabs necessitated a lot of "paint" work in order to fill in the background.

The midrange cab is going to be set in a slow rolling motion off the left side of the frame, so I had to add its own reflection and brake lights layers (Figure 12.24). Because I want to move the front cab through the entire width of the frame, I had to rebuild it in its entirety and make the associated reflection and light layers match, much wider than the project frame size (Figure 12.25).

Figure 12.24 I added the cab on the left back in with reflections and a brake light layer that will be animated while the cab rolls out the left side of the frame.

Figure 12.25 The foreground cab had to be reconstructed in its entirety and made wider than the project frame so it could be animated to pass by quickly.

I imported the PSD file into a custom-sized, vertical After Effects project file as a composition and centered it in the Comp 1 window. The layers are all arranged in order front to back, and the foremost cab layers are hidden. While working on the motion of the midrange cab on the left (and with a bit of trial and error), I discovered that it should be scaled down as well as moved just to the left. To give a little more action to the cab's movement, I added the brake lights about halfway through the motion. I applied the Easy Ease In Keyframe Assistant to both the Scale and Position markers in the Timeline and increased the Keyframe Velocity to 50%, which slows down the vehicle a bit sooner (Figure 12.26).

Figure 12.26 Both Scale and Position are adjusted to create the illusion of motion in the correct perspective path.

The additional layers, such as the reflection and brake lights, must move and scale precisely as the Mid Cab layer does, so choosing the Parenting feature in this case does the job perfectly (Figure 12.27).

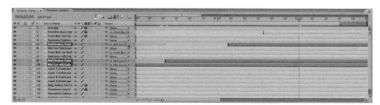

Figure 12.27 Choosing the Mid Cab layer as a parent to the reflection and brake light layers creates precise alignment in motion and scale.

To create some motion in the surface of the wet pavement, I needed a moving displacement map. I made a file about twice the width of the Project window in Photoshop and applied the Noise filter, level 15, Gaussian (Figure 12.28). I then imported this file into After Effects and created a new composition to hold the noise file layer. Then I moved the layer from the left to the right, duplicated it, and reversed the motion path to move from right to left. I inverted the top layer so that the noise patterns don't match up when they cross each other, and I set the Blending Mode to Darken. This will enable the black points of the noise to be visible in both directions (Figure 12.29).

Figure 12.28 First I generated a displacement map with a noise file in Photoshop.

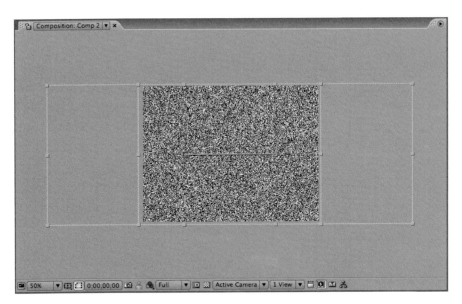

Figure 12.29 Then I created a new composition and inverted the noise file layers and moved them in both horizontal directions.

I placed the new composition into the bottom of the Timeline of Comp 1 and hid it. Then I applied the Displacement Map filter to the pavement texture and the building reflection layers (Figure 12.30). I used a RAM Preview to get a real-time view of the animated ground surface, which simulates rain on the wet surface.

Figure 12.30 The new composition is used as the displacement map for the rainy, wet surface on the ground.

Next, I made the front cab visible and selected the reflection and brake lights layers, placing them off-screen to the right in the beginning of the motion path. I then attached the reflection and brake layers to the front cab layer as the parent, selecting them from the Timeline window. Once I determined the motion path and made some scale adjustments, I applied a Directional Blur of 10 pixels at 93° to enhance the quick drive-by effect of the cab (Figure 12.31) and set the brake layer to become visible just past the halfway point of the motion path. I then applied the Easy Ease In Keyframe Assistant to the markers in the Timeline window to slow down the cab toward the end.

Finally, to create the effect of rain coming down, I placed the noise file layer at the top of the Timeline window and rotated it to a 10° angle. Then I set the Blending Mode to Screen and the Opacity to 10%. I configured the motion path to run from top to bottom at a 10° angle and applied a Directional Blur filter at 10° to match and set it to 10 pixels in length (Figure 12.32). Then I ran a RAM Preview to make sure all layer motions, scale effects, and timings were set correctly and all adjustments made.

Figure 12.31 A Directional Blur is added to the front cab layer to enhance the drive-by effect.

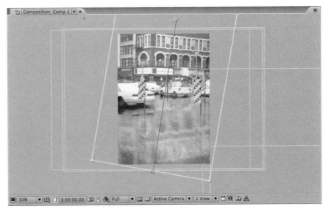

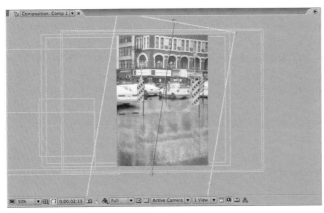

Figure 12.32

A motion blur is also used to create the effect of falling rain.

Advanced Movie Magic

You're now making animations and composites—but what are some of the details and fine-tuning you need to apply to make them believable? These chapters cover some tips and tricks in applying some finesse to your projects. Understanding a few basic principles in adjusting speed, color, atmosphere, and film-like titling will help you put the finishing professional touches on your projects.

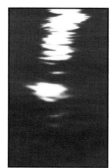 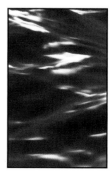 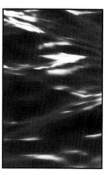

Scale and Speed

Making a composite of motion layers believable takes more than just using well-blended pixels. Perspective, scale, and speed of the object layers also need to be taken into consideration. Moving objects in the distance will appear slower than those moving at the same speed in the foreground. Larger characters will appear to be more lumbering and lethargic than smaller characters in the same scene. This is in part why Godzilla actually looks like a man in a rubber suit next to all the tall buildings with tiny people running around, but the T-Rex in Jurassic Park appears more lifelike in its movements. The man in the Godzilla suit was filmed at the same speed as the people running around, so no matter how well the building models were made, how the set was lit, or even how detailed the monster suit was, the speed of the motion did not match the scale of the creature.

13

Chapter Contents

Distance, Perspective, and Speed

What happens to an object in the distance that is traveling at the same rate of speed as another identical object closer to you? If you look up a city street and watch the cross traffic several blocks away, you will see that the perspective view not only makes the cars appear smaller, but it makes them appear to travel a shorter distance.

Look at the diagram of three cars in Figure 13.1. If you draw perspective lines that represent approximately the same distance of travel for the car in the background as the car in the foreground, this will help you determine what the rate of speed should be to correctly match them.

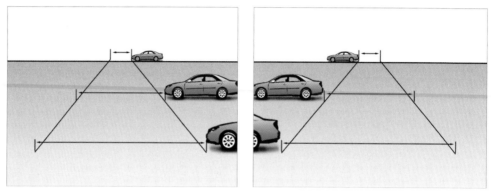

Figure 13.1 Determine the distance a far object travels to match its rate of speed with that of the foreground objects.

By setting the position key frames for the beginning and end points of all three cars along the same amount of time on the Timeline, you apply the appropriate speed to each layer (Figure 13.2). I've animated this simple three-car scene in DistanceRelativity.mov, which is included on the companion DVD. This is a pretty easy method of figuring a layer object's motion in perspective when you have a similar foreground object with which to compare it.

Figure 13.2

Set the beginning and end position key frames for all layers in motion along the Timeline to determine the rate of speed.

Size, Mass, and Speed

Why do larger objects and characters need to appear to move slower than smaller ones? It's because of the effect that the Earth's gravity and atmospheric pressure have on objects that have a large mass. Have you ever noticed how easy it is for a humming-bird to fly and dart around? Imagine a condor trying to keep up with a hummingbird! Picture an elephant trying to keep up with a cheetah. Size, mass, and weight affect how we perceive visual scale and motion speed in special effects and composite shots.

In the DinoCity.mov example, I added a layer of DV footage of a dinosaur puppet to a cityscape foreground and background. To make the small puppet appear to be a huge and ominous creature, I slowed down the playback speed of the footage. By select-ing the layer and adjusting the Time Stretch amount (Layer > Time > Time Stretch), you can increase or decrease the playback speed of any motion layer (Figure 13.3). In this case, I adjusted the Stretch Factor to 200%; it could be slower, but then it might not appear as smooth in movement because of the lower playback frame rate. If you have no reference to match the scale and speed to, then you'll need to make adjustments until they look right to you.

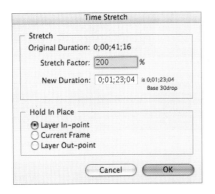

Figure 13.3

Adjust the Time Stretch on a motion layer to set the correct speed for the scale of the object in motion.

Adjusting motion layers to account for the scale of creature effects in motion pictures is common practice. However, the layers are normally shot at a higher film speed to create a smoother motion at a reduced speed.

My next example (Small-LargeDinos.mov) uses the same dinosaur puppet footage to simulate both an adult and a juvenile raptor in a cave. The original scale of the puppet was actually about 3 feet in height, but it had to appear to be about 5 or 6 feet in height for the adult in this example composite (Figure 13.4). I adjusted the Scale of the two layers of puppet footage accordingly, as well as the Stretch Factor for the speed in which they appear to move in playback. I set the adult layer to 150%, and I set the juvenile raptor to 50% of the original footage length. The adult raptor appears to move slower than it did in the original footage to give it some visual mass, while the juvenile raptor's motions, in comparison, appear rapid and darting.

Figure 13.4
Adjust the Time Stretch and Scale of duplicate layers of the same footage to make both the adult and juvenile dinosaurs appear to be in the same scene.

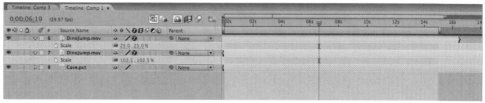

Distance and Speed

Have you ever noticed, while driving down a long straight road, that a sign or landmark doesn't appear to be getting closer until you are almost right on it? It's as if you aren't traveling very fast until the last couple of hundred yards. Although objects in the distance don't really move slower, they frequently appear to—especially if they are moving toward the camera.

If you examine my video footage of Times Square in New York City, you'll notice that the truck and bus that I've placed arrows over appear to be moving very slowly for the first half of the clip and then they appear to speed up in the last second or two toward the end. You can find this QuickTime movie, DistanceSpeed.mov, in the Chapter 13 folder on the DVD.

This clip shows two one-way streets of oncoming traffic at a steady pace, with no slowing or stopping. The first 8 seconds of the 15-second clip show very little travel in the two marked vehicles (Figure 13.5). Only slight variations in movement and scale are apparent.

Figure 13.5 Between the first frame and the 8-second mark, very little travel distance or increased scale is apparent.

Between the 8-second and 12-second marks, the rate of travel for both the truck and the bus increases dramatically (Figure 13.6). Notice that they increase in scale as well as speed as they approach the camera and more details on both vehicles become visible.

Figure 13.6
The vehicles appear to be approaching faster in the next 4 seconds of the clip.

In the last 3 seconds of the 15-second clip, the truck and bus run off the edges of the screen (Figure 13.7). This is the greatest amount of increase in scale and motion of the entire piece of footage. Note that the truck on the right is actually moving faster than the bus on the left. This is noticeable only in the final few seconds of the clip.

Figure 13.7
The final few seconds of the clip show the greatest amount of motion and increased scale, and the truck is traveling noticeably faster than the bus.

Water Mass and Distance

Using the Psunami plug-in for After Effects, you can study how water moves in relation to the distance from the camera and its mass. You can also see how environmental conditions such as wind and swells can affect the appearance of the surface of the water.

The examples I used in this section (including water color, light source, and atmospheric conditions) were all derived from the same basic Psunami plug-in settings. The only changes I made were in the height and size of the waves, wind speed, and camera height.

Note: You can install and use the Psunami Demo plug-in, which is available on the DVD, to follow along and make adjustments to the After Effects file, WaterMassProject.aep, and to view the appropriate QuickTime movies mentioned in each example.

This first example makes the water surface appear as if it's a calm lake with gentle ripples that have been filmed only a couple of feet above the water (Figure 13.8). In fact, the camera was set at 10 meters above the water and angled down about 110° in most of these examples. This example appears so smooth because the Smoothness was set at 1.000 and the Vertical Scale of the wave was set at 0.500. Also, the wave Grid Size was set larger so the wave appears to be closer to the camera. You can view the QuickTime movie of this effect by opening the file Psunami-test1.mov in the Chapter 13 folder.

When I reduced the wave Course Grid Size to 1.000, the Fine Grid Size to 0.300, and the wave Smoothness to 1.000, the camera seemed to be higher from the water's surface; however, the image still appears to be a lake or small body of water instead of an open ocean (Figure 13.9).

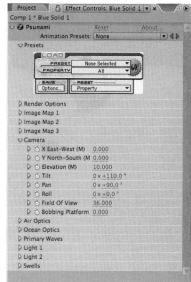

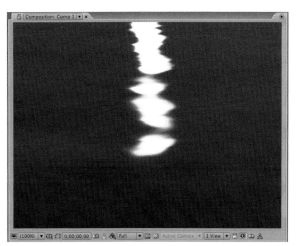

Figure 13.8 Even though the camera is 10 meters above the water surface, it appears as though it is zoomed in only a foot or two above a calm lake surface.

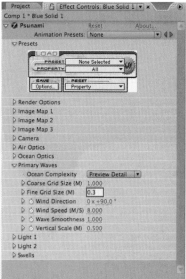

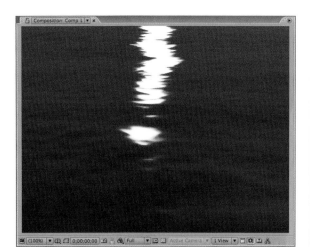

Figure 13.9 Reducing the wave Grid Size gives the appearance of more distance and adds more mass to the water surface.

Next, I increased the wave Vertical Scale to 3.000 and the Wind Speed to 8.000, and the waves started to really swell up and roll. This is definitely starting to look like a larger body of water, such as a large lake or ocean surf (Figure 13.10). Notice, though, that the camera still appears to be fairly close to the water's surface. View the QuickTime movie of this stage of the effect, Psunami-test2.mov, in the Chapter 13 folder. Adding more height and a swell to the waves increased the ocean-like appearance in the Quick-Time movie sample Psunami-test3.mov.

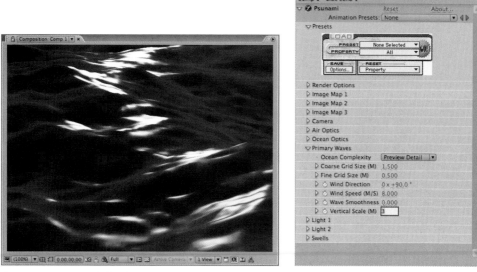

Figure 13.10 Increasing the height of the waves and the wind speed makes them roll more violently.

Increasing the camera Elevation to 100.000 meters and decreasing the Grid Sizes gave the appearance of a more distant body of water, such as an ocean or a large flowing river (Figure 13.11). Notice that an active swell is still applied to the effect, which causes the motion to be more ocean-like. View the QuickTime movie Psunami-test4.mov to see the effect in motion.

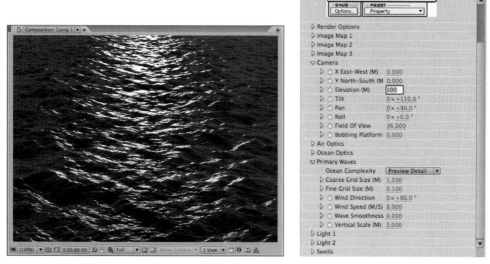

Figure 13.11 Moving the camera up and away while reducing the grid size will create the appearance of a rapidly moving larger body of water.

Moving the camera to an even higher elevation of 500.000 meters revealed an even greater expanse of flowing water (Figure 13.12). The QuickTime movie Psunami-test5.mov shows you how slow the wave motion is, which gives the illusion of either an ocean current or a very large river flowing rapidly from a distance. The settings are similar to the ones that I used to create flowing water in the example movie, Water-Matte.mov, in Chapter 9, "Static Matte 'Painting' in Photoshop."

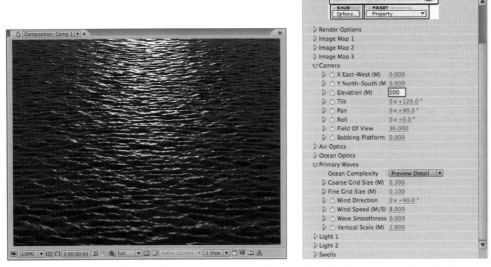

Figure 13.12 Higher camera elevation with a constant wave speed and regeneration gives the appearance of a rolling river or ocean current.

Creating Time-Lapse Footage

You can easily use digital video footage to create the speed-up effect of time-lapse shots, provided you have enough source footage. Animators often need more than 5 minutes of video footage to get only 10 seconds of time-lapse. This source video needs to be shot from a locked-off position on a tripod so it doesn't appear jumpy when played back in fast motion.

> **Note:** Unfortunately, because of the size and length of the files used in this section, the original footage files are not included on the DVD as examples. However, the finished results are available on the DVD in the Chapter 13 folder.

The sample footage I chose was a 5½ minute shot I took from the roof of a building right after a storm, when the clouds were really beautiful and full of motion and character.

I applied Time Stretch to the movie layer and set the Stretch Factor to 3.5%, which made the new duration of the video clip just over 10 seconds (Figure 13.13). This is a fairly exaggerated amount, but it lends itself well to the subject matter. You can view the resulting QuickTime movie in the Chapter 13 folder on the DVD.

Figure 13.13 Use Time Stretch to modify the movie clip to a fraction of its original length.

Sometimes, you can use a shorter clip to create a fast-motion or time-lapse clip that can be looped to simulate a longer piece of footage. This works especially well for repeating traffic patterns such as those seen on a freeway or at a traffic signal.

This original footage was only 45 seconds long, but when I applied the Time Stretch at 10%, it ended up only 4½ seconds in length (Figure 13.14). I then looped the final rendered QuickTime movie and played it back as a fast-motion clip, Time-Lapse-Traffic1.mov, available on the DVD in the Chapter 13 folder. Notice how the traffic signal changes in the loop.

Figure 13.14 Apply Time Stretch, and loop the QuickTime movie to create a longer clip.

To create a better time-lapse effect of the same footage, I applied a Time Stretch of 5% and created a clip that was just over 2 seconds in length (Figure 13.15). Being such a short clip, the motion is so fast that when the QuickTime movie is looped, you can't tell that it's stretched right away—even the traffic signal is still legible.

Figure 13.15
Looping a small time-lapse clip can still work visually.

Color, Light, and Focus

14

When you're compositing objects into a scene, you must make sure they look as though they really belong there; you can help achieve that goal by concentrating on color and lighting as well as distance and focus. An object's placement needs to match the focal length of the original footage or it will stand out as fake.

Chapter Contents

Distance, Focus, and Light

When you add new objects in the distance in a scene, you need to study the footage to see what other effects the surrounding areas have. If you're putting mountains into a background, they must match not only in scale but also in focus in proportion to the background. If the horizon is hazy and slightly blurry, then the added mountains should be also.

The same is true for moving objects, such as the planes I've added to this old film footage. I placed a DC-3 in the background and scaled it down to fit the approximate scale I wanted for the composite (Figure 14.1). Notice how crisp and clear the plane is in relation to the rest of the scene—let alone how hazy and blurred the buildings in the background are.

Figure 14.1
The DC-3 looks quite out of place in the background of this archival footage.

 Note: You can open this project file, DistAirplaneProject.aep, in the Chapter 14 folder on the DVD and follow along with the production steps. You can also view the rendered QuickTime movie, CityPlanes320.mov.

I zoomed in to 200% in the Comp window so the plane could be more easily viewed. I adjusted the exposure levels (Effects > Color Correction > Brightness & Contrast) of the plane layer to lighten the image and make the contrast less harsh, so it will better match the buildings in the background. (I pushed the Brightness up to 50 and the Contrast down to –50.) To further blend the plane image into its surroundings, I applied a Gaussian Blur (Effects > Blur and Sharpen > Gaussian Blur) with a Blurriness of 25.0. This step combined with the lightening really makes the plane appear as if it is part of the original footage (Figure 14.2).

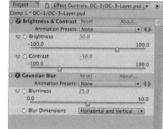

Figure 14.2 Lighten the plane to better match the background surroundings, and add a Gaussian Blur to the plane to blend it into the background of the original scene.

I created a mask layer of the opening between the buildings in the horizon and made the flight path of the plane match the angle of its direction (Figure 14.3).

Figure 14.3
Create a mask in Photoshop to keep the planes flying behind the buildings in the scene.

I duplicated the plane layer with the mask layer several times to create a few planes flying in the distance (Figure 14.4). The farther away a plane is in the scene, the lighter and blurrier it needs to be. It also needs to be scaled down accordingly.

I moved the plane layers in the same direction, although I moved the planes in the foreground slightly faster than those in the distance to add dimension, as discussed in Chapter 13, "Scale and Speed." The final composite now appears as if the planes were actually in the original footage (Figure 14.5).

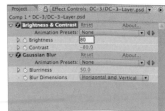

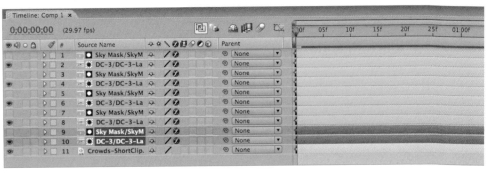

Figure 14.4 Duplicate the plane layers, rescale the copied planes, lighten them, and blur them. The farther back they appear in the scene, the more you should blur them.

Figure 14.5
If only FedEx had a fleet of DC-3s back in the 1940s!

Matching Color, Lighting, and Focus

Colored objects composited into a scene require special attention because the colors need to be adjusted to match the surrounding area. The lighting and focus of the composited objects must also be modified to blend in well with camera zoom and scene depth. Composited objects and footage are often shot in different lighting situations, such as a studio, natural bright daylight, or overcast skies, and need to be color adjusted.

For this composite, I used the original footage of an old English castle on a hill that zoomed out, plus a layered Photoshop file with still images of sheep on a hill. These two shots were taken in different locations under different lighting conditions and resolutions. Fortunately, the smaller still images of the sheep to be composited into the video footage were of a higher resolution, so they could easily be altered to match.

I started with a new After Effects file and a composition 320 × 240, 15 seconds in length (approximately the same as the original video footage). I imported the layered Photoshop file, placed the layers on top of the video footage layer in the Timeline, and resized them down to match the scale of the scene at Frame 1 (Figure 14.6). Notice how much bluer the grass and rocks around the sheep layers look against the original footage. This project file, Color_Focus.aep, can be found in the Chapter 14 folder on the DVD.

Figure 14.6

Composite the still images on top of the original footage and scale them to match at Frame 1.

Because the original footage has a greenish cast and spills on the rocks in the grass, I needed to adjust the color balance of the sheep layers to take on the same green spill. I applied the Color Balance effect (Effects > Color Correction > Color Balance) to the two sheep layers and set the Shadow Blue Balance to –30. This reduced the amount of blue in the low end of the RGB channels, which caused more yellow to appear—yet the warmer midtones and highlights remained the same. To match the resolution of the original footage, I applied a Gaussian Blur to the two sheep layers at Frame 1. Because these two layers are scaled independently, I needed to apply a slightly different amount of blur to each. The two-sheep layer received a Blurriness of 8.0 pixels, and the one-sheep layer received a 10.0 pixel setting (Figure 14.7). This amount would increase over time as the camera zoomed out and the scale became smaller.

CHAPTER 14: COLOR, LIGHT, AND FOCUS ■

Figure 14.7
Use the Color Balance adjustment to remove blue from the shadow areas of the composited layers and apply a Gaussian Blur to match the resolution of the composite layers to that of the original footage layer.

To match the camera zoom out of the original footage, I set the Stopwatch for both Scale and Position on the Timeline for each composite layer at Frame 1, and then I moved to a point where the camera stopped zooming out (Frame 15;01) and rescaled and repositioned both layers to match (Figure 14.8). Because the original camera zoom had an ease in and out with its movement, I applied the Easy Ease Out Keyframe Assistants for both Position and Scale on both layers at Frame 1 and Easy Ease In at Frame 15;01. I increased the Gaussian Blur on both layers by 2.0 pixels as well.

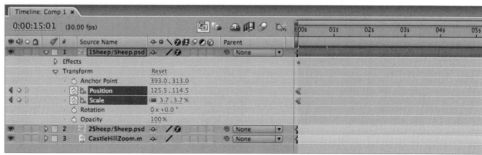

Figure 14.8 Use the Easy Ease In and Out Keyframe Assistants to match the camera zoom motion.

Exposure, Lighting, and Transparency

Some of the most difficult composites to "fake" are objects that need to be backlit by a light source in the background footage. How do you handle the exposure and lighting of the foreground objects that you are compositing in a sunset image or a shot that's looking directly into the light source? Other than merely creating a complete silhouette of the object in front of the light source, you can light it in After Effects so it will show some of the details, edge glows, and transparency or translucency.

To illustrate this problem composite, I used a still image layer of a hot air balloon composited over stock footage of a high altitude shot (above the clouds), looking directly into the sun (Figure 14.9). As you can see from the initial placement, the balloon looks obviously out of place and not lit the same as the stock video footage.

> **Note:** You can view the project file, BalloonColorProject.aep, in the Chapter 14 folder on the DVD. For this project, you will need to install the demo versions of the Shine and Starglow effects plug-ins from the Trapcode folder on the DVD.

Figure 14.09
The hot air balloon looks obviously out of place in this scene.

To give the composite a better feeling of focus and distance, I first applied a 1.0 pixel Gaussian Blur to the balloon layer. I then used Levels to lower the exposure of the hot air balloon. I first brought up the Input Black level to 20.0 and the Gamma to 0.50. I then brought the Output White level down to 70.0 (Figure 14.10). This gave the basic overall exposure of the balloon surface that would correctly match what would be seen in the composite in a semi-silhouette.

Because the original footage is very cool and void of any warm spectral light, the balloon had to be desaturated to match the scene. I used Hue-Saturation (Effects > Color Correction > Hue/Saturation) and set the Saturation down to –50 (Figure 14.11). Notice how the balloon takes on a colder look when the brighter warm colors are removed.

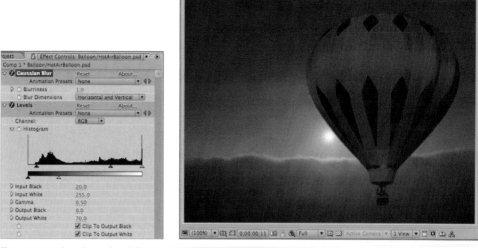

Figure 14.10 Adjust the Levels and Gamma to correct the base exposure.

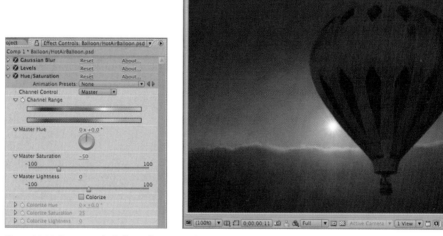

Figure 14.11 Desaturate the balloon of its warm colors to more closely match the background footage.

Next, I wanted to select areas of the balloon that would be affected by passing in front of the sun as the balloon moved across the screen. The balloon's material is somewhat translucent, so it will show some light through it and cause it to slightly glow through the center and show some of its warmer colors. I duplicated the balloon layer and removed the Levels and Hue/Saturation effects from it. I then created a new solid layer that was the full size of the comp and applied an elliptical mask to it (Figure 14.12). I then feathered the mask 50.0 pixels and positioned it in the center of the balloon over the duplicated balloon layer.

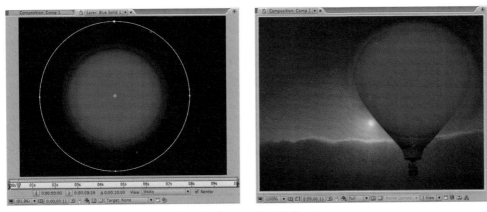

Figure 14.12 Create a feathered mask layer above a duplicate unadjusted balloon layer.

I wanted the balloon to travel from right to left, so I selected the two balloon layers and the mask layer and pressed the P key to make the layer position visible on the Timeline. With the Indicator set at the first frame, I clicked the Stopwatch to set the right-most position for all three layers. I then moved the Indicator to the last frame and dragged the layers in the Comp window to the left where I wanted the balloon to end.

I used the new mask layer to matte the balloon layer (Layer > Track Matte > Alpha Matte), and I set the Blend Mode to Hard Light (Figure 14.13). I also set the Transparency of the balloon layer to 25% at the extreme left and right of the frame and 50% where it was directly in front of the sun.

Figure 14.13 The balloon takes on a somewhat 3-D effect when the slight glow is added.

Creating a Backlit Glow

When the balloon is directly in front of the sun, it will take on a bright, harsh backlight and the edges will glow. I duplicated the second balloon layer and adjusted the Hue/Saturation to a maximum Master Saturation of 100 (Figure 14.14). I then added a

Gaussian Blur of 2.0 to spread the glow layer. I positioned the layer underneath the original balloon layer, and I set the Opacity to 100% when the balloon passes in front of the sun. I set it to 0% when it reaches the far sides of the frame.

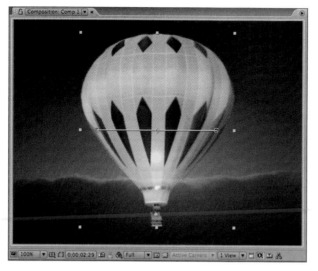

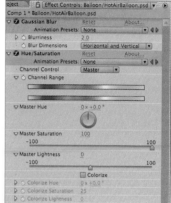

Figure 14.14
Create a glowing backlight layer by oversaturating the duplicate balloon layer.

To create a brighter glow directly in front of the sun as the balloon passes, I duplicated the top balloon layer once again and positioned it above the solid mask layer. I set the Opacity to 100%. I then duplicated the matted solid layer and readjusted the size of the mask to a smaller diameter and positioned it at the top directly in front of the sun, clicking off the Position Stopwatch in the Timeline so it wouldn't move (Figure 14.15). The top balloon layer already had the Track Matte applied, so it will show the glow through the balloon as it passes.

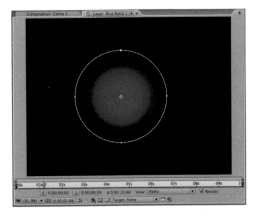

Figure 14.15
Make a direct glow pass with a duplicated balloon layer.

Third-Party Plug-Ins Enhance the Effect

A pinpoint white light was needed to overlap the edges of the balloon as it passes in front of the sun, so I created a new solid layer in white and added an elliptical mask. I adjusted the mask shape to about 200 pixels in diameter and set the Mask Expansion to –60.0 pixels and the Mask Feather to 15.0 pixels. Next, I set the Blend Mode to Screen and the Opacity to 100% at the sides, and then I reduced the Opacity to 65% when the balloon passes over the sun.

For a very realistic effect of the sun's light refraction and streaking as the balloon passes in front of it, I used Trapcode's Shine and Starglow plug-in effects. I rarely use third-party plug-ins in my example projects, but these really punch up the effect. The demo version of these plug-ins is available to you on the DVD.

I first applied the Shine effect to the white solid layer and adjusted the Ray Length to 3.0 (Figure 14.16). I then applied the Starglow effect and set the Streak Length to 25.0 to create a natural flare effect that would occur on film.

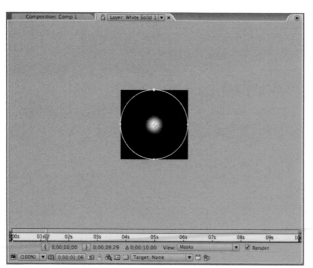
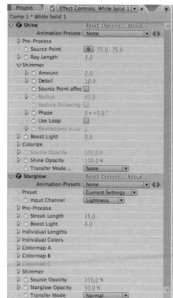

Figure 14.16 Apply the Shine and Starglow effects to give the bright sun a realistic streaking appearance.

Because the Opacity of the white layer lowers to 65%, the effect automatically softens as the balloon passes in front of the sun (Figure 14.17).

Figure 14.17 The realistic streaking and rays of sunlight soften as the Opacity of the layer lowers.

Using a Mask to Create Depth

Because of lighting and focus, some footage may include both foreground and background points of interest, which might make it difficult to concentrate on the foreground objects. In some cases, de-accentuating the background elements with a depth of field blur and diffused lighting or exposure can rectify this.

This example footage is a beautiful shot of San Francisco, with the cable car coming toward the camera in the foreground. Unfortunately, because of the lighting of the scene, the focus is on the bay in the background, where the island of Alcatraz is sharply lit and detracts from the subjects in the foreground (Figure 14.18).

Figure 14.18 The background of this video footage detracts from the moving subjects in the foreground.

In After Effects, I duplicated the footage layer and manually applied a Bezier Mask to the top half with the Pen tool to separate the bay background from the foreground elements (Figure 14.19). I then applied a 50-pixel Feather to the mask and applied a 3.0 pixel Gaussian Blur to the layer to slightly soften the focus.

Figure 14.19 Use a Bezier mask to isolate the brighter background from the underexposed foreground areas.

To give the layer a more diffused appearance and create a little mist in the background, I set the layer's Blend Mode to Screen (Figure 14.20). At this point, it actually looks as if the foreground appears darker—almost a silhouette in front of the brighter, diffused background. However, an adjustment to the foreground will balance it out.

Figure 14.20
Set the Blend Mode of the diffused masked layer to Screen to create the misty bay.

I corrected the foreground color using Curves (Effects > Adjust > Curves), which balanced the lightness and color more closely with the background (Figure 14.21). This gave the cable car and foreground elements more definition against the lighter, diffused background.

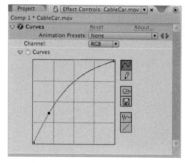

Figure 14.21 By adjusting the original footage layer with Curves, you place the focus on the approaching cable car instead of the background.

Atmosphere, Film, and Noise Effects

Whether you need to match the natural noise and film grain of your original footage with composited images or add smoke or fog to a scene, you can create most of these useful effects with layers created in Photoshop. It's just a matter of using creative masking, layer Blend Modes, and layer motion to provide realistic results.

Chapter Contents

Film and Video Noise

Often, when you composite still images along with video, you will need to add some "noise" to the still image layer so it more readily blends in with the natural noise in the film or video footage over which you're compositing. I've found a couple of methods that work extremely well. One method is to create a noise loop movie that can overlay the still image with variable noise grain size, density, and Blend Modes. Another is to use a third-party plug-in from Digital Film Tools, called 55mm Faux Film, which gives you optimal control over the noise size and color balance.

Creating a Noise Loop Movie

As mentioned previously in this book, I've created a noise loop using only a few Photoshop layers and animating them in ImageReady and QuickTime Pro. You can easily follow along with this simple process.

Note: You need to have QuickTime Pro installed for this technique, not QuickTime Player; otherwise, you will not be able to copy and paste the movie into itself.

1. Start with a new Photoshop file that is full NTSC 720 × 480 and 72 dpi, with the background set to white.

2. Apply the Add Noise filter (Filter > Noise > Add Noise), select Gaussian and Monochromatic, and adjust the amount of noise, or film grain, you want to create (Figure 15.1). You can set the Amount to 3% for a simple yet effective grain pattern, although a higher percentage may be necessary to more closely match your footage.

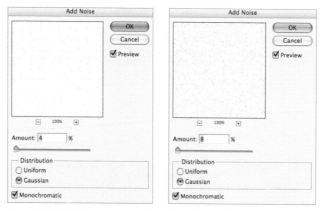

Figure 15.1 Adjust the amount of noise you're applying to closely match how much grain is in your original footage.

3. Duplicate the background layer and fill the duplicate layer with solid white. Apply the Add Noise filter to the duplicate layer by simply keying ⌘/Ctrl+F. Because the application of noise is completely random each time you apply it, the pattern of the noise applied will never look the same way twice. Repeat this step until you have created at least six complete layers (Figure 15.2).

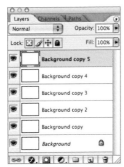

Figure 15.2
Duplicate the layers and apply the Add Noise filter to each layer.

Note: Usually, I'd recommend giving layers more meaningful names than these. But we're talking about only random noise here!

4. Jump to ImageReady, and select Make Frames From Layers from the Animation palette menu. This will create a different frame for each layer in the file (Figure 15.3).

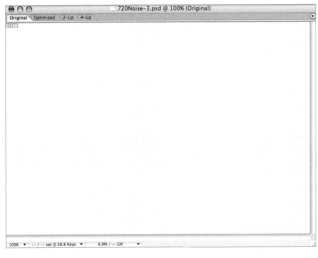

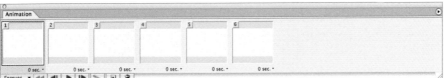

Figure 15.3
Make frames from the layers in the file and export the original as an uncompressed QuickTime movie.

Export the original as an uncompressed QuickTime movie (File > Export > Original Document). Set the options in the Save dialog, and select None as a Compression option.

6. Open your new noise movie in QuickTime Pro and play it. You'll notice that it's barely distinguishable at only six frames, so you'll need to lengthen it. Select All and copy, and then paste back into the movie file (⌘/Ctrl+V). Continue pasting the copied movie repeatedly until you have approximately 10 seconds of the noise loop (Figure 15.4).

Figure 15.4 Copy and paste the movie into itself repeatedly until it is 10 seconds long.

7. Play back the movie and notice how smooth it appears. The loop will not be noticeable because we're looping only random noise.

Applying the Noise Loop in After Effects

As discussed in Chapter 11, "Motion Matte 'Painting' in Photoshop," I used the noise loop movie to add noise to the static image layers in After Effects. I simply imported the movie as footage and placed it in the Timeline just below the blue-screen video footage layer and adjusted the Opacity to 50% (Figure 15.5). To turn the layer into only visible noise, I set the layer Blend Mode to Multiply and made the layers above visible to check for a match in the grain.

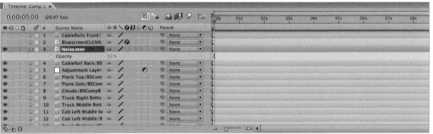

Figure 15.5
Place the noise layer above the static layers in After Effects, and set the Blend Mode to Multiply.

Adding Noise with the 55mm Faux Film Effect

On the After Effects project file labeled BreaMatteProject.aep in Chapter 10, "Static Matte 'Painting' in Photoshop," I used a third-party filter from Digital Film Tools called 55mm Faux Film. This filter offers a lot of controls, such as grain color, size, and brightness.

 Note: A demo version of the 55mm Faux Film plug-in from Digital Film Tools has been provided for you on the accompanying DVD.

In the After Effects project, I selected the static image layer that has both detailed and wide area coverage across the frame and applied the 55mm Faux Film effect (Figure 15.6). It's pictured here isolated from the rest of the composite to show which areas will be affected by the plug-in.

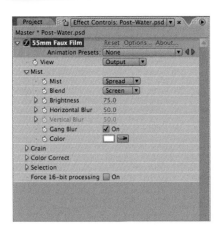
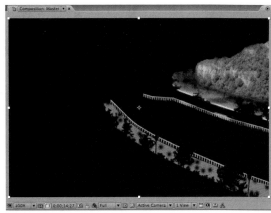
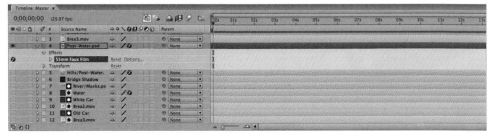

Figure 15.6 The static image layer of this composite has both detailed and wide area coverage.

With the Comp window magnified to 400%, you can see the amount of film grain that is being applied to the layer. The default film Grain size is 0.8, but that was too heavy for this composite, so I adjusted it down to 0.5 in all three RGB color channels (Figure 15.7). I left the rest of the plug-in effect at the default.

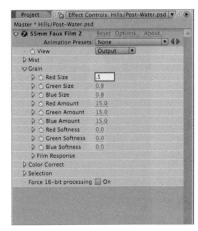

Figure 15.7 Adjust the Grain down to 0.5 in all three RGB color channels.

The final composite is well blended and no static elements appear to stand out (Figure 15.8). You can view the QuickTime movie, Water_Matte.mov, in the Chapter 10 folder on the DVD.

Figure 15.8
Apply the film grain effect to the static layer to make it blend in well with the original footage.

Creating TV Noise

Similar to the noise loop created earlier in this chapter, TV noise is random, only in negative. A blank black-and-white TV screen is black, so the noise, or "snow," created on the picture tube is the *absence* of information in a signal. This is why a strong TV signal is clear and the contrast is sharp, but a weak signal has this noise over the broadcast picture. Of course, the absence of any broadcast signal at all generates just noise.

1.   Open the multilayer noise Photoshop file 720Noise-3.psd, in the Chapter 15 folder on the DVD, in ImageReady. Invert each layer (Image > Adjustments > Invert), so you have white noise on a black background (Figure 15.9). The frames in the Animation palette will automatically update.

2.   Export the inverted original as a QuickTime movie.

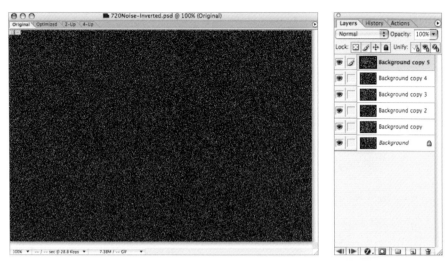

Figure 15.9 Invert the noise layers so the noise is white on a black background.

3. Create a longer loop in QuickTime Pro, as you did earlier in this chapter.

4. Import your loop into a new After Effects project along with the Photoshop composite file, TV.psd, found in the Chapter 15 folder on the DVD.

5. Turn off the screen layer from the Photoshop composite. Place the inverted noise layer on top of the TV background layer, and set the layer Opacity to 75% to see the outline of the TV behind it (Figure 15.10).

 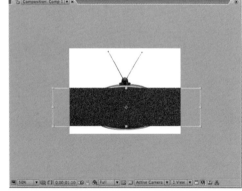

Figure 15.10 Resize the inverted noise movie layer over the TV background layer to fit the screen vertically, and leave the layer width alone.

6. Resize the layer using the Transform handles, and squeeze it vertically so that the noise dots become horizontal dashes.

7. Apply the Track Matte option as Alpha Matte to the inverted movie layer, and the screen layer above will mask it automatically (Figure 15.11).

Note: Layer "transparency" and layer "opacity" are very different. Transparency is the void on a layer surrounding the layer object; opacity is the density of the entire layer. Adobe uses ⌘/Ctrl+T for the Opacity settings though, which can be confusing.

Figure 15.11 Apply an Alpha Matte to the inverted movie layer so that the screen layer above will mask it.

8. Place a scene on the TV screen and duplicate the inverted noise movie layer (for this sample project, I used a still image, Cowboy.jpg, found in the Chapter 15 folder on the DVD). Duplicate the noise and TV screen layers once more and place them on top in the Timeline. To give the appearance that the signal is wavering (Figure 15.12), adjust the opacity of the top noise layer that is applied over time in the Timeline. Leave the first noise layer alone, but vary the duplicated layer's Opacity on the Timeline from 0% to 100%.

Figure 15.12 Duplicate the inverted noise layer positioned over a scene layer on the TV, and vary the Opacity to simulate a weak signal.

Creating Clouds and Fog from Photoshop Layers

Moving or distorting Photoshop layers in After Effects can produce realistic clouds and fog. By using the Clouds filter in Photoshop, you can create random cloud layers that can be used to float over one another to create 3-D effects—or you can Liquify layers to produce swirls in motion. These clouds can be composited into the background of a scene or screened lightly into the foreground to create fog effects.

1. Start with a new Photoshop file, NTSC 720 × 480 with the default white background and black foreground.

Note: The process of making cloud layers is somewhat similar to making the initial noise loop. Because the Clouds plug-in randomizes the pattern every time it is applied, you can reapply the filter over itself on a layer and it will not multiply or "build up" as the Add Noise filter does. As a result, you can keep applying the filter effect until you see a desirable cloud pattern.

2. Apply the Clouds filter (Filter > Render > Clouds) to the background layer; then duplicate the layer and reapply (Figure 15.13). Keep duplicating and reapplying the filter by keying ⌘/Ctrl+V until you are satisfied with the result on each layer.

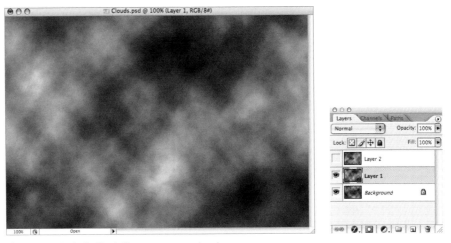

Figure 15.13 Apply the Clouds filter to as many as three layers.

3. Create a new project file in After Effects, NTSC 640 × 480 with a 10-second composition, and import the Photoshop file as a composition to retain the layers.

4. Drag the layers to the Timeline and set the Blend Mode of the top two layers to Screen. Then adjust the Scale of each layer to 160%. This will allow position movement of the layers over time (Figure 15.14).

5. Drag the layers to opposing diagonal corners. Set the Indicator to the first frame on the Timeline, and click the Position Stopwatch for each layer to set the starting position.

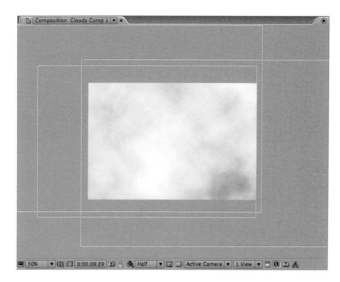

Figure 15.14
Import the cloud layers, increase their scale, and move each layer to prepare for motion.

6. Go to the last frame on the Timeline and move each layer to the opposite side or corner from its starting position (Figure 15.15). This will create the animation of the different layers and give a 3-D appearance to the clouds in motion.

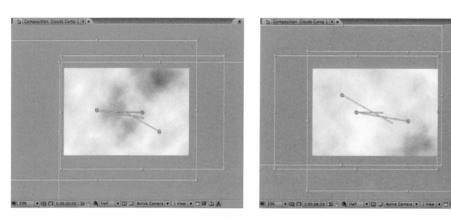

Figure 15.15 Move each layer's position to the opposite side or corner to create the effect of 3-D clouds in motion.

You can adjust the length of time or the distance each layer moves to control the speed of the cloud animation. This cloud animation can now be used as a background or screened over another scene.

Using Liquify to Move Clouds

In addition to moving a layer's position across the frame, you can use the Liquify option to further distort it to create motion and flow. You can also control the amount of distortion over time in the Timeline, which will give you the effect in motion.

Start by duplicating just one layer of the clouds project, and hide the original three layers. Move the Indicator to the first frame on the Timeline, and open the Liquify palette (Effect > Distort > Liquify). Apply only a small amount of one of the Liquify distortion tools to a section of a cloud to set the keyframe. Set the Stopwatch in the Effects option on the Timeline to set the first keyframe. Then move the Indicator to the last frame, and apply various distortions to the clouds in the frame, such as Grow, Shrink, Move, or Twirl (Figure 15.16). You can go back along the Timeline and make other distortions if you like, and it will automatically tween. Play a RAM Preview or render out your animation to see the moving cloud effect that was so easy to make!

Figure 15.16

Use the Liquify tools to distort the clouds over time.

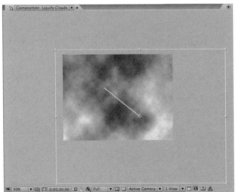
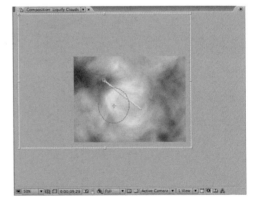

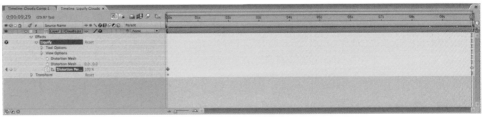

Adding Mist or Fog to Your Footage

The multiple cloud layer method works well for adding a misty marine layer or moving a fog bank into your scene. To make the effect more subtle, you need to lower the layer Opacity and use some of the background footage base colors when making your clouds.

In this example, I used QuickTime Pro to open the footage to which I was going to add the mist and fog. I then created a new Photoshop file and changed the foreground color using the Color Picker to match the green water in the visible Quick-Time movie (Figure 15.17). I then applied the Clouds filter and repeated the process on another layer.

I then imported the original footage and the Photoshop cloud layer files into an After Effects project. I created a mask for each cloud layer, resized the mask, and applied a 150-pixel feather (Figure 15.18). This allowed the bottom edge of the clouds to be soft while the clouds still went past the edges of the frame.

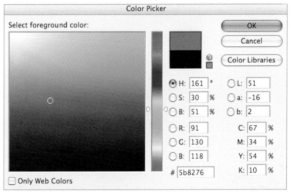

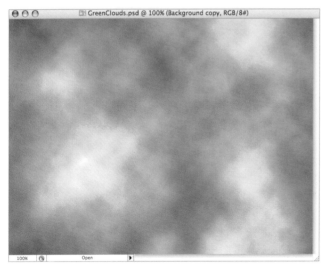

Figure 15.17

Sample the original footage base color to use as the foreground color for your cloud layers.

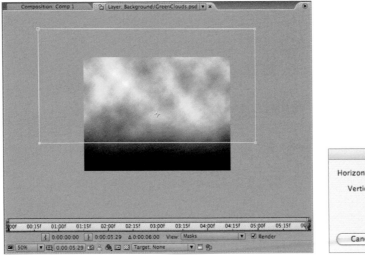

Figure 15.18 Add a feathered oversize mask to the cloud layers to create a soft bottom gradation.

Because my original video footage was 320 × 240 and my cloud layers were 720 × 480, I had to resize them to better fit the scale of the video footage layer. I made them two different sizes so they could move independently and still follow the direction the camera moves in the footage layer (Figure 15.19). I scaled them much shorter vertically and the top layer much longer horizontally to match the movement of the camera. I adjusted both layers in Opacity as well, setting the top layer to 50% because it will be the fog layer that moves along with the camera. I set the lower layer to 35% to create a mist effect.

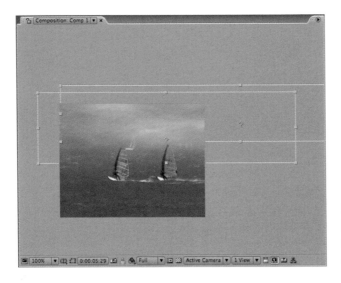

Figure 15.19
By stretching out the cloud layers, you can move them to follow the camera motion in the video clip.

I set the two cloud layers off to the left of the frame in the beginning of the clip and then set the position to the extreme right at the end of the clip (Figure 15.20). Because the lower cloud layer is shorter in horizontal scale, it moves less and makes the effect appear more 3-D.

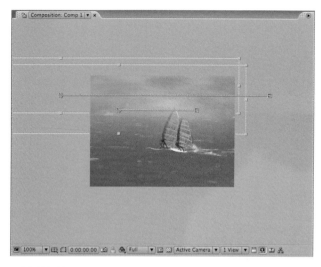

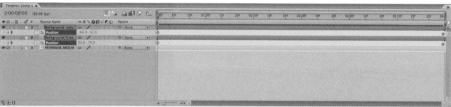

Figure 15.20
Move the cloud layers' position to the opposite side of the frame to create the motion.

Making Smoke: A Real Barnburner

By combining several techniques in this chapter with video alpha channels, you can add realistic smoke effects to stock footage. This effect uses only one Photoshop cloud layer and two stock video clips of fire with a mask copy. You can follow along with these steps or simply open the After Effects file, BarnBurnerProject.aep, to use for reference.

Create a new After Effects project with a composition, NTSC 640 × 480, and import the QuickTime video files RedBarn-Corn-ShortClip.mov (the background footage), RF108.mov (the fire clip), and RF108M.mov (the fire mask clip). Position all three files on the Timeline. Then select both the fire and fire mask clips, scale them down to 19.4%, and move them onto the right corner of the barn (Figure 15.21). Make sure that you keep both layers selected as you scale and reposition them.

Figure 15.21 Scale and reposition the two fire clips exactly the same over the corner of the barn.

Hide the fire mask layer and select the fire layer. Then apply a Track Matte (Layer > Track Matte > Luma Matte) to reveal just the fire without the black background around it (Figure 15.22). Run a RAM Preview to verify that the two layers match exactly.

Figure 15.22

Apply a Track Matte, Luma Matte to the fire layer to reveal only the fire.

The two layers seem a bit too sharp and crisp for the background footage of the barn, so you'll need to apply a 5.0-pixel Gaussian Blur on the fire layer and a 20.0-pixel Gaussian Blur on the fire mask layer. Then apply Brightness & Contrast with the Brightness adjusted to −50 to soften the edges of the flames (Figure 15.23).

Figure 15.23 Apply a Gaussian Blur and adjust the Brightness of the fire mask layer to soften the flames' edges and match the resolution of the barn footage.

Duplicate the fire mask layer and move it below the fire layer. Change the layer Blend Mode to Silhouette Luma. This is going to become the first smoke layer, and it needs to move slower than the flames, so stretch the movie length out 300% (Layer > Time > Time Stretch). Use Transform to stretch the layer vertically to 43.3%, leaving the horizontal dimension the same. Move it off to the left in the Timeline to take it out of sync with the flame layer, so it doesn't appear to be a duplicate (Figure 15.24). Increase the Gaussian Blur to 50.0 pixels and remove the Brightness & Contrast effect from this layer. Adjust the Opacity to 20% and play back the RAM Preview to see the effect.

Figure 15.24 Create a moving dark smoke layer from the original fire mask clip.

> **Note:** Move the new smoke layer on the Timeline to put it slightly out of sync with the beginning of the fire layer to make it appear more random.

Import the file Smoke.tif into the project file. This is a single-layer Photoshop cloud file that has been blurred slightly. Apply a feathered mask to the layer, and adjust the Bezier handles to create a tall, narrow shape around the brighter section of the image (Figure 15.25). Set the layer Blend Mode to Lighten and the layer Opacity to 20%.

To make the smoke cloud gently rise, click the layer Position Stopwatch at Frame 1 on the Timeline; then go to the last frame and drag the layer up slightly to set the keyframe. Now, to animate the smoke, return to the first frame and apply Liquify with a small amount of the Twirl tool. Go to the last frame again and use larger Twirl and Shift Pixels tool brushes to create upward swirls of the smoke (Figure 15.26). Run a RAM Preview to test the animation of the smoke cloud and adjust the Liquify effects as necessary.

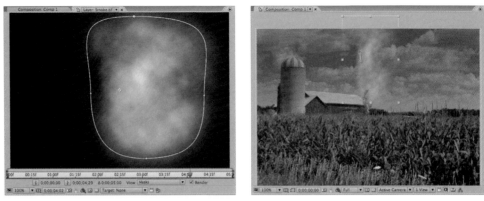

Figure 15.25 Position the smoke cloud behind the first smoke layer and move it subtly against the background.

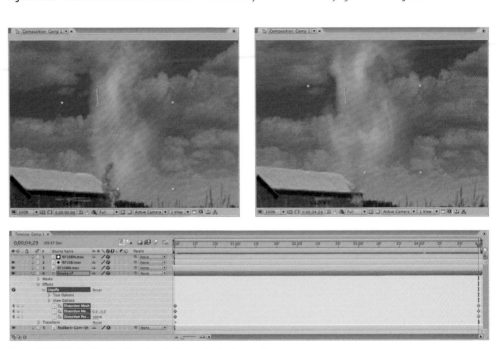

Figure 15.26 Use the Liquify effects to swirl the smoke cloud upward.

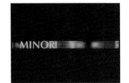

Motion Titling Effects

Titling is probably the most overlooked aspect in video production. Frequently, producers just add some text to the screen and add dissolves or scrolling as an afterthought. Recently, motion picture studios have been producing visually appealing and creative opening titles and credits to entertain, open up the story of the picture, or just provide eye candy. A whole book could be devoted to the subject of titling. In this limited chapter, I hope to provide you with a few ideas to get your creative juices flowing and make you think about how your next motion-titling project can be enhanced with simple techniques.

16

Chapter Contents
Titles from Photoshop Layers
Using 3-D Layers to Simulate 2-D Titling
Animating Text Layers in After Effects
Creating Dynamic Lower Thirds

Titles from Photoshop Layers

I've seen a lot of opening movie titles that obviously required thousands of man-hours to create with sophisticated motion-tracking hardware and 3-D software. You can create a very believable 3-D rendered title that can rival those of the big studios. In many cases, you can create simple text layers with layer style effects in Photoshop and composite them into your After Effects project. In this first project, I wanted to combine the classic feel of the kind of titling used in old western movies from the 1950s with a modern 3-D composite effect. The text is a simple Photoshop layer with layer style effects applied, but it is then transformed to match the angle of the scene in the background to give it a more integrated look. You can follow along with this project by using a different font if you prefer, or you can download the same Freeware font I used, called *Pointedly Mad 2.0*, from http://www.1001fonts.com.

Open the QuickTime movie file Desert Vista Time Lapse.mov in the Chapter 16 folder on the DVD. Copy and paste the first frame of the movie to the clipboard. You'll use this frame as a template for designing the 3-D title. Create a new file in Photoshop from the clipboard and add a large font title text layer. I used the font named Capitals for this example.

Apply a Drop Shadow layer style, with the Global Angle set to 135°, the Distance to 25 pixels, and the Size to 5 pixels. For this example, I added a Color Overlay of orange (Figure 16.1). Apply Bevel and Emboss with the default settings and set the Size to 1 pixel.

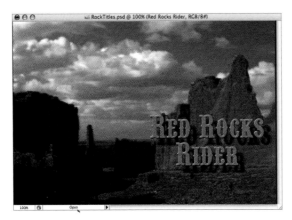

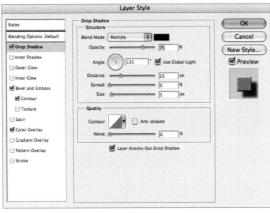

Figure 16.1

Apply drop shadows and bevels to the text layer.

Duplicate the text layer and rasterize it in the Layers palette so it can be transformed in any direction or shape. Disable the Layer Style so you see only the plain text (Figure 16.2) and then Select All and Cut the layer contents to the clipboard.

Figure 16.2
Rasterize the text layer and cut the layer contents to the clipboard.

Open Vanishing Point and create a grid in front of the red rocks on the right. Once you've configured your grid, paste the clipboard into the window and drag the text over the grid so it automatically snaps into perspective (Figure 16.3). You will need to further flatten the text layer prior to importing it into After Effects. If you don't, the layer style effects will not remain with the layer. Do this by creating a new layer, linking it with the text layer, and then choosing Link Merged from the Layers palette menu.

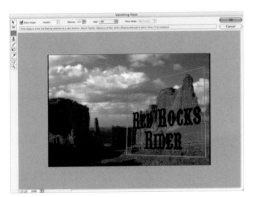
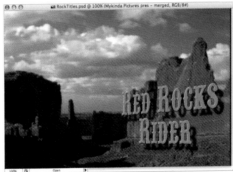

Figure 16.3 Use Vanishing Point to set the correct perspective on the rasterized text layer and reapply the Layer Style.

Repeat this text layer process for subsequent titling, such as for actors, subtitle descriptions, and production companies. When you are finished, you can save the Photoshop file as it is for additional editing or save it as a copy and delete all of the non-merged text layers (Figure 16.4). This will give you a simple layered Photoshop file that will be easy to import into After Effects.

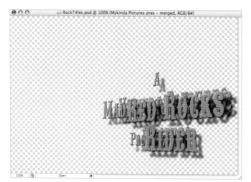

Figure 16.4 Remove the unwanted layers, and save the Photoshop file for easier layer import into After Effects.

Create a new project file in After Effects, NTSC 640 × 480, and import the QuickTime movie footage file and the Photoshop text layer file as a composition to retain the individual layers. Stack the text layers in the order in which you want them to appear on the screen in the Timeline, and adjust the Opacity of each layer to create fade-ins and fade-outs (Figure 16.5). The text layers already have shadow transparency, so you can leave the Blend Mode in Normal mode.

Figure 16.5 Adjust the Opacity of the text layers in the Timeline to create fade-in and fade-out key frames.

You'll notice that as the clouds pass by the rocks, they get darker and the text stands out more. When the clouds clear, the shadows are more predominant and the 3-D effect appears more integrated into the footage (Figure 16.6). You can review the rendered QuickTime movie of this titling composite in the Chapter 16 folder on the DVD.

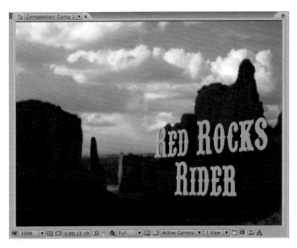

Figure 16.6
The 3-D effect is enhanced by the
lighting and shadows on the rocks
in the background.

Using 3-D Layers to Simulate 2-D Titling

Sometimes you have to animate text running at an angle or hugging the face of a building
or wall. By making comps with animated text that gets integrated into the master composition, you can apply the 3-D layer option and rotate the text to match the footage below.
This allows you to match perspectives without affecting the quality of the animated text
layer, but it does not provide a 3-D effect because no lights, shadows, or layer movement
is involved.

In this example, I wanted to create a Wall Street–style running ticker board sign
that wraps around the building in the QuickTime movie footage. Because the footage
was shot in a locked-off position and time-lapsed, the process was a simple matter of
matching the text layer comps to the lines of the building.

I started by creating a narrow Photoshop file with a black background and
applied a line of text with a dot-matrix style font in bright green (Figure 16.7). I then
flattened the file and saved it as a single-layer JPEG.

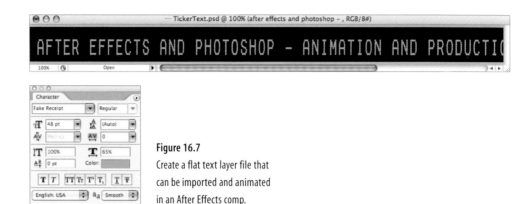

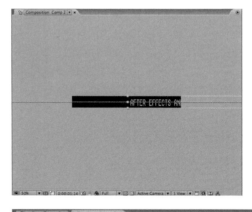

Figure 16.7

Create a flat text layer file that can be imported and animated in an After Effects comp.

After I created a project file in After Effects and imported the original footage file, CloudsInBuilding.mov in the Chapter 16 folder on the DVD, I placed it into Comp 1. I then created a new comp in which to animate the running ticker text, 640 pixels wide, 64 pixels high, and 20 seconds in duration. I added a new solid black layer for the background so it wouldn't appear transparent in the final composite. I then placed the text layer in the comp, positioned it off the right side at Frame 1, and clicked the Position Stopwatch in the Timeline. This animation was 10 seconds long, so I moved the Indicator to the 10-second mark and moved the text layer off the left side of the frame (Figure 16.8). This left 10 seconds of pure black at the end that I'd need for the final composite.

Figure 16.8

Before compositing with the main comp, create a separate comp in which to animate the text layer.

I returned to Comp 1 and created a new camera (Layer > New > Camera) and used the default setting with a 50mm lens preset to prevent a wide-angle distortion or excessive flattening (Figure 16.9). I then selected the Camera 1 view at the bottom of the Comp window.

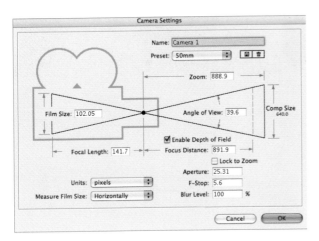

Figure 16.9
Create a new camera layer and use
the default lens length of 50mm.

With the Comp 2 layer selected, I clicked the 3-D box in the Timeline to convert
the layer to three-dimensional space so it could be rotated and moved along the X-, Y-,
and Z-axes. I then rotated and moved the layer in all axis directions until the layer fit precisely onto the right side of the building in the original footage layer below (Figure 16.10).
I used the sliders in the axis adjustments on the Timeline to fine-tune the positioning.

Figure 16.10
Convert the animated text comp to a 3-D
layer and rotate and move it along the X-,
Y-, and Z-axes to the desired angle.

I duplicated the Comp 2 layer and repositioned it for the left side of the building, making sure that the edges of the text comp layers just touched and did not overlap. I also had to resize the layer slightly to match the depth of the building.

By moving the Indicator down the Timeline a few seconds, I could see that the
ticker board was starting at the same time on both sides of the building instead of
wrapping around it in a continuous stream. To rectify this, I duplicated the Comp 2
layer and moved it along the Timeline to the left, just until the text animation was finished, leaving only the 10 seconds of black (Figure 16.11). I then moved the top Comp 2
layer to the right on the Timeline until the timing properly matched for the text to
wrap around.

Figure 16.11
To correct the mismatched timing of the ticker board wrapping around the building, duplicate the text layer and adjust the start and end points on the Timeline.

For the finishing touch, I wanted the black areas to take on some of the shininess and reflectivity of the glass on the building so they would blend in better. I duplicated the original footage layer and moved it to the top layer in the Timeline. I set the Blend Mode to Lighten and the layer Opacity to 25% (Figure 16.12). The end result was a slight reflection over the ticker board areas, and that completed the composite.

Figure 16.12
Create a slight reflection on the sign by duplicating the original footage, overlaying the text layers, and adjusting the Opacity and Blend Mode to Lighten.

Animating Text Layers in After Effects

After Effects has some powerful text animation capabilities that don't require any external resources or graphics in order to create eye-catching title animations. Using text layer animation tools, you can divide words into individual letters that can zoom, pan, wiggle, and fly around as if they were individually programmed in a 3-D application. The big difference is that the After Effects text animators are so simple and easy to use.

The examples I've chosen for this part of the chapter barely scratch the surface of the endless possibilities of the After Effects Wiggly and Range text animators. All of these example projects are easy to follow and reproduce, and none of them uses third-party plug-in effects or imported files. I wanted to demonstrate some production titling effects that may appear somewhat familiar to you but aren't the actual animations for the names or titles I've chosen. I hope they can spur you on to experiment with your own projects. You'll discover that making fine adjustments to the animation settings can produce very different results.

Fly-In Zoom Titling

This effect is a simple yet effective motion-titling animation that works great with short titles or names, and it looks much more difficult to produce than it really is. With only a couple of settings of the text animator, it will break a word into separate letters and have them fly in from the camera's perspective and zoom down to form the word on screen:

1. Start with a new After Effects project file and create a new composition, NTSC 640 × 480.

2. Use the Text tool to create a text layer by clicking in the middle of your Comp 1 window. Using a large sans serif font, such as Arial, type a name or short title that fits well inside the width of the frame (Figure 16.13).

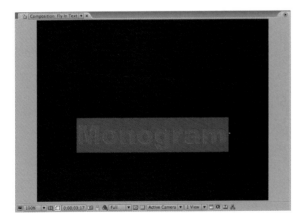

Figure 16.13
Type a short name or title using a large sans serif font.

Note: If you want simply to review the following completed After Effects titling examples, you'll find them all inside one project file, Wiggly-Range.aep, located in the Chapter 16 folder on the DVD. You can also find most of the fonts used in this chapter's examples for free at http://www.1001fonts.com.

3. To set up the animation of the text, apply the Range text animator (Animation > Add Text Selector > Range). Spin down the text layer arrow on the Timeline and then spin down the Range Selector arrow. Click the Add selector, choose the Scale property (Figure 16.14), and then choose the Opacity property. These are the two parameters that will cause the text to zoom in.

Figure 16.14 Apply the Range Text Selector, and select the Scale and Opacity properties from the text layer in the Timeline.

4. Set the layer Opacity to 0% and the Scale to 1000%. This will be the largest state of the letters prior to zoom in, because they will also fade in from 0% to 100%.

5. Next, spin down the Advanced arrow and adjust the Ease High setting to 0%. This gives the animation its amount of motion (Figure 16.15).

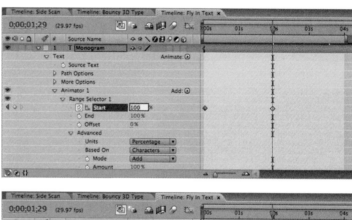

Figure 16.15 Set the parameters for the Range Selector to create this simple title animation.

6. Click the Range Selector Start percentage Stopwatch and set the amount to 0%. Move the Indicator down to the 2-second mark and set the Start amount to 100%.

7. Render a RAM Preview to see the animation. To make speed adjustments, simply move the Start percentage key frame back or ahead on the Timeline. Notice how the letters scale down and fade in to create the zooming effect (Figure 16.16).

Figure 16.16 Adjust the Start percentage key frame to speed up or slow down the animation rate.

8. To finish off the title animation, make it fade out at the end by adding key frames to the layer Opacity and setting them to fade from 100% to 0% (Figure 16.17).

Figure 16.17
Create an Opacity fade-out at the end of the titling animation to finish it.

Bouncy 3-D Titles

This is a fun titling effect that really shows off the 3-D effect because of the constant bouncing motion. By applying the Wiggly animator to the text, you can make it bounce and wiggle slightly while the 3-D layer projects shadows on the wall behind it. This playful title animation can be used for comedic effect or just as an eye-catcher:

1. In a new composition, create a text layer with the Text tool in the Comp window. Select a large fun-styled font (I used a TrueType font called Pokemon for this example), and enter a title or name that fits within the width of the frame (Figure 16.18).

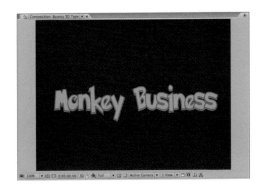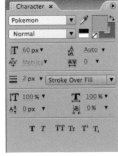

Figure 16.18
Create a colorful text layer with a fun font.

2. Apply a bright orange color for the text fill and a 2-pixel red outline to give the text definition from the background.

3. Create a new solid layer with a light-green background to contrast with the orange and red text, and place it below the text layer. Set both layers to 3-D in the Timeline window.

4. Apply the Wiggly text animator (Animation > Add Text Selector > Wiggly), and spin down the text layer arrow on the Timeline to make adjustments for the animation.

5. Click the Add selector and choose the Position and Rotation properties. Set the Rotation for 0 × +20.0°, the maximum amount of rotation the letters will get, and set the Position to 5.0, 10.0 for X- and Y-axis movement (Figure 16.19). Set the Wiggles/Second to 6.0 for a gentle motion. Increase or decrease the amount, and then use a RAM Preview to see how the various amounts affect the type.

6. Change the Comp view to Left view and position the two layers apart from each other. Check the positioning in the Active Camera view—if you move the green solid layer back too far, simply increase its scale in the Timeline or in the Comp window.

7. Create a new Light layer, a Spot light with a 90% Intensity, the Cone Angle set to 130°, and a 50% Cone Feather. Set the Shadow Darkness level to 65%, and be sure that the Casts Shadows check box is selected (Figure 16.20).

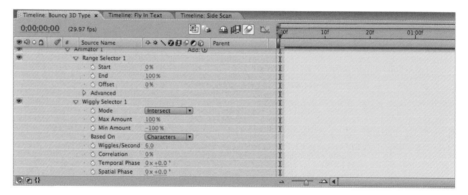

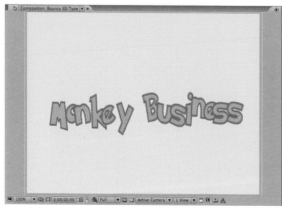

Figure 16.19
Apply a Wiggly text animator
and set the parameters to
create the animation.

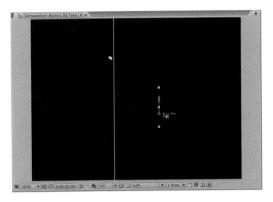

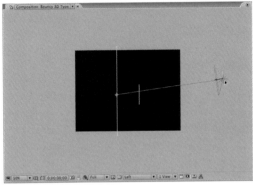

Figure 16.20
Move the 3-D layers apart to create depth and create a new Spot light to cast shadows.

8. Return to the Left view on the comp and reduce the view scale to 50% so you can move the light back away from the text and background. Be sure that you do not move the light's Point of Interest when positioning the light. If you do, make sure you reposition it in its original location.

Render a RAM Preview to see the animation in motion. Select the Motion Blur check box in the Timeline and see the effect it has on the rapidly moving letters—it helps give the animation a softer and gentler motion (Figure 16.21).

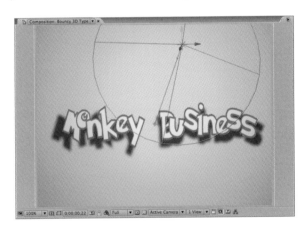

Figure 16.21
Apply Motion Blur to the text animation to give it a more realistic 3-D effect.

Horizontal Scanning Title

This is a popular effect for movie promos and titling, and it can be done without using any third-party plug-in effects. The individual letters of the title do a random scanning along a horizontal line and slowly build up the title. Adding additional blurred layers gives the effect some smoothness and depth, while adding a light burst in motion finishes off the animation:

1. Create a new comp and add a line of text for the title.

2. Apply the Wiggly text animator and spin down the text layer arrows in the Timeline to make adjustments to the Wiggly animator settings. Click the Add selector and choose the Position parameter. To make the animation maintain its horizontal-only motion, set the Position X-axis to 300.0 and leave the Y-axis at 0.0 (Figure 16.22). Set the Wiggles/Second to 25.0 and the Correlation to 50% to keep the letters from moving around too wildly.

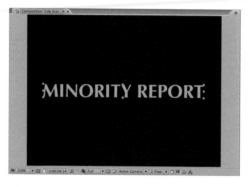

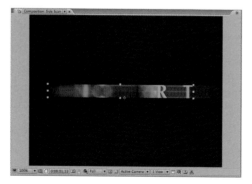

Figure 16.22

Create a text layer and apply the Wiggly text animator to it.

3. Add a Range Selector animator and move the Indicator on the Timeline to the 2-second mark. Click the Start Stopwatch and set the parameter to 0%. Move the Indicator down toward the 4-second mark and set the Start parameter to 100%

(Figure 16.23). This will allow the animation to continue scanning back and forth for 2 seconds and then start to build in the title letter by letter.

Figure 16.23 Set the Range Selector to animate past 2 seconds and slowly build in the title.

4. Duplicate the text layer and move it below the original.

5. Remove the Range Selector key frames so the animation continues.

6. Apply a 16.0-pixel Gaussian Blur to the duplicate layer to add a soft glow to the letters in motion (Figure 16.24). This gives the animation another level of depth and light.

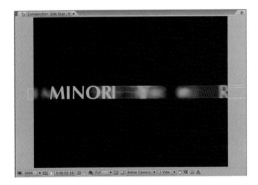

Figure 16.24 Duplicate the text layer, blur it, and position it below the original.

7. Create a new solid layer in white. Add an elliptical mask to the layer and set the Mask Feather to 100.0 pixels and the Mask Expansion to −80.0 pixels.

8. Duplicate the original text layer and position it above the masked solid layer.

9. Apply a Track Matte, Alpha Matte to the solid layer to constrain the glow to inside the title lettering (Figure 16.25).

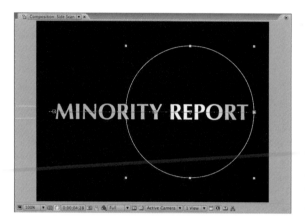

Figure 16.25
Add an internal glow to the text by masking a solid layer on top of the original text.

10. Duplicate the solid layer, position the duplicate at the top level, and rescale it down to 50% (Figure 16.26). Move the Indicator to Frame 04;23 and click the layer Scale Stopwatch to set the key frame. Move the Indicator one frame to the left and set the Scale to 15%; repeat this one frame to the right.

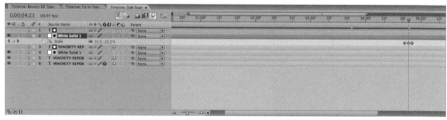

Figure 16.26 Create a light burst by duplicating the solid layer and positioning it on top.

To give the effect another layer of motion and interest, let's animate the solid burst layer to move along the length of the text layer and change the Opacity to create a single-frame "flash." The solid layer starts centered in the letter Y and remains there until Frame 04;02; then it moves to the left of the first letter and changes Opacity along the path (Figure 16.27). Apply the Position and Opacity settings from Table 16.1 to see how the patterns line up with the Scale of the layer.

▷ **Table 16.1** Final Solid Layer Position, Opacity, and Scale

Transform	03;00	03;13	04;00	04;06	04;11	04;12	04;21	04;23	04;25	05;02
Position X,Y			327.0, 241.0		50.0, 241.0					600.0, 241.0
Scale %							15.0	50.0	15.0	
Opacity %	0	100	0		0	100			100	0

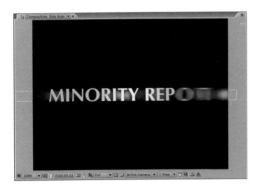

Figure 16.27
Animate the burst's movement along the length of the line of text, and adjust the Scale of the solid layer to correspond with the set Opacity.

What's the Buzz?

When you experiment with the Wiggly and Range text animators, you'll discover some really great effects that will spark your imagination. I stumbled across this next animation by accident and thought it would be great to create a title from an older classic movie opener. The pattern reminded me of a swarm of bees, so I thought the movie title *The Swarm* would be a great example. The buzzing, flying letters came to rest one at a time, but then I took one letter out of a name or the title to buzz back out quickly and return. I created the lead character actors' names in sequence before the actual title in this project. Follow along with the After Effects project file TheSwarm-Title.aep, and check out the final rendered QuickTime movie in the Chapter 16 folder on the DVD.

I started with a new After Effects comp and placed a line of large text in the Comp window. For this title project, I chose a creative font called Embossing Tape 1 and gave it a yellow fill color (Figure 16.28). The text in this figure appears blue because it is selected and shows only the complementary color of the applied color.

Figure 16.28
Create a new comp and place a line of bright text in a large font in the center.

I applied the Wiggly text selector to animate the text layer, and then I added a Position parameter of 400.0 horizontal and 300.0 vertical for movement that stays inside the Comp window frame (Figure 16.29).

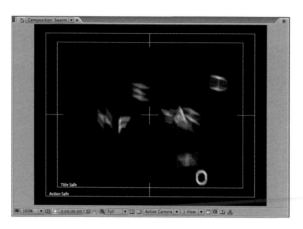

Figure 16.29
Add a Wiggly text selector to animate the letters.

I then adjusted the Start range to 0% for the first couple of seconds and set key frames for the letters to end at 100%, for about 15 frames (Figure 16.30). I wanted the last letter to quickly fly up and buzz around for a few frames and then get back in line again, so I added some key frames and set the next key frame to 90% and then switched back to 100% a few frames later. I also added an Opacity fade-out to the end of each name in the sequence.

Figure 16.30 Set the Start range key frames to control the amount of "flight" the letters take.

To keep from repeating the same animation pattern on every actor's name in the title sequence, I varied the Offset rate by sliding the amount on the Timeline until only one letter at a time moved (Figure 16.31). I then changed this amount for each of the names and the main title.

Figure 16.31
For variation in the title sequence, adjust the Offset rate to select different letters to animate.

Creating Dynamic Lower Thirds

In video and television, the term "lower thirds" refers to the lower portion of the frame that contains graphical information such as names, titles, logos, station IDs, etc.

In a talking-head shot, the lower-third graphics sit somewhere below the subject's shoulders, but still within the Title-Safe region. They don't really take up a complete third of the frame.

If you plan to display only a name or short title in the lower third, you don't need as much space and you have more room for creativity and possible animations. In recent years, some cable companies and corporate videos have been positioning a translucent "bug," or station/corporate identifier logo, in the bottom-right corner throughout the duration of the program or video. In this section, we'll discuss topics such as static lower-thirds graphics, static lower thirds with an animated layer, static graphics with an animated displacement map, and lower-thirds multiple layers in motion.

Static Lower-Thirds Graphics

The most common lower-thirds element in broadcast production is a static graphic that allows text to be placed over for titling. This kind of graphic can be saved into a library database and called up in a production control room prior to the broadcast. Many TV newsrooms will use these graphics repeatedly when a similar topical graphic is required for a breaking story or sports feature.

For this project, I started with a new Photoshop file. I selected a preset for NTSC DV 720 × 480 (with guides) and the pixel aspect ratio correction preset for D1/DV NTSC (0.9) (Figure 16.32). As you create your designs, the guides created in this file will show you where the Title-Safe and Action-Safe areas are. I also created a static bar design across the bottom, just inside the Action-Safe line on its own layer above the background.

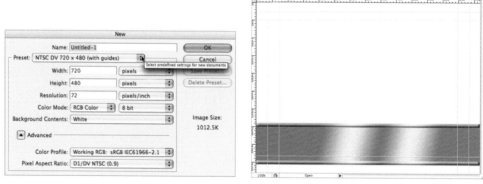

Figure 16.32 Create a new Photoshop file with the presets for NTSC DV and Pixel Aspect Ratio Correction.

Note: You can follow along with all of the lower-thirds projects in this chapter section by opening the LowerThirds.aep file in the Chapter 16 folder on the DVD. I've provided all of the Photoshop production files and rendered movies for you as well.

Next, I imported a single-layer graphic of a baseball to position in the lower-left corner, just inside the Action-Safe zone (Figure 16.33). This layer can be merged with the bar layer and used as part of the static graphic element or left on its own layer that can be animated in After Effects.

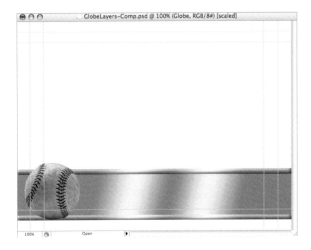

Figure 16.33
Position a graphic element on a
layer above the bar graphic.

Because we have created a file with Pixel Aspect Ratio Correction enabled, the
ball appears to be round on the screen. However, if we turn off the correction (View >
Pixel Aspect Ratio Correction), the ball appears to be elongated horizontally because
we are viewing the file in the original 720 × 480 NTSC (Figure 16.34).

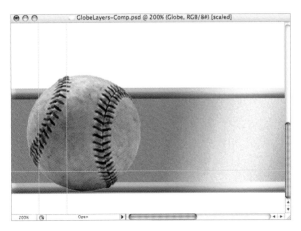

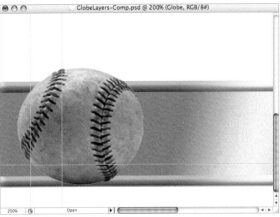

Figure 16.34
Turning on and turning off the
Pixel Aspect Ratio Correction will
affect symmetrical images, especially spherical or round objects.

To give the ball graphic more depth and a three-dimensional look as if it's floating above the bar, I applied a Drop Shadow and Bevel and Emboss layer style (Figure 16.35). The ball already had some highlights and shading on the image, so I applied only a subtle amount of lighting.

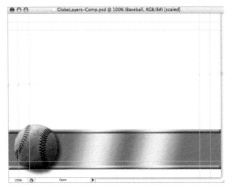
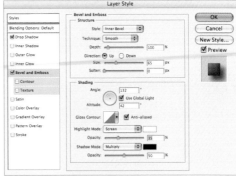

Figure 16.35 Applying a layer style to the ball will create depth and 3-D realism over the background.

To start building a library of elements for use with this graphic, I added a few more elements on their own layers and applied the layer style to them (Figure 16.36). These elements can be left as individual layers in your master Photoshop file, or they can each be merged with a copy of the bar graphic layer as static graphics.

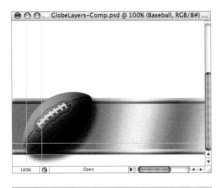
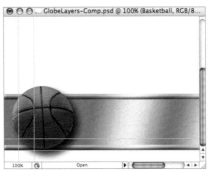

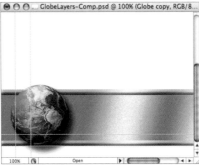

Figure 16.36
You can layer several different elements in the master Photoshop file to create a library that you can animate in After Effects.

I duplicated the bar graphic and globe layers and merged them into one layer (Figure 16.37). I renamed the layer so it would be easily identified when I import it into After Effects.

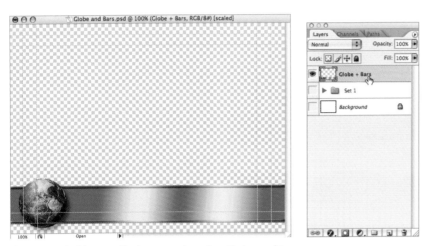

Figure 16.37 Position a graphic element on a layer above the bar graphic.

The static graphic can be alpha-keyed and used in broadcast, or it can be imported into After Effects and the titling and video footage can be composited in post production (Figure 16.38).

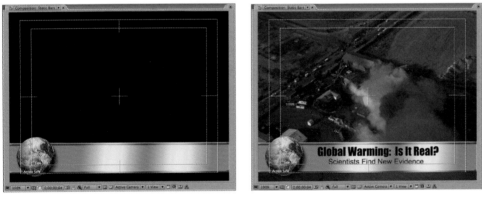

Figure 16.38 The static graphic bar can be composited over video footage in After Effects with text animated or simply displayed over it.

Static Lower Thirds with Animated Layer

Using the same Photoshop file that was used with the previous project, we can animate the globe onto the static bar graphic in After Effects. However, as I mentioned in Chapter 2, "Photoshop Layers and After Effects," Photoshop's layer styles won't import into After Effects properly, so we need to merge a copy of the globe layer to a new blank layer to contain the Drop Shadow and Bevel and Emboss layer style information.

Import both the bars layer and the globe merged layers from the master Photoshop file and position them similarly to the previous project (Figure 16.39).

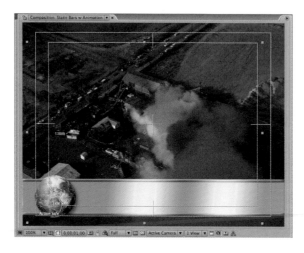

Figure 16.39
Position the globe above the bar graphic layer in After Effects.

On the globe layer in the Timeline, move the Indicator down to the 1-second mark and click the Position Stopwatch. This will add a key frame for the resting position of the globe layer. Hold down the Shift key to keep it horizontally locked in position (Figure 16.40), move the Indicator back to Frame 1, and click-drag the globe layer off the right side of the screen. Apply the Easy-Ease-In Keyframe Assistant to the 1-second key frame, and select the Motion Blur option on the Timeline.

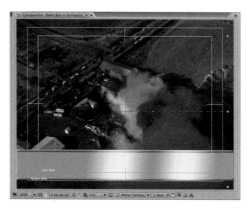
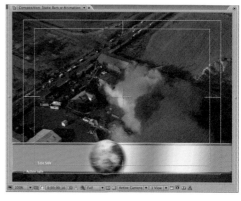

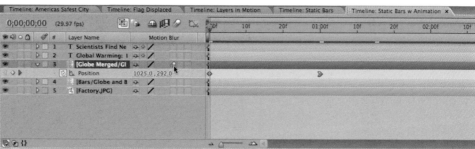

Figure 16.40 Position the globe layer to fly in from the right side of the window and apply Motion Blur.

To make the title fade in after the globe flies into frame, move the Indicator down to the 1:15 mark and click the Opacity Stopwatch for both title layers on the Timeline to set the 100% key frame. Move the Indicator back 15 frames, and set the opacity to 0% (Figure 16.41). This will produce a smooth fade-in of the title and complete the simple animation for a more compelling titling effect.

Figure 16.41

Adjust the opacity of the title layers to fade in after the globe flies into frame.

Static Graphics with Animated Displacement Map

Another effective lower-thirds animation involves static graphic elements using the moving displacement map technique, as described in Chapter 2, "Photoshop Layers and After Effects." The moving displacement map technique will create the illusion of motion without actually using stock video footage or rendered animations.

Using a tiled wavy texture file I imported into After Effects, I duplicated the layer several times and set the layers into motion from right to left in its own composition (Figure 16.42).

In a new comp, I imported the animated wave comp and the flag image. I scaled down and masked it with a feathered edge into the lower-third region of the frame (Figure 16.43). I also scaled down the animated wave layer to closely match the proportions of the flag layer.

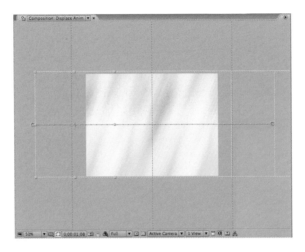

Figure 16.42
I duplicated a tiled wavy pattern layer and put it into motion from right to left in its own composition.

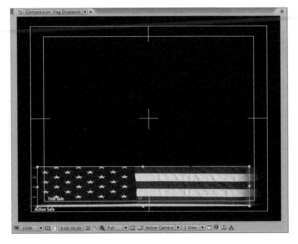

Figure 16.43
Create a feathered mask around the flag layer so it softly blends into the background.

With the animated wave comp layer hidden, apply the Displacement Map effect to the flag layer and choose the animated wave comp as the source (Figure 16.44). I set the horizontal and vertical displacement both to 25 pixels for this effect.

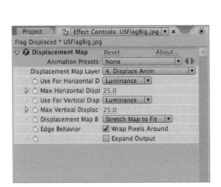

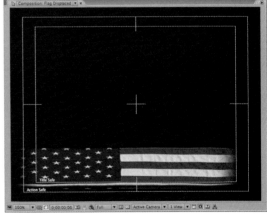

Figure 16.44 Apply the Displacement Map effect to the flag layer.

To add more realism to the waving flag, I made the wave animation comp layer visible and set the Blending Mode to Multiply. This allows the shadows to show up on the flag surface in sync with the displacement animation (Figure 16.45). Instead of creating another mask for this layer to match the flag layer, I duplicated the flag layer (with its mask intact), positioned it above the wave animation comp layer, and made it invisible. I selected the wave animation comp and applied a Track Matte Alpha, which allows only the inside of the feathered flag layer matte to show up.

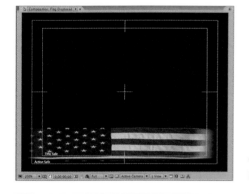

Figure 16.45
I used the animated wave layer as an overlay, creating more depth and realism to the flag animation.

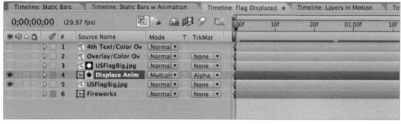

Finally, I added a fading solid color to the right side of the flag as an underlay to the text layer so that the text would be clearer and more legible (Figure 16.46).

Figure 16.46
Add a fading solid color over the animation to give a place for the text to remain visible.

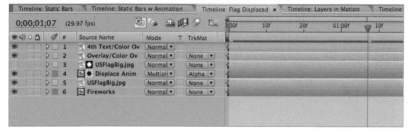

Note: Don't put too much animation underneath or too close to any text because it will be distracting and make the text hard to read.

Lower-Thirds Multiple Layers in Motion

A common lower-thirds technique used today involves putting several layers in motion as the background and then floating text and other objects above the animation. This technique creates subtle motion and a sense of depth, which really makes the foreground objects stand out.

In this project, I create a multilayered Photoshop file with simple shapes that are modified on each layer and then rotated in a separate comp in After Effects. The results served as my animated background layer.

I started with a solid blue background and added a layer with dots painted in a vertical row down the center (Figure 16.47). I duplicated the layer several times and applied increasingly more intense Radial Blur filters to layers.

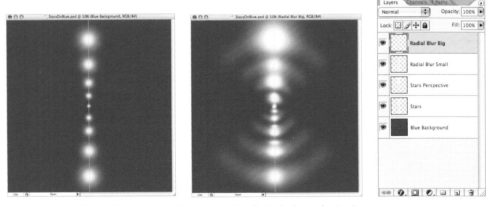

Figure 16.47 A multilayered Photoshop file will serve as the basis for the background animation.

Once I imported the multilayered Photoshop file into After Effects, I created a comp to animate each layer individually; I alternated speed and amount of rotations across the Timeline (Figure 16.48). This creates more separation in the layers and depth to the final animation.

I created a new comp and imported the animation comp and scaled it down to the lower-third region of the frame. I applied a mask with only horizontal feathering off the sides (Figure 16.49).

I placed the text and photo object layers on top of the animated background layer, which provided a visually stimulating lower third for this project (Figure 16.50). Because the title text is large enough, it does not appear illegible nor does the underlying animated background detract from it.

CHAPTER 16: MOTION TITLING EFFECTS

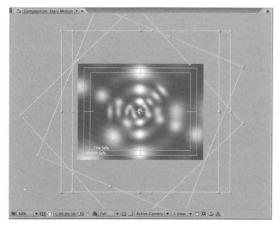

Figure 16.48
I rotated all of the layers individually at different speeds.

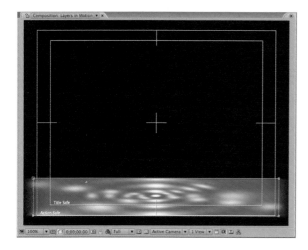

Figure 16.49
I imported the animation comp into the main comp window, scaled it, and applied a feathered mask.

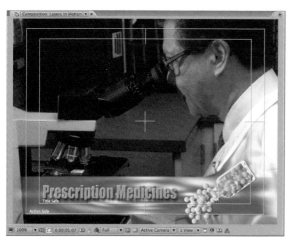

Figure 16.50
The final composite illustrates depth and interest in the lower-third graphic title.

Custom Scene Transitions

Traditionally, video and film transitions have been achieved by making quick cuts and fades between camera positions or scenes. Since the introduction of desktop video, we've been inundated with a myriad of transition wipes, grids, multipliers, and so forth, but all of them start to look the same after a while. In this final chapter, I'd like to introduce you to a few creative concepts that you can run with, modify, and customize to create your own original transitions.

Chapter Contents
Luminance Mattes from Movies
Painting a Transition
Animating 3-D Layers for a Cube Transition
Animating Photoshop Layers for Sophisticated 3-D Transitions

Luminance Mattes from Movies

This is a great effect to use as a transition or just a composite. The effect is similar to applying an Alpha Matte with a mask layer; it uses a high-contrast movie as a luminance matte that allows the top and bottom layers to show through in the highlights. You can achieve this effect with both video and still image layers.

I used two video clips and one still image for this example. You can follow along with or review them in the After Effects project file LuminanceMatteProject.aep in the Chapter 17 folder on the DVD:

1. Start with a new AfterEffects project file, create a comp (320 × 240, 15 seconds), and import the three source files from the Chapter 17 folder on the DVD (Figure 17.1): CloseFireClip.mov, FirefighterClip.mov, and BurntWood.jpg.

 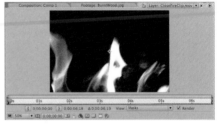

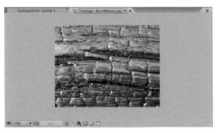

Figure 17.1

Import the source files into a new After Effects project.

2. Drag all three files into the Comp window, rescale them to fit, and set them in order with the close-up fire clip on top and the burnt-wood image on the bottom.

3. Select the firefighter layer in the Timeline and apply a Luma Matte (Layer > Track Matte > Luma Matte). The shape of the fire in the top layer will now be the mask for the firefighter layer (Figure 17.2). Although the effect isn't all that impressive at first in single-frame mode, you can run a RAM Preview to see the effect in motion.

Figure 17.2

Apply the Luma Matte to the middle layer to be masked, and allow the flames to mask the image.

You can use this as an interesting transitional effect, but because the flames aren't very large and are moving quite rapidly, the section of the middle layer isn't exposed long enough to distinguish what it is right away. Another technique is to reverse the Luma Matte (Layer > Track Matte > Luma Inverted Matte), which shows the firefighter layer below in the black space of the close-up fire clip (Figure 17.3).

Figure 17.3

Apply a Luma Inverted Matte to make the background behind the flame be the mask.

To get the most out of the close-up flame clip, you need to zoom in on it over the Timeline to make it take up more space inside the frame. To turn this into a transition, you need to zoom up the scale of the flame until it takes up nearly the entire frame. This requires applying an increase in scale as well as a change in position over time:

4. Select the top fire layer and move the Timeline Indicator just past the 2-second mark. Click the Scale and Position Stopwatches to set the current keyframe for both. To make it easier to see the fire clip by itself and make it visible while scaling along the Timeline, click the eyeball icon for that layer.

5. Move the Indicator down just before the 4-second mark, rescale the layer to about 250%, and position it until the flame covers most of the frame (Figure 17.4).

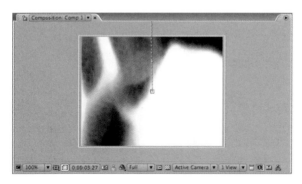

Figure 17.4

Resize and reposition the flame mask layer over time to create a transition motion in the matte.

Next, to create a smooth transition, you'll need to fade the mask layer into the matte effect and then back out at the end, revealing the background layer in its entirety. At approximately 1 second before the layer starts its increase in scale, you'll need to fade in by making the layer start out black and then ease into the full exposure. You can do this most easily by changing the Channel values in Hue/Saturation:

6. Go to about the 1-second mark in the Timeline and apply the Hue/Saturation and adjust the Master Lightness to –100. Click the Stopwatch in the Timeline to set the key frame.

7. Move the Indicator up to the 2-second mark and set the Master Lightness back to 0 (Figure 17.5).

8. Move the Indicator down to the 4-second mark and click the Set check box to set the keyframe at 0. Then move it down to the 5-second mark, and set the Master Lightness to 100.

Render a RAM Preview to see the finished effect. Refer to Table 17.1 for all of the fading, Scale, and Position settings used in this project example.

▷ **Table 17.1** Hue/Saturation, Scale, and Position Settings

Transform	01;01	01;26	02;05	03;27	04;02	04;23
Master Lightness	–100	0			0	100
Scale %			50%	250%		
Position X, Y			160.0, 120.0	154.0, –283.0		

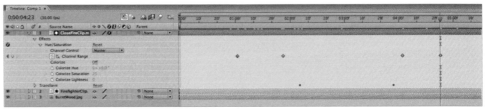

Figure 17.5 Use Hue/Saturation over time to create a fade-in and fade-out of the transition.

Painting a Transition

After Effects has a paint layer capability; with it you can animate the brush strokes from the start of a stroke to the finish over time. Using this animated paint layer as a mask and some imagination with your brush strokes will provide you with an unlimited amount of creative custom transitions.

Start with an After Effects project, 320 × 240, 8 seconds in length. Import two clip layers (BostonChurch.mov and Lighthouse.mov) or open the project file Paint-TransProject.aep from the Chapter 17 folder on the DVD.

Create a solid-black layer on top, double-click the layer in the Timeline, which opens it in its own window, and apply the paint layer effect (Effects > Paint > Paint). Open the Paint palette (Window > Paint), select the Paintbrush from the Tools palette, and create an angled, feathered brush of about 45 pixels. Then select white for the paint color, and select the Paint On Transparency option. Draw a squiggly line from the upper-left corner down through the middle, increasing in size and thickness if you are using a drawing tablet (Figure 17.6).

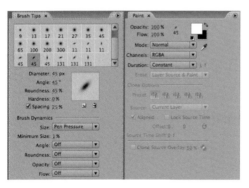

Figure 17.6
Use a soft brush to paint a squiggly line down through the center of the frame.

Note: Have you ever tried to draw or paint with a bar of soap? Drawing with a mouse is just about as difficult. I find it much easier to use a drawing tablet with a pen to draw the lines. Select Pen Pressure for the Size, Angle, and Flow settings, and you'll have natural, smooth strokes.

Each brush stroke you make becomes independently animatible over time in the Timeline. There's a start and end of each stroke and a path that represents the direction of the stroke. To view the path of each brush stroke, you must select the individual brushes in the Paint effect on the Timeline (Figure 17.7).

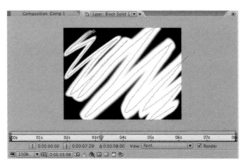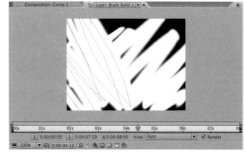

Figure 17.7 Each stroke has its own path that can be animated.

Spin down the paint layer, then the Brush 1 settings, and then the Stroke Options. Move the Indicator down to the 1-second mark and click the End Stopwatch. Adjust it to 0.0%, which is actually the very beginning of the stroke—or 0% of the finished stroke. Move the Indicator down to over 3 seconds and adjust the End setting to 100.0%—the end of the stroke (Figure 17.8). For a smoother, more natural brush stroke, apply an Easy Ease Out and Ease In on the beginning and end of the stroke path animation. Move down the Timeline and apply the beginning and end key frames for the additional brush strokes.

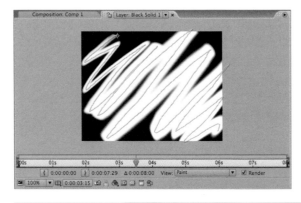

Figure 17.8
Create key frames for the beginning and end of the stroke path animation.

Select the top movie clip layer that is positioned just below the paint layer, apply the Alpha Matte (Layer > Track Matte > Alpha Matte), and move the Indicator down the Timeline to see the transition revealing the lower clip layer (Figure 17.9).

Figure 17.9

Apply the Alpha Matte to the top movie clip to reveal the animated paintbrush transition.

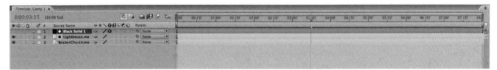

Note: The paint layer will automatically hide itself when you select the Alpha Matte option.

To control the playback speed of the strokes, adjust the distance between the beginning and end key frames for each brush stroke.

Animating 3-D Layers for a Cube Transition

By utilizing some of the animation techniques we covered in Chapter 3, "3-D Layers from Photoshop Layers," you can create interesting scene transitions from one video clip to another. Depending on which shapes and how many layers you use to complete the transition, your animation possibilities are virtually limitless.

Animating only the movie layers in After Effects can also produce simple 3-D transitions. Similar to using some third-party plug-ins, you can make a simple simulated cube rotation by connecting the two movie layers at right angles and rotating them in front of the camera. This example uses just two movie file layers and a single camera:

1. Create a new After Effects comp, NTSC 640 × 480, 10 seconds.

2. Import the two movie files SkyClouds.mov and 747Airborne.mov, provided in the Chapter 17 folder on the DVD. Drag the movies to the Timeline, convert them to 3-D layers in the Timeline, and add a camera layer (Layers > New > Camera) using the default settings.

3. Put the 747 movie on the bottom layer in the Timeline, and set the Y Rotation to –90°. Set the X-axis Anchor Point to 0.0 and the X Position to 640 (Figure 17.10).

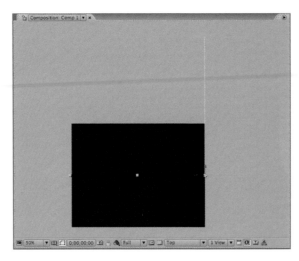

Figure 17.10
Select the Top view on the Comp window to see the joining angle of the two movie layers.

4. Set the X-axis Anchor Point for the clouds movie layer to 640.0 and the Y-axis Orientation to 270.0. Select the 747 movie layer as its parent. This will group the two layers in this configuration so that whatever movement is applied to the parent layer, the child layer will automatically follow.

5. Move the Indicator to the 2-second mark and click the Y Rotation Stopwatch on the 747 movie layer. Move the Indicator down to the 5-second mark and set the Y Rotation to 0.0.

6. To make the transition rotate correctly in front of the camera, you need to reposition the movie layers along a straight X-axis path. Move the Indicator to the 2-second key frame and click the Position Stopwatch on the 747 movie layer, which sets the current X-axis position at 640.0. Move the Indicator down to the 5-second key frame and set the X-axis position to 0.0.

7. Grab the right-side path handle and pull down toward the bottom middle of the frame to create a smooth arc in the position path (Figure 17.11). This will give the illusion that the point of rotation is the center of the imaginary "cube" as the transition revolves.

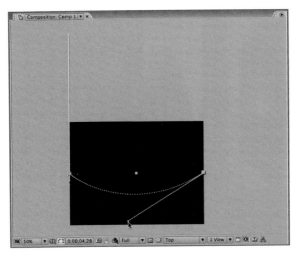

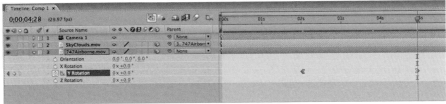

Figure 17.11
Adjust the curvature of the X-axis position path to create a smooth rotation around the imaginary "cube."

8. While still in Top view, zoom out of the Comp window so you can see the entire camera layer. Position the camera so it is back far enough from the movie layers to fill the frame (Figure 17.12). Be sure that the camera is correctly centered and angled at 90° to the movie layers so the transition works smoothly. Switch back and forth between the Top view and the Camera 1 view on the Comp window to check the alignment.

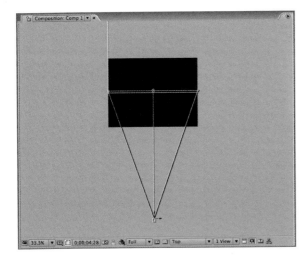

Figure 17.12
Center the camera to aim directly at the middle of the movie frames and fill the Comp window.

Render a RAM Preview to check the 3-D transition effect for timing and motion (Figure 17.13). You can add more movies to complete the cube or a larger geometric connected shape that can rotate. It's also possible to position this comp inside another comp containing other movies and traditional transitions or effects.

Figure 17.13 The rendered transition appears to be a 3-D rotating cube.

Animating Photoshop Layers for Sophisticated 3-D Transitions

You can use a multilayered Photoshop file to create individually masked movie comps. You can then place these comps inside a master comp and animate them independently, although the same running footage can be shown simultaneously on the individual pieces.

To demonstrate this, I created a 30-piece puzzle file in Photoshop with each piece sequentially placed on its own layer (Figure 17.14). The layers are numbered by row and are in the correct position within the frame for easy alignment in After Effects.

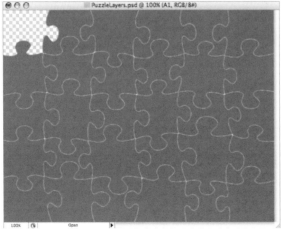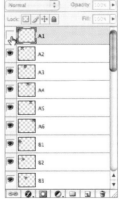

Figure 17.14 The 30-piece Photoshop puzzle has all of the layers aligned.

Note: You can follow along with the completed After Effects project file, 3-DPuzzleTrans.aep, which can be found in the Chapter 17 folder on the DVD. All of the required source files and rendered QuickTime movies are also available in the Chapter 17 folder.

I created an After Effects project and imported the Photoshop puzzle file as a composition to retain the layers, plus the 747Airborne.mov and SkyClouds.mov Quick-Time movies. I then created a comp, NTSC 640 × 480, 15 seconds, and dragged the 747 movie into the Timeline. I opened the Photoshop puzzle layer file folder in the Project window and dragged the first puzzle piece, A1, into the Timeline on top of the movie clip (Figure 17.15). I then applied an Alpha Matte to the movie layer to create a mask of the puzzle piece.

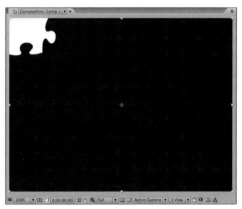

Figure 17.15 The puzzle piece becomes a mask for the movie layer and is correctly aligned in the frame.

Note: Selecting Alpha Mattes from the Timeline columns is the easiest selection method. If you don't have the Modes column visible by default, then right-click/Ctrl+click the Timeline menu bar and select Columns > Modes, as shown in the following graphic.

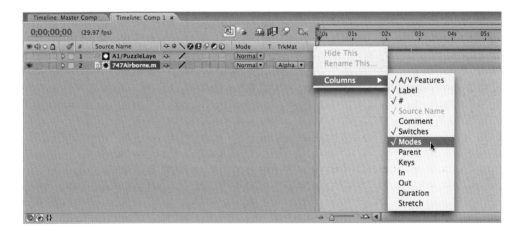

I duplicated Comp 1 and replaced the A1 puzzle layer with A2, and I repeated this process until I had all 30 comps created (Figure 17.16). Because the movie layer already had the Alpha Matte applied in each duplicated comp, everything lined up perfectly for each layer and it was a quick process.

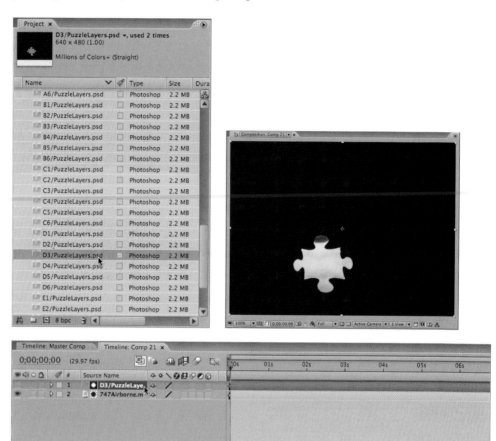

Figure 17.16 Repeatedly duplicate Comp 1 and replace the puzzle layer for each comp until all the pieces are used.

I created a new master comp and dragged the puzzle comps into the Timeline in sequential order. This made it much easier to keep track of the layers and puzzle pieces as they were animated. Once I placed all of the comps in the Timeline, I dragged in the clouds movie and placed it at the bottom. I then converted all of the comps and movie layers to 3-D layers by clicking the check box in the Timeline (Figure 17.17).

I created a new Spot Light, increased the Intensity to 100% and the Cone Angle to 150°, and made it white in color. I then selected all of the comp layers, spun down the Material Options settings, and turned on the Casts Shadows option (Figure 17.18). Even though I changed the setting on only one layer, all of the selected layers responded to the setting. I then set the Master Comp view to Left and dragged the light up and to the right so it would shine down on the center of the layers.

Figure 17.17 Sequentially drag the comps into the Timeline and convert them to 3-D layers.

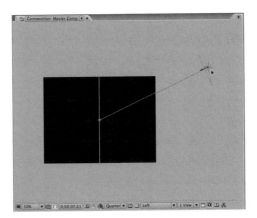

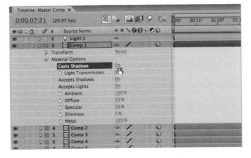

Figure 17.18

Create a new Spot Light and turn on the
Casts Shadows option on all comp layers.

Next, I moved the Z-axis of the background Clouds movie 9 pixels so the puzzle pieces cast a shadow on it as they fall to rest against it (Figure 17.19). You can hide several of the comp layers to see the slight drop shadow effect onto the background layer.

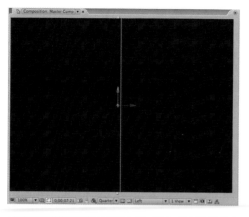

Figure 17.19

Move the background layer back slightly to allow the puzzle pieces to cast a shadow on it.

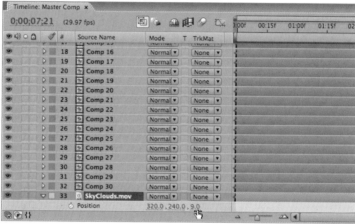

Because it's easier to take a puzzle apart than it is to line it all up in the end, I made the animation in reverse. With the comp layers still selected, I moved the Indicator down to the 10-second mark and pressed P to spin down the Position settings. I clicked the Stopwatch to set the final key frame for the transition animation (Figure 17.20). I then selected only the A1 comp layer, moved the Indicator back to the 3-second mark, and moved the layer up and to the left of the frame. I continued with the remaining layers, moving ahead a few frames for each layer and moving the layers outside the frame.

I moved back the last key frame for each layer so they would animate at a rate of about 2 seconds each—creating a cascading effect. I needed to make the 3-D layer effect more predominant, so I had to adjust the height of each puzzle piece so that it would fly down onto the background, casting shadows on the pieces below as they fall in sequence. I then applied a Z-axis position of –200.0 at the beginning key frame for each layer animation (Figure 17.21). I set them all to return to 0.0 at the end key frame and appear to be on the same plane.

To create a smooth transition out of the puzzle composites and into the running footage of the 747 in flight, I added the movie layer to the top in the Timeline and created an Opacity fade-up from the layers below (Figure 17.22). The movie layer covers all of the layers below, so I did not have to convert it to a 3-D layer.

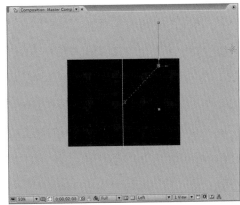

Figure 17.20 Set the final key frame and move back in the Timeline to position the layers outside the comp frame one at a time.

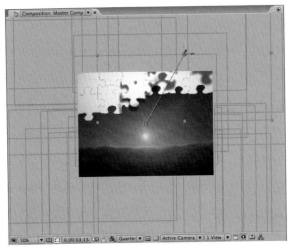

Figure 17.21
Set the Z-axis position at the beginning of each layer animation to give the effect of flying into the scene.

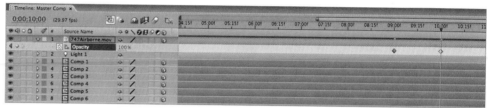

Figure 17.22 Add a new movie layer to the Timeline and fade up the Opacity to complete the transition effect.

By using other 3-D layer animation techniques covered in Chapter 3, such as moving cameras or spinning layers, you can come up with an unlimited number of 3-D layer transitions for your projects.

Appendix

Adobe Photoshop and After Effects Resources

On the following pages are some resources that I have referred to in the book or that you might find of interest. I've also provided a hand-selected list of references for further training and software application education.

Art Center College Library
1700 Lida St
Pasadena, Ca 91103

Third-Party Plug-ins, Stock Imagery, and Footage

Many of these software and stock providers have allowed me to include their samples and demo version software on the enclosed DVD-ROM. Be sure to check them out on the DVD and online!

Ambrosia Software Snapz Pro X 2.0 screen and movie capture software and utilities

www.AmbrosiaSW.com

ArtBeats Stock images, textures, and video footage

www.artbeats.com

Boris FX Continuum complete 3-D effects filters for After Effects and more

www.borisfx.com

BuyoutFootage.com Professional royalty-free stock video footage

www.buyoutfootage.com

Digital Anarchy Plug-in effects for After Effects and Photoshop: Psunami, Primatte Keyer 2.0 for Photoshop, and more

www.digitalanarchy.com

Digital Film Tools Plug-in effects for After Effects and Photoshop: Composite Suite, 55mm, zMatte, and more

www.digitalfilmtools.com

dvGarage dvMatte Pro AE: Keyer plug-in for DV footage

www.dvgarage.com

PhotoSpin.com Professional royalty-free photographic and illustrated image library, downloadable by subscription

www.photospin.com

RE:Vision Effects Plug-in effects for After Effects: Twixtor, Video Gough, ReelSmart Motion Blur, and more

www.revisionfx.com

Red Giant Software Plug-in effects for After Effects: Primatte Keyer, Knoll Light Factory, and more

www.redgiantsoftware.com

SmartSound Audio creation and editing software for After Effects, plus stock music and audio tracks

www.smartsound.com

TimeImage Professional royalty-free stock video footage

www.timeimage.com

Tools for Television Products for video production and graphic design

www.toolsfortelevision.com

Trapcode Plug-in effects for After Effects: Shine, Starglow, 3D Stroke, and more

www.trapcode.com

Ultimatte AdvantEdge: Keyer plug-in for After Effects and Photoshop

www.ultimatte.com

Walker Effects Plug-in effects for After Effects: Alpha Tool, Color Fill, Gradient Designer, Fast Tracker, and more

www.walkereffects.com

Technical and Training References

Do you need more technical help with Photoshop or After Effects? Do you need to learn the tools in more detail? Are you looking for advanced video formatting, optimization, and compression? These references are from the best of the best in Adobe book authors and training organizations.

Organizations

NAPP National Association of Photoshop Professionals

www.photoshopuser.com

www.photoshopworld.com

DVPA Digital Video Producers Association

www.dvpa.org

MGLA Motion Graphics Los Angeles

www.mgla.org

dvGarage Downloadable DV production techniques and training tutorials

www.dvgarage.com

Books

Creating Motion Graphics with After Effects, Volume 1: The Essentials: Trish Meyer and Chris Meyer (CMP Books, 2004)

Adobe After Effects 6.0 Classroom in a Book: Adobe Creative Team (Adobe Press, 2003)

Adobe Photoshop CS Classroom in a Book: Adobe Creative Team (Adobe Press, 2003)

Photoshop CS Savvy: Stephen Romaniello (Sybex, 2004)

Photoshop CS Killer Tips: Scott Kelby and Felix Nelson (New Riders Press, 2004)

The Hidden Power of Photoshop CS: Richard Lynch (Sybex, 2004)

The Photoshop CS/CS2 Wow! Book: Linnea Dayton and Jack Davis (Peachpit Press, 2005)

Photoshop Secrets of the Pros: Mark Clarkson (Sybex, 2004)

Photoshop CS at Your Fingertips: Jason Cranford Teague and Walt Dietrich (Sybex, 2004)

Index

Note to the Reader: Throughout this index **boldfaced** page numbers indicate primary discussions of a topic.